365 Tasty Steak and Chop Recipes

(365 Tasty Steak and Chop Recipes - Volume 1)

Paula Stone

Content

4

8

365 Awesome Steak And Chop Recipes

***

1. A Marine's Memory Of Monkey Gland Steak Recipe

Serving: 6 | Prep: | Cook: 1hours | Ready in:

Ingredients

- 3lbs cube steak(preferably 1 steak per person)
- 3T olive oil
- 1 large onion, diced
- 4 cloves garlic, minced
- 1t red pepper flakes
- 12oz fresh mushrooms, sliced
- 14oz diced tomatoes
- 8oz tomato sauce
- 1/2-3/4 cup beef broth
- 1/3 cup worcestershire sauce
- 4oz peach or mango chutney or other chunky fruit spread
- 2T red wine vinegar
- 1/4 cup red wine
- kosher or sea salt and fresh ground pepper
- 1/2lb of sliced, rustic, bread
- 1/2 stick butter
- garlic powder or minced garlic/herb combo
- or, fresh garlic, minced

Direction

- Heat oil in large, deep skillet or Dutch oven. (I used cast iron).
- Brown steaks over medium high heat for about 2-3 minutes, each side.
- Remove from pan and reduce heat to low.
- Add onion and cook about 5-7 minutes, until softening.

- Add garlic, red pepper flakes, tomatoes, tomato sauce, beef broth, Worcestershire sauce, chutney, vinegar, wine and salt and pepper.
- Mix well and let return to simmer.
- Simmer about 15 minutes, without stirring.
- Add mushrooms.
- Add steaks back to the pan, covering with the sauce as much as possible.
- Let simmer, uncovered, for at least 30 minutes, or longer, until steaks are tender.
- Meanwhile, melt butter and add whatever garlic component you are using and brush over 1 side of each slice of bread.
- Bake at 450 for 7-10 minutes until golden brown and crunchy.
- Serve steak and gravy over a slice of bread.

2. Adobong Kangkong Recipe

Serving: 3 | Prep: | Cook: 15mins | Ready in:

Ingredients

- kangkong
- pork/beef (chopped)
- soy sauce
- vinegar
- black pepper
- brown sugar
- onion (chopped)
- garlic (minced)
- vegetable oil

Direction

- Marinate chopped meat for 30mins to 1hr in soy sauce, a little sugar and black pepper.
- Blanch kangkong for 90secs. Drain then set aside.
- Heat pan and put oil.
- Add onions and garlic.

- Once garlic is lightly brown and onion is transparent, add the marinated meat.
- When meat is a little brown, set heat on low.
- On a separate pan stir fry kangkong. Then add kangkong in the pan with meat.
- Add a little vinegar, soy sauce, and black pepper. Mix well. Serve with rice. (^_^)

3. Alsatian Pork With Sauerkraut Recipe

Serving: 4 | Prep: | Cook: 40mins |Ready in:

Ingredients

- 4 slices bacon cut into 1 inch pieces
- 1 medium onion chopped
- 2 cans sauerkraut drained
- 2 TBS packed brown sugar
- 4 med potatoes cut into fourths
- 2 tart apples sliced-Granny Smith works well (She is getting kind of long in the tooth and hard of hearing but she will still work pretty good)
- 12 juniper berries (optional)
- 6 Whole peppercorns
- 2 whole cloves
- 1 sprig parsley
- 1 bay leaf
- 4 smoked pork chops, 1/2" thick
- 4 frankfurters, slashed diagonally
- 2 Cups chicken broth

Direction

- Cook and stir bacon and onion in Dutch oven or 12" skillet until bacon is crisp; drain.
- Stir in Sauerkraut and brown sugar.
- Add potatoes and apples
- Tie all spices in cheesecloth bag or a tea ball; add to Sauerkraut
- Add pork and frankfurters
- Pour chicken broth over meat
- Heat to boiling

- Reduce heat cover and simmer until meat is done and potatoes are tender, about 30 minutes.
- Remove Spice bag
- Place the dish on a platter and enjoy.

4. Applebees Bourbon Street Steak Recipe

Serving: 4 | Prep: | Cook: 15mins |Ready in:

Ingredients

- 1/2 cup bottled steak sauce
- 1/4 cup bourbon whiskey
- 1 tablespoon honey
- 2 teaspoons prepared mustard
- 4 beef rib, round, or chuck steaks (10 ounces each)

Direction

- Combine all the ingredients except the steaks in a baking dish or resealable plastic storage bag; mix well. Add the steaks; cover (or seal) and refrigerate for 2 hours, or overnight. Preheat the grill to medium−high heat. Grill the steaks for 12 to 15 minutes, or until desired doneness, turning them over halfway through the grilling.

5. Aromatic And Spicy Kebabs Recipe

Serving: 6 | Prep: | Cook: 5mins |Ready in:

Ingredients

- 1 lb boneless skinless chicken breast halves, cut into 1-inch pieces
- 1/2 lb. beef top sirloin, cut into 1 inch cubes
- Marinate Ingredients:

- 4 garlic cloves, mashed
- 1/2 red onion, cut into 1-inch pieces .
- 4 tbsp fresh lemon juice .
- 1 bunch fresh mint .
- 1/4cup extra-virgin olive oil .
- 2 tsp crushed lemongrass
- 1 tsp ground cinnamon .
- 1/4 tsp. ground cardamom
- 1 tsp ground ginger
- 1/4 tsp allspice
- 1/4 tsp. ground cloves.
- 1 tsp fresh ground black pepper .
- 1 tsp salt
- To insert into skewers:
- Onion chunks
- Red peppe pieces
- Chopped cilantro to garnish.

Direction

- Put chicken breast pieces in one bow and beef sirloin cubes in other bowl and set aside.
- Mix the marinate ingredients in the blender and pour over chicken and sirloin; mix well and let marinate for 12 hours.
- Alternate chicken, onion, sirloin, red bell pepper on skewers; sprinkle with salt & pepper.
- Grill until chicken and sirloin are just cooked through, turning & basting every once.
- Serve and enjoy.

6. Asian Beef Kebobs Recipe

Serving: 4 | Prep: | Cook: 20mins |Ready in:

Ingredients

- 1 pound beef top sirloin steak
- 6 green onions cut into 1-1/2 inch pieces
- 1/4 cup packed brown sugar
- 3 tablespoons dry sherry
- 3 tablespoons soy sauce
- 2 teaspoons dark sesame oil
- 2 cloves garlic crushed

- 1/2 teaspoon ground ginger
- 16 bamboo skewers

Direction

- Trim all fat from steak then cut crosswise into 1/4" thick strips.
- Make marinade by combining brown sugar, sherry, soy sauce, sesame oil, garlic and ginger.
- Place beef and half of the marinade mixture in plastic bag turning to coat.
- Close securely and marinade in refrigerator 20 minutes.
- Reserve remaining marinade.
- Meanwhile soak 16 bamboo skewers in water 10 minutes.
- Remove beef from marinade and discard marinade.
- Alternately thread beef and green onion onto skewers.
- Place kabobs on rack in broiler pan so surface of kabobs is 3-4 inches from heat.
- Broil 5 minutes turning once.
- Brush kabobs with reserved marinade during last 2 minutes.

7. Asian Honey Pork Chops Recipe

Serving: 4 | Prep: | Cook: 60mins |Ready in:

Ingredients

- 2-4 pork chops, 1/2 inch to 3/4 inch thick
- 1 tbsp toasted sesame oil or olive oil
- 1/2 cup chicken broth
- 1/2 cup honey
- 1/4 cup soy sauce or Bragg's Liquid Aminos
- 2 tablespoons ketchup
- 1/4 teaspoon crushed red pepper flakes
- 1/4 teaspoon garlic salt, plus some extra for seasoning the chops

Direction

- Preheat oven to 350. Sprinkle chops with garlic salt and brown in oil. Place in a greased casserole dish. Mix all remaining ingredients and pour over the chops. Bake uncovered for one hour. Serve extra sauce over rice.

8. Asian Style Pork Chop Bake Recipe

Serving: 4 | Prep: | Cook: 45mins | Ready in:

Ingredients

- 1/2 cup teriyaki sauce
- 1/2 cup orange juice
- 1/4 cup dry sherry
- 2 teaspoons minced fresh ginger root
- 2 cloves garlic minced
- 1 teaspoon freshly ground black pepper to taste
- 1 dash ground allspice
- 6 thick pork chops

Direction

- In a glass dish combine teriyaki sauce, orange juice, sherry, ginger root, garlic, pepper and allspice and mix well.
- Add pork chops to dish then cover and marinate in refrigerator for 6 hours turning occasionally.
- Preheat oven to 400.
- Remove chops and marinade from refrigerator.
- Remove cover and bake in preheated oven for 40 minutes.

9. Austins Bourbon Sirloin Recipe

Serving: 4 | Prep: | Cook: 20mins | Ready in:

Ingredients

- 1/2 cup soy sauce
- 3/4 cup brown sugar
- 1 cup Dijon mustard
- 1 tbsp black pepper
- 2 tbsp worcestershire sauce
- 1/4 cup bourbon
- 1/4 cup honey
- 24 oz sirloin steak (either one huge one or (4) 6 oz ones)

Direction

- Whisk all ingredients together in a bowl.
- Pat the steak dry with a paper towel.
- Pour the marinade in a gallon size zipper bag and add the steak(s)
- Marinate a minimum of 8 hours, turning the meat now and then.
- Remove steaks and discard marinade. Preheat grill to high heat.
- Cook to desired doneness turning only once if possible.

10. Authentic Mexican Arracheras Recipe

Serving: 12 | Prep: | Cook: 30mins | Ready in:

Ingredients

- 2-1/2 pounds trimmed beef skirt steak
- 2/3 cup lime juice
- 1/4 cup minced Jalapeños en escabeche
- 2 tablespoons minced garlic cloves
- 1 teaspoon salt
- 2 large onions; sliced into rings
- 1/2 cup peanut oil
- 12 warmed flour tortillas

Direction

- Note: In Northern Mexico, the Mexican vaqueros, driving cattle North into Texas, ate this tasty but tough cut of beef, marinated to tenderize and flavor, then grilled over the coals of their camp fires. Arrachera was the original forerunner of the famous Tex-Mex Fajita. "Fajita" is the diminutive form of the Spanish word "faja" which translates to "belt" or "girdle" in English. The word was used to mean the diaphragm muscle of a steer or what we call "skirt" steak. Restaurateurs, all on their own, decided to call charbroiled chicken, pork and shrimp "fajitas" to expand their menus. While these items are delicious in their own right; they are not fajita.

- Trim and place the whole skirt steak in a shallow non-reactive pan. Combine lime juice, jalapénos and garlic. Mix well, then pour over the meat. This works even better enclosed and sealed in a large Ziploc bag.
- Refrigerate for at least 8 hours, turning the meat occasionally. Remove the meat from the refrigerator and drain it. Salt the meat and let it sit at room temperature for about 45 minutes.
- Coat the onions well with oil.
- On an outdoor grill, prepare enough charcoal to form a single layer of coals beneath the meat. When the coals are covered with gray ash, place the steaks directly over the fire and the onions a little to the side.
- Grill the meat medium-rare, about 6 minutes per side. Turn the onions occasionally, taking them off when soft and some edges are browned and crispy.
- Allow the steaks to sit for 5 minutes before slicing across the grain diagonally into finger-length strips. Pile a platter high with the meat and grilled onions, garnished with lime wedges, and serve warmed flour tortillas on the side.

11. BEEF FAJITAS Recipe

Serving: 10 | Prep: | Cook: 15mins |Ready in:

Ingredients

- 1 can 10 oz rotell diced tomatoes and green chilies
- 1 cup budweiser
- 1/4 cup lemon juice
- 3 tbl. veg oil
- 2 cloves garlic minced
- 1/8 teas. blk pepper
- 1-2 lbs skirt steak trim excess fat
- 2 medium onions sliced 1/4 thick
- 2 medium bell peppers sliced 1/4 " thick
- pam no stick spray
- 10 8" flour tortillas
- 1 cup 4 oz shredded cheddar cheese
- 1/2 cup sour cream
- 1 cup guacamole
- 1/2 cup taco sauce

Direction

- In a 9x12x2" baking dish, combine rotell, beer, lemon juice, oil, garlic, pepper; place meat in dish.
- Add the onions and bell peppers; cover and refrigerate overnight or no less than 6 hours.
- Remove from marinade.
- Broil 3" from the heat source for 8 minutes.
- Pull out, baste in marinade and put back in for 7 minutes the other side, medium doneness.
- Slice the beef across the grain into thin strips.
- Spray the skillet and sauté the veggies till tender.
- For a fajita on tortillas, layer meat, onions, peppers, cheese, sour cream, guacamole and taco sauce; roll to close. Makes 10.

12. BISTRO BEEF STEAK Recipe

Serving: 4 | Prep: | Cook: 30mins |Ready in:

Ingredients

- Ingredients:
- 1 Lb boneless beef top sirloin steak ¾ -inch thick
- 2 Tbs. chopped fresh Italian parsley

- 2 cloves garlic, crushed
- ½ tsp. pepper
- 1 large red onion
- 1 Tbs olive oil
- ¼ cup dry red wine
- 1 ½ Lb. new potatoes, steamed
- 2 cups steamed vegetable medley (green beans & sliced yellow bell pepper)

Direction

- 1) Trim fat from beef steak. Cut steak lengthwise in half then crosswise into ½ inch thick strips. In a medium bowl, combine beef, parsley, garlic and pepper; toss to coat. Set aside.
- 2) Cut onion into ¼ inch thick slices; separate into rings. In a large nonstick skillet, heat oil over medium-high heat until hot. Add onion; cook and stir 3 to 5 minutes or until crisp-tender. Remove to serving platter; keep warm.
- 3) In the same skillet, add beef and stir-fry 2 minutes or until outside surface is no longer pink. Place beef on top of onion.
- 4) Add wine to skillet; cook and stir until browned bits attached to skillet are dissolved and liquid thickens slightly. Pour sauce over beef and onions. Serve with vegetables.
- Calories per serving: 419

13. BROWN GRAVY CABBAGE ROLLS Recipe

Serving: 8 | Prep: | Cook: 30mins | Ready in:

Ingredients

- 2 heads cabbage
- 1 c. cooked rice
- 1 c. seasoned bread crumbs
- 2 eggs, beaten
- 1 lb. ground beef or pork
- 1 c. chopped onions
- 1/4 c. chopped parsley
- 1 clove garlic, crushed

- 1/4 tsp. thyme
- 4 tsp. sage
- salt and pepper

Direction

- Parboil large leaves of cabbage for a few minutes until pliable.
- Brown meat in a little oil, remove meat; brown onions, remove them.
- Drain off excess oil, add water to make a light brown gravy.
- Pour out and reserve.
- Put meat, rice, bread crumbs and all seasoning in pan.
- Mix thoroughly while heating through, turn off heat; add eggs, and mix again.
- Place correct amount of stuffing in centre of each cabbage leaf.
- Fold in sides of leaf, roll up tightly and place in a 9x13 pan.
- If they are packed tight and fill the pan, they will usually not need to be secured with toothpick. Heat brown gravy which you make from reserved drippings and pour over rolls.
- Bake at 350 until bubbly.
- I do not use the home made gravy because of fat. I purchase 2 packages of brown gravy mix and use that.
- Hope you enjoy.

14. Bacon Wrapped Lamb Chops With Garden Fresh Veggies Recipe

Serving: 6 | Prep: | Cook: 30mins | Ready in:

Ingredients

- 6 to 8 small lamb chop ends
- bacon
- 1 garlic clove
- fresh beans, yellow and green beans
- fresh carrots

- brown rice
- 4 green onions
- 3 tbsp soya sauce
- balsamic vinegar
- 1 lemon
- 2 tsp sugar

Direction

- In a skillet, add 2 tbsp. olive or canola oil
- Wrap a slice of bacon around each chop, securing with toothpick
- Place French-cut sliced green onions into the skillet, and allow to caramelize. Remove onions and set aside
- Add garlic, finely chopped
- French-cut the beans
- Add the chops, and then add the carrots and beans. Cook over low to medium heat until the chops are done and the bacon is crisp
- In the meantime, cook one cup of brown rice, with the soya sauce in the water, and drain...
- Make a balsamic vinegar reduction:
- In a small saucepan, combine:
- 5 tbsp. balsamic vinegar
- Juice of one whole lemon
- Reduce this to ½ the original quantity.
- Take some of the zest of the lemon and reserve.
- When ready to serve, plate as follows:
- Place a bed of rice on the plate first;
- Add the chops on top;
- Drizzle with the balsamic reduction;
- Sprinkle lemon zest on top of chops;
- Add the vegetables around the meat and rice;
- Drizzle a little of the balsamic reduction around the plate.
- ENJOY!

---

15. Bacon Wrapped Pork Chops With Blue Cheese Mashed Potatoes Recipe

---

Serving: 4 | Prep: | Cook: 30mins | Ready in:

Ingredients

- 4 (6-7 ounces each) boneless pork loin chops, 1 1/4-inch thick (I use Niman Ranch all natural pork, the best!)
- 4 slices thick-cut applewood smoked bacon
- 4 small sprigs of fresh rosemary
- Balsamic rosemary butter (recipe follows):
- 8 tablespoons (1 stick) chilled unsalted butter, room temp
- 1/4 cup aged balsamic vinegar
- leaves from 1 rosemary sprig, finely chopped (about 2 tbsp)
- kosher salt and freshly cracked black pepper to taste
- blue cheese mashed potatoes (recipe follows):
- 4 large idaho potatoes (about 3 pounds)
- 1 3/4 teaspoons salt
- 1/2 cup heavy cream
- 4 tablespoons unsalted butter (I used Kerrygold butter)
- 1/4 teaspoon freshly ground black pepper
- 6 ounces Roquefort, or other French blue cheese such as Bleu d'Avergne or Fourme d'Ambert (I used Creamy Danish Blue and it was delicious)
- 2 tablespoons minced fresh parsley leaves

Direction

- For the rosemary butter: Place softened butter in bowl and whisk in remaining ingredients. Remove butter mixture from bowl and spoon onto parchment paper or plastic wrap. Roll into a log, using the edge of a baking sheet to form a tight log. Chill for 2 hours before serving.
- For the mashed potatoes: Peel and quarter the potatoes lengthwise, then cut into 1-inch wedges. Put in a heavy medium saucepan with 1 teaspoon of the salt and add enough cold water to cover by 1-inch. Bring to a boil over high heat. Reduce the heat to medium-low. Simmer until the potatoes are fork-tender, about 25 minutes. Drain in a colander. Put potatoes through a ricer and return the potatoes to the saucepan. Add the cream,

butter, the remaining 3/4 teaspoon salt, and the pepper. With the heat on medium-low and stir the mixture until well blended, 4 to 5 minutes. Mix in 4 oz. blue cheese and mash to incorporate (use remaining blue cheese for garnish).

- For the pork chops: Dry the chops with paper towels and season generously with salt and pepper. Place a sprig of rosemary down on each chop and wrap a strip of bacon around each one, securing with a toothpick if needed. Prepare medium-hot fire in grill; grill chops over direct heat for 6-7 minutes; turn and grill 5-6 minutes more for medium doneness. Transfer to plate, tent with foil and let rest for 10-15 minutes.
- To serve: Remove toothpick and rosemary sprig (leave bacon on, of course!) Serve each chop with a pat of rosemary balsamic butter and side of blue cheese mashed potatoes garnished with left over blue cheese and chopped fresh parsley.

16. Bahama Mama Pork Chops Recipe

Serving: 4 | Prep: | Cook: 30mins | Ready in:

Ingredients

- 1 (8 ounce) can pineapple chunks, reserve juice
- 2/3 cup tomato-based chili sauce
- 1/3 cup raisins
- 1 tablespoon brown sugar
- 1/8 teaspoon ground cinnamon
- 4 pork chops
- 1 tablespoon vegetable oil

Direction

- In medium bowl, blend reserved pineapple juice with cornstarch; stir in pineapple, chili sauce, raisins, sugar and cinnamon and set aside.

- In large skillet lightly brown chops in oil and drain. Pour pineapple mixture over chops. Cover and simmer 30 minutes or until pork is cooked throughout.

17. Baked Pork Chops With Apple Raisin Stuffing Recipe

Serving: 4 | Prep: | Cook: 35mins | Ready in:

Ingredients

- 1 C. applesauce
- 1/2 C. water
- 2 Tbs. margarine OR butter, melted
- 1 stalk celery, chopped (about 1/2 cup)
- 2 Tbs. raisins
- 4 C. Herb seasoned Stuffing such as Stove Top
- 4 boneless pork chops, 3/4 inch thick (about 1 pound)
- paprika OR ground cinnamon
- apple slices for garnish

Direction

- Mix applesauce, water, margarine, celery and raisins.
- Add stuffing.
- Mix lightly.
- Spoon into 2-quart shallow baking dish.
- Arrange chops over stuffing.
- Sprinkle paprika over chops.
- Bake at 400°F for 35 min. or until chops are no longer pink.
- Garnish with apple slices.

18. Balsamic Glazed Skirt Steak With Parmesan Grits And Southwest Garlic Lime Butter Or Blue Cheese Walnut Butter Recipe

Serving: 4 | Prep: | Cook: 40mins | Ready in:

Ingredients

- 2 pounds inside skirt steak
- 1/2 cup olive oil
- 1/3 cup balsamic vinegar
- 2 large cloves garlic
- 3 tablespoons dark brown sugar
- _____
- Parmesan grits
- 4 cups water
- 3/4 teaspoon salt
- 2 tablespoons unsalted butter
- 1 cup coarse stone-ground white grits
- 1 cup half-and-half
- 1/4 teaspoon black pepper
- 1/2 cup parmesan cheese
- _____
- blue cheese walnut butter
- 6 ounces blue cheese, crumbled
- 4 tablespoons butter, room temperature
- 2 tablespoons chopped Italian parsley
- 1 teaspoon fresh chopped thyme
- 1/4 cup chopped toasted walnuts
- 1 teaspoon fresh ground pepper
- _____
- Southwest garlic lime butter
- 2 tablespoon unsalted butter (softened)
- 2 tablespoon chopped cilantro
- 1 clove garlic (finely chopped)
- 1 tablespoon fresh-squeezed lime juice
- 1 teaspoon chipotle chili powder
- 1/4 teaspoon sea salt

Direction

- In a blender, put in oil, balsamic, garlic and sugar and puree.
- Pour over skirt steak and allow to marinate for 2 hours.
- Heat cast-iron skillet over medium heat.
- Remove skirt steak from marinade and dry with a towel.
- Place in cast-iron skillet and cook for 3-4 minutes on each side.
- Slice thinly across the grain of the meat.
- Top with blue cheese walnut or southwest garlic lime butter and serve with grits.
- Parmesan grits:
- Bring water, salt, and 1 tablespoon butter to a boil in a 3-quart cast-iron sauce pan, then add grits slowly, stirring constantly with a wooden spoon.
- Reduce heat and cook at a low simmer, covered, stirring frequently, until water is absorbed and grits are thickened, about 15 minutes.
- Stir in 1/2 cup half-and-half and simmer, stirring occasionally for 10 minutes.
- Stir in remaining 1/2 cup half-and-half and simmer, partially covered, stirring occasionally, until liquid is absorbed and grits are thick and tender, about 35 minutes.
- Stir in Parmesan, pepper and remaining tablespoon butter.
- Southwest garlic lime butter
- Combine ingredients in a mixing bowl and mix well. Chill
- Bring butter to room temperature before using
- Blue cheese walnut butter
- Combine cheese, butter, parsley and 3/4 teaspoon rosemary in medium bowl.
- Stir to blend well. Mix in walnuts.
- Season to taste with salt and pepper. Transfer blue cheese butter to small bowl.
- Cover and refrigerate.
- Bring butter to room temperature before using
- You can use either the Walnut butter or Garlic Lime butter with these steaks.

19. Barbecue Cube Steaks Recipe

Serving: 8 | Prep: | Cook: 35mins | Ready in:

Ingredients

- 4 pounds cubed steak
- 1/4 cup flour seasoned with salt and pepper
- 3 tablespoons fat
- 1 medium white onion
- 1/4 teaspoon pepper
- 1 tablespoon vinegar
- 2 tablespoons lemon juice
- 1/2 cup catsup
- 2 tablespoons worcestershire sauce
- 1/2 teaspoon salt
- 1/2 cup water
- 1 tablespoon brown sugar

Direction

- Flour and season steak then brown in fat then add chopped onion and brown lightly.
- Combine remaining ingredients and pour over steak then cover slowly.
- Cook slowly for 35 minutes.

20. Bbq Beef Sandwiches Recipe

Serving: 4 | Prep: | Cook: 15mins | Ready in:

Ingredients

- 1 POUND beef sirloin steak OR BEEF TOP ROUND GET VERY THIN SLICES OR HAVE BUTCHER CUT VERY THIN
- 1 MEDIUM onion SEPARARTED INTO RINGS
- 1 TABLESPOON cooking oil
- 2/3 CUP BOTTLED OF YOUR FAVORITE BBQ SAUCE ME I THINK THE BEST IS HEAD COUNTRY BBQ FOUND IN PONCA CITY OKLAHOMA YOU CAN ORDER IT ON LINE IT IS THE BEST IVE

TASTED..
.....
- 1 TEASPOON lemon juice OR VINEGAR
- 4 HOAGIE buns, SPLIT AND toastED
- 4 SLICES jalapeno pepper JACK cheese, OR ANOTHER IF YOU DONT LIKE THIS ONE..............QUARTERED
- ******* OPTIONAL -YOU CAN ALSO TENDERIZED THE beef SOME BEFORE COOKING

Direction

- TRIM ANY SEPARABLE FAT FROM BEEF, CUT INTO BITE SIZE STRIPS OR CHUNKS
- IN A LARGE SKILLET COOK ONION IN HOT OIL OVER MEDIUM -HIGH HEAT ABOUT 3 MINUTES UNTIL ONIONS ARE TENDER
- ADD BEEF STRIPS OR CHUNKS.
- COOK AND STIR FOR 4- 5 MINUTES TO DESIRED DONENESS, AND IS TENDER.
- STIR IN BBQ SAUCE AND LEMON JUICE OR VINEGAR,
- COOK OVER MEDIUM HEAT UNTIL HEATED THROUGH, STIRRING OCCASIONALLY.
- SPPON BEEF MIXTURE OONTO THE HOAGIE BUN BOTTOMS.
- TOP WITH THE CHEESE AND PUT THE TOP OF HOAGIE ON AND SERVE.
- MAKES 4 SERVINGS

21. Beef Fajita Bowls Recipe

Serving: 4 | Prep: | Cook: 30mins | Ready in:

Ingredients

- 1 cup uncooked regular long-grain rice
- 1 pound boneless beef sirloin steak
- 2 tablespoons vegetable oil
- 1 flour tortilla for burritos (8 inch) (from 11.5-ounce package), cut into 4x1/2- inch strips

18

- 1 (1 pound) stir-fry bell peppers and onions
- 1/2 cup frozen whole kernel corn
- 1 cup Thick 'n chunky salsa
- 2 tablespoons lime juice
- 2 tablespoons chili sauce
- 1/2 teaspoon ground cumin
- 2 tablespoons chopped fresh cilantro

Direction

- 1. Cook rice as directed on package.
- 2. Meanwhile, cut beef with grain into 2-inch strips; cut strips across grain into 1/8-inch slices.
- 3. Heat 12-inch nonstick skillet over medium-high heat. Add oil; rotate skillet to coat bottom. Cook tortilla strips in oil 1 to 2 minutes on each side, adding additional oil if necessary, until golden brown and crisp. Drain on paper towel.
- 4. Add beef to skillet; cook and stir over medium-high heat 4 to 5 minutes or until beef is no longer pink. Remove from skillet.
- 5. Add bell pepper mixture and corn to skillet; cook and stir 1 minute. Cover and cook 2 to 3 minutes, stirring twice, until crisp-tender. Stir in beef, salsa, lime juice, chili sauce and cumin. Cook 2 to 3 minutes, stirring occasionally, until hot. Stir in cilantro. Divide rice among bowls. Top with beef mixture and tortilla strips.

22. Beef Sauerbraten From Germany Recipe

Serving: 8 | Prep: | Cook: 344mins | Ready in:

Ingredients

- 4 pounds beef Rump Or sirloin Tip
- 1-1/2 cup vinegar
- 1 cup Coca-Cola
- 3/4 cup water
- 3 medium Sliced onions
- 3 Stalks celery, Sliced
- 2 Sliced carrots
- 3 cup drippings Plus
- Strained marinade
- 8-10 Whole black peppers
- 2-3 whole cloves
- 1-2 bay leaves
- 2 tablespoon sugar
- 1-1/2 teaspoon salt
- flour
- 3 tablespoon oil
- 5 tablespoon flour
- 5 tablespoon ginger snap Cookie Crumbs
- Note: The recipe doesn't call for garlic but I like to mince 2 garlic cloves and toss them in.

Direction

- GRAVY:
- Two to three days before serving, wipe the meat with a damp cloth, then place in a large plastic bag. In a large bowl, thoroughly combine vinegar, Coca-Cola, water, onions, celery, carrots, pepper, cloves, bay leaves, sugar and salt; pour over meat.
- Fasten bag tightly and lay flat in a 9 X 13 pan.
- Refrigerate, turning bag each day. (If you like sour sauerbraten, allow it to marinate for 4 days.)
- When ready to cook, remove meat (saving marinade) and dry well.
- Rub the surface lightly with flour.
- In a Dutch oven, heat oil and slowly brown the meat well on all sides.
- Add 1 cup of the marinade liquid plus some of the vegetables and bay leaves.
- Cover tightly and simmer on surface heat or in a preheated 350 degrees F oven for 3 to 4 hours until the meat is fork tender.
- If needed, add more marinade during the cooking time to keep at least 1/2 inch liquid in the Dutch oven.
- Remove the meat and keep warm until ready to slice.
- Into a large measuring cup, strain the drippings.
- Add several ice cubes and let stand for a few minutes until the fat separates out.

- Remove the fat, then make the gravy.
- TO MAKE THE GRAVY:
- In the Dutch oven, combine the gravy ingredients, stir and cook for about 5 minutes over medium heat until gravy has thickened.
- Taste for seasonings and adjust if necessary.
- This makes about 3 cups of gravy.

23. Beef Souvlaki Recipe

Serving: 4 | Prep: | Cook: 10mins | Ready in:

Ingredients

- beef Souvlaki
- +
- 1 lb. sirloin tip steaks or round steaks
- 2 teaspoons dried oregano
- 2 teaspoons minced garlic
- 1/2 teaspoon ground black pepper
- 2 teaspoons oil
- 1/4 cup lemon juice
- Sauce:
- 1/3 cup plain yogurt
- 1/2 teaspoon dried dill
- 1 teaspoon red wine vinegar
- 1 teaspoon minced garlic

Direction

- Combine spices and oil and press into meat of both sides. Cut meat into 1-inch cubes and toss with lemon juice and let stand for 5 minutes. Thread on skewers. Broil or grill for about 5 minutes, turning once. Do not overcook. Combine sauce ingredients and serve with Souvlaki.

24. Beef Steak And Vegetables In Fresh Corn Tortillas Recipe

Serving: 3 | Prep: | Cook: 15mins | Ready in:

Ingredients

- Ingredients
- corn tortillas
- 2 cups / 300g masa harina
- 1 1/3 cup water
- steak and vegetables
- 7 oz / 200g beef steak (e.g. 1 new york strip steak)
- ¼ tsp dried ground cumin
- freshly ground black pepper
- 1 tbsp olive oil
- 2 tbsp brown sugar
- 1 onion, coarsely chopped
- 2 fresh poblano peppers (often sold as pasilla peppers), cut into ½ in / 1cm pieces
- 1 red bell pepper, cut into ½ in / 1cm pieces
- 2 plum tomatoes, cut into ½ in / 1cm pieces
- 1/8 tsp cumin
- ¼ tsp salt or to taste
- ¼ cup / 60ml white wine
- ½ cup / handful cilantro, coarsely chopped
- a few cilantro leaves as garnish

Direction

- Corn Tortillas:
- 1. Combine masa harina with water. Mix well until you get a smooth dough. Add water in tablespoon increments if necessary.
- 2. Divide dough into 6 equal parts. Shape each part into a ball.
- 3. Use a tortilla press to make tortillas. I find it works best to press the tortillas between two sheets of parchment paper (most instructions seem to recommend plastic foil but I find that too flimsy).
- 4. Carefully peel each tortilla off the parchment paper.
- 5. Place on ungreased hot cast iron griddle (or in a cast iron pan).
- 6. Cook ca. 30s from one side, flip over, cook for 60s, flip back and cook for another 30s.
- 7. Keep tortillas warm (in oven set to low temperature or wrapped in a clean kitchen towel)
- 8. Repeat until all tortillas have been made

- Steak, Vegetables and Assembling the Tortillas:
- 1. Sprinkle steak with freshly ground pepper and cumin.
- 2. Place heavy fry pan over medium-high heat. Add olive oil. Cook steak until done, ca. 6 minutes per side for medium-rare. Remove steak from pan and set aside.
- 3. Place heave sauté pan over medium-high heat. Add olive oil and brown sugar. Cook until the sugar starts to darken.
- 4. Add onion, cook until onion starts to brown. Add poblano and bell peppers, chopped tomato and ground cumin. Cook until the peppers start to soften, stir frequently.
- 5. Add salt and white wine. Cook until liquid has mostly evaporated. Adjust seasoning with salt and freshly ground black pepper.
- 6. Stir in chopped cilantro.
- 7. Cut steak into thin slices. For all six tortillas, place steak and vegetable mix on one half of a tortilla. Fold over. Garnish with a few cilantro leaves. Serve.
- I find freshly prepared corn tortillas to be a real treat. They are most easily shaped with a tortilla press. I have an 8in (ca. 20cm) press which is available from many sources for less than $20.
- Yields 6 tortillas

25. Beef Stroganoff Recipe

Serving: 6 | Prep: | Cook: 45mins |Ready in:

Ingredients

- 1 lb round steak
- 1/2 cup chopped onions
- 1-2 cans cream of mushroom soup
- 1/4 cup water
- 2 cups cooked egg noodles
- 2 tblsp margarine
- 1/2 cup sour cream

Direction

- Cut steak into thin strips
- Brown steak and onion in butter
- Stir in soup, water and sour cream
- Cover and cook over low heat for 45 mins (or until tender)
- Stir often
- Serve over cooked noodles

26. Beef Stroganoff Sandwich Ci Recipe

Serving: 6 | Prep: | Cook: 20mins |Ready in:

Ingredients

- 2lb round steak("cubed" at the supermarket or butcher, or very thoroughly tenderized at home), and sliced into 1in pieces
- 1 onion, thinly sliced
- 3-4 cloves garlic, minced
- 12oz fresh mushrooms, sliced
- 1/2 cup beef stock
- 2t worcestershire sauce
- 2t dijon
- 1t paprika
- 1/2 cup flour
- 2T butter
- 2T olive oil
- salt and pepper
- 1/4 cup fresh parsley, chopped
- 1/2 cup milk or half and half
- 8oz sour cream
- 8 slices mild white cheese(swiss, jack, farmer's, etc)
- 1 large loaf, or 2 small loaves, baked ciabatta bread
- 2T butter, melted

Direction

- Slice bread into 8 equal portions, then cut each portion through the middle to create sandwich halves.

- Brush inside of each half with melted butter and place in 250 oven to "toast" while preparing meat.
- Combine flour, salt, pepper and paprika in large bowl.
- Add meat and toss to coat.
- In LARGE skillet, brown meat in butter and oil and add garlic, onions and mushrooms about halfway through.
- When cooked, add beef stock and bring to boil, stirring often so as to prevent any lumps.
- Add milk, Worcestershire sauce, Dijon and parsley and continue to cook to thicken and heat through. Add more salt and pepper, if needed
- Add sour cream and mix to combine.
- Top half of bread with a slice of cheese then spoon on the meat mixture. Top with remaining bread pieces.

27. Beef Strogonoff Recipe

Serving: 6 | Prep: | Cook: 30mins | Ready in:

Ingredients

- 3 Tbs. olive oil
- 1-1/2 lb. top sirloin, cut into thin strips about 1" wide and 2" long
- salt and freshly ground pepper, to taste
- 3 Tbs. unsalted butter
- 4 green onions, sliced in 1/4" pieces or 1/2 cup yellow sweet onion
- 1 lb. cremini mushrooms, brushed clean and sliced
- 1 Tbs. Worchestershire sauce
- 2 Tbs. all-purpose flour
- 2-1/4 cups beef stock
- 1/3 cup crème fraîche or sour cream
- 2 tsp. Dijon mustard
- 2 tsp. fresh lemon juice
- Finely chopped fresh flat-leaf parsley for garnish
- wide egg noodles

Direction

- In a large fry pan over high heat, warm 1 Tbs. of the olive oil. Pat the beef dry with paper towels and season with salt and pepper. Add half of the beef strips (do not overcrowd the pan) and sauté until nicely browned but still a little pinkish on both sides, about 1 minute per side. Transfer to a bowl. Repeat with 1 Tbs. of the oil and the remaining meat.
- In the same pan over medium heat, melt the butter with the remaining 1 Tbs. oil. Add the green or yellow onions and sauté until softened and lightly browned, about 5 minutes. Add the mushrooms and sauté until nicely browned, about 5 minutes more. Season with salt and pepper.
- Stir in the Worcestershire sauce and cook until blended in, about 1 minute. Sprinkle the flour over the vegetables and stir to incorporate. Increase the heat to high, add the stock and bring to a boil, stirring with a wooden spoon to scrape up the browned bits from the pan bottom. Boil for 1 minute, then reduce the heat to medium. Add the crème fraiche or sour cream, mustard and lemon juice and cook for 1 minute more to allow the flavors to blend. Taste and adjust the seasonings.
- Return the meat and any accumulated juices to the pan and cook just until the beef is heated through, about 2 minutes. Garnish with parsley and serve immediately. Serves 6.
- Serving Tip: Stroganoff, though not technically a braise, has a similar consistency when finished. It is traditionally served over wide egg noodles.

28. Beef Tapa Recipe

Serving: 0 | Prep: | Cook: 30mins | Ready in:

Ingredients

- 1 kilo beef tenderloin or sirloin, cut into strips
- white vinegar

- sugar
- salt
- pepper
- soy sauce
- oil for frying

Direction

- Combine ingredients in a large bowl. Use your hands to mix evenly. Marinate for 30 minutes.
- Heat the pan in low heat, add the crushed garlic and fry it until it turns golden brown. Set aside.
- In the same pan, add the beef and fry it over medium high heat. Adjust the heat until beef turns brown. Add roasted garlic on top.
- Garnish with chives or spring onions.

29. Beef Tips With Mushrooms Recipe

Serving: 4 | Prep: | Cook: 60mins |Ready in:

Ingredients

- 1 1/4 lb sirloin, cubed 1 inch
- 1 clove garlic, minced or pressed
- 1 1/2 lb fresh mushrooms, sliced
- 2/3 cup beef broth
- 1 cup dry red wine
- 2 tsp soy sauce
- 2 tsp Dijon style mustard
- 2 tsp cornstarch
- 1 cup whipping cream
- chopped parsley

Direction

- Heat wide skillet, with a little oil in it, and brown the meat. Add the garlic, stir for a few minutes and remove all the meat and garlic to a casserole with cover.
- Add 1/2 cup of red wine to skillet and sauté the mushrooms till slightly wilted. Pour over

the meat in the casserole dish. Cover and bake at 275 degrees for one hour.
- Meanwhile, add broth, remaining wine and soy sauce to the skillet and bring to a boil, scraping up anything stuck to the pan. Boil till reduced by half - about 10 min. In another bowl, mix the cream, mustard and cornstarch; add this to the skillet; boil till thick.
- Remove casserole from oven, pour off any juices into the cream sauce and whisk till smooth. Add the meat back into the skillet and mix well, serve over rice or noodles sprinkled with parsley.

30. Beef And Snow Peas Recipe

Serving: 4 | Prep: | Cook: 10mins |Ready in:

Ingredients

- 3 tablespoons soy sauce
- 2 tablespoons rice wine
- 1 tablespoon brown sugar
- 1/2 teaspoon cornstarch
- 1 tablespoon vegetable oil
- 1 tablespoon minced fresh ginger root
- 1 tablespoon minced garlic
- 1 pound beef round steak, cut into thin strips
- 8 ounces snow peas
- 1 small can of waterchestnuts
- Your favorite white rice cooked
- sesame seeds

Direction

- In a small bowl, combine the soy sauce, rice wine, brown sugar and cornstarch. Set aside.
- Heat oil in a wok or skillet over medium high heat. Stir-fry ginger and garlic for 30 seconds. Add the steak and stir-fry for 2 minutes or until evenly browned. Add the snow peas and stir-fry for an additional 3 minutes. Add the soy sauce mixture and water chestnuts, bring to a boil, stirring constantly. Lower heat and simmer until the sauce is thick and smooth.

Place large scoop of rice in a bowl, a scoop of beef and snow peas on top and sprinkle with sesame seeds. Serve!

31. Beefy Stroganoff Recipe

Serving: 6 | Prep: | Cook: 45mins | Ready in:

Ingredients

- 2 lbs.(1kg) beef tenderloin or top sirloin grilling steak
- Note: I also like using beef short ribs
- 1/2 tsp.(2 mL) salt
- 1/4 tsp.(1 mL) freshly ground black pepper
- 1/2 cup(125 mL) all-purpose flour
- 1/2 cup(125 mL) butter, divided
- 2 tbsp.(30 mL) olive oil
- 2 onions, chopped
- 2 garlic cloves, minced
- 8 oz.(250 g) mushrooms, halved (optional)
- 1 cup(250 mL) beef stock
- 1 cup(250 mL) sour cream
- salt and freshly ground black pepper
- Serve over egg noodles or a pasta of your choice
- *Fresh chopped parsley. spring onions or chives to sprinkle overtop.

Direction

- Cut beef into thin strips or if using short ribs cut between the ribs.
- Sprinkle with salt and pepper.
- In a bag, working in batches, shake beef strips in flour.
- Discard excess flour.
- Set beef aside.
- In a large skillet, melt 2 Tbsp. (30 mL) of the butter over medium-high heat.
- Cook onions, stirring, until softened and browned.
- Transfer to large pot.
- In same skillet, melt some of the remaining butter and half of the oil over medium heat.

- In small batches, brown beef, stirring constantly, adding more of the butter and oil between batches as necessary.
- Transfer beef to pot with onions and garlic.
- If using mushrooms, add to skillet and cook, stirring, until browned. Add to beef mixture.
- Pour stock into pot and bring to boil over medium-high heat, stirring often.
- Reduce heat and simmer for about 5 minutes or until sauce thickens slightly.
- Stir in sour cream and cook, stirring, just until heated through. Season to taste with salt and pepper.
- Makes 6 servings.

32. Bengal Chili Best Youll Ever Have Recipe

Serving: 6 | Prep: | Cook: 240mins | Ready in:

Ingredients

- 1 Tbsp olive oil
- 2 1/2 lb ground sirloin
- 1 can (46 oz) tomato juice
- 1 can (15 oz) tomato sauce
- 1 cup water
- 4 Tbsp instant minced onion
- 4 Tbsp chili powder
- 4 Tbsp celery flakes
- 2 tsp salt
- 1 tsp oregano leaves
- 1 Tbsp garlic powder
- 1 tsp ground cumin
- 1 tsp powdered mustard
- 1/2 tsp curry powder
- 1/2 tsp garlic salt
- 1/4 tsp ground red pepper
- 2 cans (4 oz) green chilies (mild), drained/chopped
- 1/2 tsp chopped, canned hot jalapeno peppers (opt)

Direction

- In a large pot, heat oil until hot. Add beef; cook and stir until browned, about 10 minutes.
- Add tomato juice, tomato sauce, water, onion, chili powder, celery flakes, salt, oregano, garlic powder, cumin, mustard, curry, garlic salt, red pepper, green chilies and hot peppers.
- Bring this all to a boil. Reduce heat and simmer.
- Cover, cook stirring frequently, until flavors are well blended; cooking about 3 1/2 to 4 hours.
- This is great served alone in bowls, served over rice and even fantastic served over spaghetti.

33. Best Bacon Cheeseburgers Ever Recipe

Serving: 8 | Prep: | Cook: 25mins | Ready in:

Ingredients

- 1 lb bacon, fried and crumbled
- 2 cups shredded havaarti cheese
- 2 cups shredded swiss cheese (or any cheeses that melt well)
- 3 lbs. ground sirloin, 85 % lean
- 1 envelope beefy oinion soup mix
- 2 T. chopped garlic
- 4 T. worcestershire sauce
- 2 T. Heinz 57 Sauce
- fresh ground black pepper
- 1/4 c. grated parmesan cheese
- 2 eggs
- 1 loaf of french or Italian bread, sliced thick, on the bias into 16 slices
- melted butter
- avacado slices
- thick, ripe red tomato slices
- red onion slices
- green leaf or romaine lettuce
- herbed Mayo (Real Mayo, garlic, chives & dill)

Direction

- The night before, or the morning of meal, combine herbs & mayo, cover and chill.
- Fry bacon and crumble.
- Mix with cheese.
- Mold 8 patties, squeezing together to make them hold.
- Wrap each in plastic wrap and place in the freezer.
- 1 hour before cooking, combine remaining ingredients from meat to eggs by hand in large mixing bowl.
- Form into 8 large patties.
- Place one cheese/bacon patty on top of each meat patty.
- Work meat around the cheese patty until it is submerged in the center of the meat, and completely covered.
- Allow patties to come to room temperature.
- Place on lightly oiled grill rack.
- Turn only once, halfway through cooking.
- Cook to internal temperature of 160.
- Lightly brush melted butter on bread and grill.
- Serve burgers with herbed mayo, avocado, tomato, onion, and lettuce.
- Good kosher deli pickles and oven roasted red potatoes make great accompaniments.

34. Best Grilled Pork Chops Recipe

Serving: 6 | Prep: | Cook: 20mins | Ready in:

Ingredients

- 1/2c. water
- 1/3c. light soy sauce
- 1/4c. vegetable oil
- 3T. lemon pepper seasoning
- 2 cloves of garlic,minced
- 6 pork chops,fat removed

Direction

- In a deep bowl, mix all marinade ingredients
- Marinate at least 2 hours

- Remove from marinade and cook over medium heat on greased grill for 15 mins. Or till done. Baste with the marinade

35. Bi Bim Bap Recipe

Serving: 8 | Prep: | Cook: 8mins | Ready in:

Ingredients

- 12 oz bean sprouts
- 1/4 c sliced white scallions
- 1/2 c sugar
- 2 T sugar
- 12 oz carrots, julienned
- 1 c soy sauce
- 1 T water
- sesame oil, to taste
- 1/4 c garlic, minced
- 6-8 eggs
- 1 T mild oil for stir-frying
- 12 oz cucumbers, julienned
- 6 c cooked rice
- 3 T sesame seeds, toasted
- salt & pepper to taste
- 1/4 - 1 c red chili bean paste (kochujang)
- 1/2 pound chicken breasts
- 1 pound top round steak

Direction

- Make a marinade by combining the soy sauce, scallion, garlic, sesame seeds, 1/2 cup sugar, and salt & pepper to taste.
- Cut the chicken and beef into small pieces.
- Marinate the meat & chicken in the marinade at least 2 hours in the refrigerator.
- Sprinkle the carrots and cucumbers with salt, set aside for 5 minutes to draw some water out of them. Rinse and dry.
- Stir fry the carrots, cucumbers and bean sprouts briefly. Set aside.
- Stir fry the chicken and beef until done.
- Combine the red chili bean paste, 2 T sugar, 1 T water and sesame oil to taste in a small pan.

Bring to a boil, stirring, then reduce heat and cook 3-5 minutes.
- Fry the eggs over-easy or over medium, to your taste.
- Arrange a mound of rice in the middle of each serving dish. Ideally, this would be a piping hot stone or cast iron bowl, alternative any deep sided vessel will do.
- Arrange the vegetables and meat around the rice.
- Top each serving with an egg.
- Place a bit of the Kochujang sauce on a small plate or bowl for each diner.
- To eat, all the ingredients are thoroughly mixed together at the table, with each person adding the Kochujang sauce to his or her own taste.

36. BistekPhilippine Style Recipe

Serving: 34 | Prep: | Cook: 15mins | Ready in:

Ingredients

- 2 pounds sirloin steak,cut into 1/4-inch pieces
- 2 tablespoons lemin juice
- 3 tablespoons soy sauce
- 1/2 teaspoon freshly ground pepper
- salt to taste
- 1 cup thinly sliced onion rings
- 1/4 cup cooking oil
- 1/2 cup water

Direction

- Marinate the meat in lemon juice, soy sauce, pepper and salt for 1 hour or more.
- Cook onion rings in oil until transparent. Transfer to a serving dish, leaving the oil in the skillet.
- Add the meat to the skillet and cook over high heat, stirring often, until tender.
- Transfer the meat to a serving dish. Add marinade and water to the skillet, simmer for

10 minutes and pour over the meat and onion rings.

37. Black Cherry Pork Chops Recipe

Serving: 2 | Prep: | Cook: 25mins | Ready in:

Ingredients

- 2 tblsp vegetable oil
- 4 (8 oZ) bone-in pork chops
- seasoning - salt and pepper
- 1/4 cp butter
- 3/4 cp sliced shallots
- 1 1/2 cps fresh black cherries, pitted and halved
- 2 tblsps red wine (table is fine)
- 1/4 cp beef stock
- 1/4 tsp dried rosemary leaves, crumbled

Direction

- Oven to 350 degrees F
- Prepare baking sheet with aluminum foil.
- Heat the vegetable oil over medium-high heat
- Season the pork chops with salt and pepper
- Brown pork chops in the hot oil (should be about 120 seconds each side)
- Place the pork chops on baking sheet.
- Bake until the pork chops are no longer pink in the centre (about 20 minutes).
- While baking, melt butter in the same skillet over medium heat
- Stir in shallot & cherries
- Cook until the shallot has begun to soften, about 120 seconds
- Mix in the red wine and beef stock and simmer
- Season with rosemary, and simmer until the sauce has reduced and thickened.
- Season to taste with salt & pepper before pouring over the pork chops to serve.

38. Bootheel Stove Top Roasted Pork Chops Recipe

Serving: 4 | Prep: | Cook: 120mins | Ready in:

Ingredients

- 6 to 8 center-cut thick pork chops
- A small bag of baby carrots, rinsed
- 1 cup broccoli, cut into small spears
- 1 medium yellow squash, diced, into 1-inch cubes
- 1 teaspoon cajun spice
- 2 teaspoons salt
- 2 heaping teaspoons corn starch
- 10 to 12 small new potatoes, rinsed
- 1 cup fresh green beans, cleaned and snapped
- 1 medium white onion, cut into wedges
- 6 ounces of beef broth
- 1 teaspoon garlic powder
- 2 tablespoons canola oil
- 2 tablespoons margarine
- 1/2 cup water

Direction

- Season pork chops with garlic powder, Cajun spice and 1 teaspoon of salt. Brown lightly in very hot skillet in 2 tablespoons canola oil. Transfer to large heavy pot. Reduce heat, cover with tight fitting lid and cook very slowly, turning pork chops every 30 minutes for first hour. Add potatoes, carrots, onion, green beans and beef broth.
- Bring back to simmer for 30 minutes. Add broccoli and squash in the last 10 minutes of cooking time. Total cooking time is 2 hours at 300 to 325 degrees. Center of pork chops must reach 160 degrees to be completely done. Sauté' mushrooms in 2 tablespoons margarine until lightly browned.
- Remove pork chops and vegetables from pot. Strain gravy; heat to boiling and add remaining salt. Add corn starch in 1/2 cup water. Mix well and add to gravy and bring

back to a boil until thickened. Arrange pork chops in the center of a platter. Arrange vegetables around edge, place mushrooms and pour gravy over the top of the entire dish.

39. Bourbon Glazed Pork Chops And Peaches Recipe

Serving: 4 | Prep: | Cook: 15mins |Ready in:

Ingredients

- 1/3 cup bourbon
- 1/4 cup honey
- 3 Tbsp low-sodium soy sauce
- 1 Tbsp vegetable or light olive oil
- 3/4 tsp ground ginger
- 1/4 tsp ground black pepper
- 1/4 tsp crushed red pepper flakes, or dash red hot pepper sauce, such as Frank's X-tra hot sauce.
- 4 thin loin pork chops (bone-in or I prefer boneless)
- 2 peaches, halved, pitted, and skinned

Direction

- In a shallow Tupperware (or other resealable) container, stir together the bourbon, honey, soy sauce, oil, ginger and black pepper and the pepper flakes or hot sauce.
- Add the pork chops and peaches and turn to coat. Cover and refrigerate for up to 2 hours.
- Preheat the grill (or place a grill pan over medium-high heat if cooking indoors). Clean and oil the grill grates well.
- Place the pork and peaches on the grill reserving the marinade. Cook, turning once, until nicely browned on both sides and cooked through, ~ 4 minutes per side.
- Meanwhile, in a saucepan on the side burner, (or indoors on the stovetop or in a microwave-safe bowl in the microwave) bring the marinade to a boil. Simmer briefly until marinade reduces slightly (have to kind of place this by sight and feel).
- Divide the pork and peaches evenly among individual plates and spoon the sauce over them.
- Serve Immediately.

40. Braggin Rights Chicken Fried Steak Recipe

Serving: 4 | Prep: | Cook: 20mins |Ready in:

Ingredients

- 2 pounds round steak, sliced 1/2 inch thick and twice-tenderized by the butcher
- 2 cups all-purpose flour
- 2 teaspoons baking powder
- 1 teaspoon baking soda
- 1 teaspoon fresh ground black pepper
- 3/4 teaspoon salt
- 1 1/2 cup buttermilk
- 1 large egg
- 1 teaspoon cayenne pepper
- 2 cloves garlic, minced
- Crisco for deep frying (I am sorry, I use lard)
- ***CLASSIC CREAM GRAVY***
- 1/4 cup pan drippings
- 3 tablespoons all-purpose flour
- 2 cups evaporated milk
- 1 cup Unsalted beef stock
- 1/2 teaspoon fresh ground black pepper
- salt to taste
- ***OPTIONAL***
- mashed potatoes
- Homemade buttermilk biscuits
- .

Direction

- Cut steak into 4 equal portions.
- Pound until each is about 1/4 inch thick.
- Place flour in a shallow bowl.

- In a second dish, stir together baking powder, soda, pepper and salt; mix in buttermilk, egg, pepper sauce and garlic.
- The mixture will be thin.
- Dredge each steak first in flour, then in batter.
- Dunk steaks back into flour and dredge well, patting in the flour until the surface of the meat is dry.
- Add enough shortening (lard) [or a combination of both!] to a deep cast-iron skillet or Dutch oven to deep fry steaks in at least 3 inches of fat. Bring temperature of shortening to 325 degrees.
- Fry the steaks, pushing them under the fat or turning them as they bob to the surface, for 7 to 8 minutes, or until they are golden brown.
- Drain steaks on paper towels and transfer to a platter.
- Keep warm while preparing Classic Cream Gravy.
- Divide steaks among 4 plates and serve with mashed potatoes and gravy. .
- CLASSIC CREAM GRAVY:
- After cooking chicken-fried steak, pour off the top fat through a strainer, leaving about 1/2 cup pan drippings in the bottom of the skillet.
- Return any browned cracklings from the strainer to the skillet before starting the gravy.
- Place skillet over medium heat.
- Sprinkle in the flour, stirring to avoid lumps.
- Add milk and stock.
- Simmer until liquid is thickened and the raw flour taste is gone, about 3 minutes.
- Stir the gravy up from the bottom frequently, scraping up any browned bits.
- Season with pepper and salt.
- Makes about 3 cups.
- .

41. Broccoli Beef Stir Fry

Serving: 0 | Prep: | Cook: |Ready in:

Ingredients

- For the beef:
- 1 teaspoon soy sauce
- 1 teaspoon Chinese rice cooking wine or dry sherry
- 1/2 teaspoon cornstarch
- 1/8 teaspoon freshly ground black pepper
- 3/4 pound flank or sirloin, sliced thinly across the grain
- For the sauce:
- 2 tablespoons oyster sauce
- 1 teaspoon Chinese rice cooking wine or dry sherry
- 1 tablespoon soy sauce
- 1/4 cup chicken broth
- For the stir fry:
- 3/4 pound broccoli florets
- 2 tablespoons high-heat cooking oil
- 2 cloves garlic, very finely minced or pressed through a garlic press
- 1 teaspoon cornstarch, dissolved in 1 tablespoon water

Direction

- Marinate the beef: Stir together the beef marinade ingredients (1 teaspoon soy sauce, 1 teaspoon Chinese rice wine, 1/2 teaspoon cornstarch, 1/8 teaspoon black pepper) in a medium bowl.
- Add the beef slices and stir until coated. Let stand for 10 minutes.
- Prepare the sauce: Stir together the sauce ingredients (2 Tbsp. oyster sauce, 1 teaspoon Chinese rice wine, 1 teaspoon soy sauce, 1/4 cup chicken broth) in a small bowl.
- Blanch or steam the broccoli: Bring a pot of water to a boil. Add the broccoli and cook until tender-crisp, about 2 minutes. Drain thoroughly.
- Stir-fry the beef: Heat a large frying pan or wok over high heat until a bead of water sizzles and instantly evaporates upon contact. Add the cooking oil and swirl to coat.
- Add the beef and immediately spread the beef out all over the surface of the wok or pan in a single layer (preferably not touching).

- Let the beef fry undisturbed for 1 minute. Flip the beef slices over, add the garlic to the pan and fry for an additional 30 seconds to 1 minute until no longer pink.
- Add sauce, cornstarch, and broccoli: Pour in the sauce and the cornstarch slurry (1 teaspoon cornstarch dissolved in 1 tablespoon of water). Stir until the sauce boils and thickens, 30 seconds. Stir in the broccoli.
- Serve immediately: Serve the stir fry immediately, either on its own or over cooked rice.

42. Burgundy Beef Recipe

Serving: 6 | Prep: | Cook: 90mins | Ready in:

Ingredients

- 3 slices bacon cut into 2-inch pieces
- 3 pound beef round steak cut into 1-inch cubes
- 2 cups Burgundy wine
- 1/2 cup water
- 1 can condensed beef broth
- 1/2 teaspoon thyme leaves
- 1 garlic clove minced
- 1 bay leaf
- 16 small boiling onions
- 16 baby carrots
- 2 tablespoons butter softened
- 2 tablespoons flour
- 2 tablespoons chopped fresh parsley
- 8 cups hot cooked brown or white rice

Direction

- Preheat oven to 350. Use a skillet to pre fry bacon until crisp. Drain out liquid fat and set aside bacon on a paper towel covered plate. Brown beef in skillet and drain out liquid fat. Stir in wine, water, beef broth, thyme, garlic and bay leaf. Cover then bake at 350 for 2 hours stirring occasionally. Add bacon, onion and carrots. Cover and continue baking 1-1/2 hours stirring occasionally. Remove from

oven and take out bay leaf. Temporarily remove meat and vegetables into a side pot and keep warm. In small bowl combine butter and flour. Gradually add about 1/2 cup of the cooking liquid stirring until smooth. Add flour mixture to remaining liquid then cook over medium heat until mixture thickens stirring constantly. Add back meat and vegetables then heat thoroughly. Spoon into serving dish and sprinkle with parsley then serve over rice.

43. CEDAR SAGE PORK CHOPS WITH WHISKEY HONEY GLAZE Recipe

Serving: 4 | Prep: | Cook: 15mins | Ready in:

Ingredients

- 4 thick center cut pork chops, I prefer bone-in, but boneless works too
- sweet Hungarian paprika
- Hot Madras curry powder
- garlic powder
- kosher salt
- ¼ cup fresh sage leaves, I prefer pineapple sage
- olive oil spray
- 1 sweet onion cut in eighths
- 8 T. bourbon whiskey
- 2 T. honey
- Cedar plank

Direction

- Rinse pork chops. Place on a large plate. Sprinkle liberally with paprika, curry powder, garlic powder and a little salt. Spray with olive oil. Press half the sage leaves into pork. Turnover and do the other side. .Cover with plastic wrap and refrigerate 2-4 hours.
- Soak cedar plank thoroughly for 2-4 hours, turning occasionally to soak both sides.

- When ready to grill, remove chops from fridge. Prepare medium fire for direct cooking. Place chops on plank interspersed with onion wedges. Carefully place the plank on the grill. Combine the bourbon and honey. Spoon half the mixture over the chops. Grill, covered, without turning about 10 minutes. Add the rest of the glaze. Cook an additional 5 minutes or so. Meat should be just off medium rare, and onions should be soft.

44. CHICKEN ATOP RICE Recipe

Serving: 56 | Prep: | Cook: 1mins | Ready in:

Ingredients

- 1 ¼ cup rice uncooked (long grain regular)
- 2 tablespoons chopped onion (optional)
- ½ teaspoon salt
- 1 stick celery, chopped (optional)
- 2 cups water
- 1 (10 ounce) can cream of chicken soup
- 2 ½ or 3 pounds of chicken breast or pork chops
- 2 tablespoons butter, melted
- ½ teaspoon salt
- ½ teaspoon paprika (optional)

Direction

- Heat oven to 375 degrees. In a 9x13 inch baking pan combine first seven ingredients, mix well. Arrange meat on rice mixture skin side up. Drizzle with the butter. Sprinkle with salt and paprika. Bake uncovered for 1 hour.
- For pork chops brown chops arrange on rice mixture and omit butter.
- Makes 5 to 6 servings.

45. CUBE STEAKS WITH GRAVY Recipe

Serving: 6 | Prep: | Cook: 68mins | Ready in:

Ingredients

- 1/3-cup flour
- 6 beef cube steaks
- 1-tablespoon vegetable oil
- 1 large onion, sliced and separated into rings
- 3 cups water, divided
- 1 envelope brown gravy mix
- 1 envelope mushroom gravy mix
- 1 envelope onion gravy mix

Direction

- Place flour in a large resalable plastic bag. Add the steaks a few at a time, and shake until completely coated. In a skillet, cook the steaks in oil until lightly browned on each side. Transfer to a slow cooker. Add the onion and 2 cups water. Cover and cook on low for 8 hours or until meat is tender. In a bowl, whisk together gravy mixes with remaining water. Add to the slow cooker; cook 30 minutes longer. Serve over mashed potatoes or noodles. If the gravy is too thick just add more water.

46. Cajun Pork Fingers Recipe

Serving: 2 | Prep: | Cook: 10mins | Ready in:

Ingredients

- 3-4 Boneless Top Loin pork chops
- 2 large eggs
- ½ cup of milk
- 4 tablespoons of Donnie's cajun seasoning Mix (or equivalent ingredients) (recipe found on my recipe page)
- 1 ½ cups of Bisquick
- salt to taste

- 1 quart and 1 gallon ziploc bag
- vegetable oil, enough to cover the bottom of pan by at least 1 ½ inch
- 1 heavy pot or pan for frying. (I use my 5 qt enamel coated cast iron Dutch oven)
- Plate lined with 3-4 paper towels

Direction

- Remove all fat from pork chops.
- Cut (lengthwise) into strips ½ - ¾ inch by the thickness of the chops.
- Wash and pat dry the strips.
- In a bowl, whisk the eggs, milk and 1 tablespoon of the seasoning mix until blended well.
- Put the egg mixture and all of the pork fingers into the quart size Ziploc bag and put onto the refrigerator for ½ hour.
- Remove from the refrigerator and allow to come to room temp. For ½ hour.
- In a bowl, whisk the Bisquick and remanding seasoning mix well, and then put into the gallon Ziploc bag.
- Remove the pork fingers one at a time from the egg mixture (shaking off excess egg mixture) and place into the gallon Ziploc bag.
- Seal bag and shake well so that all of the pork fingers are covered well with Bisquick.
- Put the oil in the pot and heat on medium-high. (Do not smoke the oil)
- Remove pork fingers from bag (shaking off excess Bisquick) and put into the oil. Do not crowd pork fingers in the oil. (Several batches will have to be done.)
- Using tongs, turn pork fingers frequently until golden brown. (This will happen in less than two to five minutes)
- Remove the pork fingers from the oil and lay on a plate covered with paper towels to allow the oil to drain.
- Sprinkle with salt.
- Enjoy!

47. Caramel Apple Pork Chops Recipe

Serving: 4 | Prep: | Cook: 10mins | Ready in:

Ingredients

- 4 boneless pork loin chops
- 1 teaspoon oil
- 2 tablespoons brown sugar
- 1 teaspoon salt
- 1 teaspoon freshly ground black pepper
- 1/8 teaspoon cinnamon
- 1/8 teaspoon ground nutmeg
- 2 tablespoons butter
- 2 medium tart red apples cored and sliced into 1/2 inch wedges
- 3 tablespoons chopped pecans

Direction

- Heat skillet over medium high heat.
- Brush chops lightly with oil and cook for 6 minutes turning occasionally until evenly browned.
- Remove and keep warm.
- In a small bowl combine brown sugar, salt, pepper, cinnamon and nutmeg.
- Add butter to skillet then stir in brown sugar mixture and apples.
- Cover and cook 4 minutes then remove apples with a slotted spoon and arrange on top of chops and keep warm.
- Continue cooking mixture in skillet uncovered until sauce thickens slightly.
- Spoon sauce over apples and chops.
- Sprinkle with pecans.

48. Caramel Apple Pork Recipe

Serving: 4 | Prep: | Cook: 20mins | Ready in:

Ingredients

- 4 thick pork chops

- 1 teaspoon vegetable oil
- 3 tablespoons brown sugar
- salt and pepper to taste
- 1/8 teaspoon ground cinnamon
- 1/8 teaspoon ground nutmeg
- 2 tablespoons unsalted butter
- 2 tart apples - peeled, cored and sliced
- 1/4 c pecans

Direction

- Preheat oven to 175°F. Place a medium dish in the oven to warm. Heat a large skillet over medium-high heat. Brush chops lightly with oil, and place in hot pan. Cook for 5 to 6 minutes each side, turning occasionally, until evenly browned. Transfer to the warm dish, and keep warm in the preheated oven. In a small bowl, combine brown sugar, salt and pepper, cinnamon and nutmeg. Add butter to skillet, and stir in brown sugar mixture and apples. Cover, and cook for 3 to 4 minutes, or just until apples are tender. Remove apples with a slotted spoon, and arrange on top of chops. Keep warm in the preheated oven. Continue cooking mixture uncovered in skillet, until sauce thickens slightly. Spoon sauce over apples and chops. Sprinkle with pecans

49. Carmel Apple Pork Chops Recipe

Serving: 4 | Prep: | Cook: 25mins | Ready in:

Ingredients

- 4 (3/4 inch) thick pork chops
- 1 teaspoon vegetable oil
- 2 tablespoons brown sugar
- salt and pepper to taste
- 1/8 teaspoon ground cinnamon
- 1/8 teaspoon ground nutmeg
- 2 tablespoons unsalted butter
- 2 tart apples - peeled, cored and sliced

- 3 tablespoons pecans (optional)

Direction

- Preheat oven to 175 degrees F (80 degrees C).
- Place a medium dish in the oven to warm.
- Heat a large skillet over medium-high heat.
- Brush chops lightly with oil and place in hot pan.
- Cook for 5 to 6 minutes, turning occasionally, or until done.
- Transfer to the warm dish, and keep warm in the preheated oven.
- In a small bowl, combine brown sugar, salt and pepper, cinnamon and nutmeg.
- Add butter to skillet, and stir in brown sugar mixture and apples. Cover and cook until apples are just tender.
- Remove apples with a slotted spoon and arrange on top of chops. Keep warm in the preheated oven.
- Continue cooking sauce uncovered in skillet, until thickened slightly. Spoon sauce over apples and chops.
- Sprinkle with pecans.

50. Carne Asada Tacos Recipe

Serving: 6 | Prep: | Cook: 45mins | Ready in:

Ingredients

- 1-1/2 lb boneless beef top sirloin,cut in thin bite-size slices
- 1/2 tsp salt
- 1` tsp fresh ground black pepper
- crushed red pepper to taste
- 2 limes
- 1 (28 oz.)can tomatillos
- 2 fresh jalapeno peppers,seeded
- 4 Tbs canola oil,divided
- 1 (10.5 oz) can beef broth
- 12 (6") corn tortillas
- 1/2 large onion,chopped
- 2 tomatoes,chopped

- 1 avocado,peeled,pitted and sliced
- 1 bunch fresh cilantro,chopped

Direction

- Place sliced meat into shallow bowl and season with salt, black pepper and crushed red pepper. Squeeze lime juice (from 1 lime) over the meat and turn till evenly coated. Cover, refrigerate 30 mins.
- In blender, combine tomatillo and jalapeno. Puree 15 to 20 seconds, or till thick. Heat 1 Tbsp. oil in large skillet over med-high heat. Carefully pour in tomatillo mixture. Cook, stirring frequently for 5 mins. Stir in beef broth. Reduce heat and simmer 20 to 30 mins or till mixture coats a spoon. Transfer mixture to serving dish.
- Heat Tbsp. oil in large skillet over high heat. Stir in 1/3 beef and sauté 1 mon. Transfer to serving dish. Repeat with remaining beef. Meanwhile, heat tortillas in oven or microwave.
- To serve, place 2 Tortillas on top of each other. Add desired amt. of meat, spoon over some tomatillo mixture. Top with onions, tomatoes, avocado and cilantro. Garnish with a wedge of lime, to be squeezed over taco before eating.
- Note: Sometimes instead of making tomatillo mixture, I use a 16 oz. jar of La Victoria Salsa Verde to make it even easier.

51. Carne Asada Y Naranjas

Serving: 46 | Prep: | Cook: 15mins |Ready in:

Ingredients

- 2 pounds beef, skirt steak
- 3 cups orange juice
- 4 ea Oranges, cut oranges cut into 1/2 inch slices

Direction

- Pound meat with side of saucer to tenderize, if needed.
- Cut meat into serving pieces.
- Place steaks in bowl; pour orange juice over meat.
- Marinate at room temperature 3 hours or in refrigerator overnight.
- Drain marinade and reserve.
- Grill meat and orange slices over hot charcoal to taste.
- Heat orange juice marinade; serve as sauce.

52. Cast Iron Skillet Chicken Fried Steak Recipe

Serving: 8 | Prep: | Cook: 35mins |Ready in:

Ingredients

- 5 lbs top or bottom round of beef, sliced 1/2 inch thick in serving size pieces
- 3 cups milk
- salt and freshly ground pepper
- 5 cups all purpose flour
- 2 eggs, lightly beaten
- 1 quart vegetable oil, for frying
- 2 cups heavy cream
- Large Cast Iron Skillet
- Meat Pounder

Direction

- In a shallow dish, steep the sliced steak in 2 cups of the milk for 1 hour.
- Drain and dry with paper towels.
- Season the meat with salt and pepper to taste on both sides.
- Sprinkle lightly with 2 tablespoons of the flour and pound to 1/4 inch with the meat pounder.
- In a shallow bowl, combine the eggs and the remaining cup of milk.
- Lightly dip the meat in the egg mixture.
- Dredge in the remaining flour, reserving 2 tablespoons, and dredge twice more, shaking away any excess.

- In a large cast iron skillet, pour in 1 inch of oil.
- Heat the oil until hot and fry the steak in batches until golden brown on each side. (The oil will have to be changed at least once for this amount of meat.)
- Continue frying until all the floured meat is cooked.
- When the meat is cooked, pour off all but 1 tablespoon of the oil.
- Off the heat, stir in 2 tablespoons flour and mix with the oil.
- Return to low heat and add the cream.
- Bring to a simmer, stirring constantly and scraping up the browned bits that cling to the bottom of the pan, until the cream thickens.
- Season to taste with salt and pepper and serve hot.

53. Cheese Stuffed Pork Chops Recipe

Serving: 4 | Prep: | Cook: 40mins | Ready in:

Ingredients

- 1/4 c sugar
- kosher salt
- 4 bone-in tghick pork chops(6 to 8 oz ea)
- 1/2 med head escarole
- 2 cloves garlic
- 4 Tbs extra vorgin olive oil,plus more for brushing
- ground pepper
- 4 slices provolone cheese(about 2 oz)
- 4 fresh sage leaves,chopped
- 1 19 oz can cannellini beans,drained and rinsed

Direction

- Dissolve 1/4 c salt and the sugar in 3 cups warm water in large bowl. Insert paring knife into curved side of each pork chop to make deep pocket, about 2 " wide. Soak the chops in the brine for about 5 mins.

- Meanwhile, finely chop the escarole and garlic. Toss with 2 tbsp. olive oil and salt and pepper to taste.
- Remove chops from brine; pat dry. Fold each cheese slice and tuck into the pocket of pork chop, then stuff with the escarole mixture. Brush the pork with olive oil, sprinkle with sage and season with salt and pepper.
- Heat remaining 2 tbsp. olive oil in large skillet over med-high heat. Sear the pork in batches, turning once, until golden brown, 3 to 4 mins. Transfer to plate. Add the beans and 1/3 c water to the skillet, scraping up browned bits; season with salt and pepper. Return pork to the skillet; cover and cook over med. heat until no longer ink, 5 to 7 mins more. Serve pork with beans.

54. Chef Als Three Layer Lasagna Bolognese Recipe

Serving: 10 | Prep: | Cook: 50mins | Ready in:

Ingredients

- 2 lbs ground round steak
- 1 lb bulk Italian pork sausage
- 6 strips bacon
- 1 medium yellow onion (chopped fine)
- 1 green bell pepper (chopped fine)
- 6 cloves garlic (minced)
- 2 Tbsp butter
- 2 Tbsp extra virgin olive oil
- 28 oz tomato sauce (2 cans)
- 14 oz Diced tomato (1 can)
- 1 lb 'NO BOIL' lasagna noodles
- 3 lbs ricotta cheese
- 1 lb mozzarella cheese (shredded)
- 1 1/2 cups parmesan cheese (grated)
- 2 large eggs (beaten)
- 3 Tbsp fresh basil leaves (chopped)
- 2 Tbsp black pepper (freshly ground)

Direction

- Fry Bacon until crispy, place on paper towel and set aside.
- Sauté Onion, Green Pepper and Garlic in Butter and Oil.
- Add Tomato Sauce and Diced Tomatoes. Simmer.
- In a separate pan, brown Ground Round and Italian Sausage.
- Drain and add to sauce. Continue to simmer.
- In a large mixing bowl, combine Ricotta, Mozzarella, Parmesan Cheeses, Eggs, Basil and Black Pepper.
- Mix well.
- In a 9x13 lasagna pan, place 1/2 of Meat Sauce on bottom.
- Cover Sauce with Lasagna Noodles (just as you would lasagna)
- Over Noodles, place all the Cheese Mixture.
- Cover Cheese with more Noodles.
- Top with remaining Meat Sauce.
- Crush crisped Bacon and sprinkle evenly over top layer of Meat Sauce.
- Cover sparsely with additional Parmesan Cheese.
- Cover with aluminum foil (tented).
- Bake in 450 degree oven for 40 min.
- Carefully remove foil and bake an additional 10 min.
- Remove from hot oven and cool 20-30 mins. before cutting and serving

55. Chicken Fried Pork Chops Crock Pot Recipe Recipe

Serving: 6 | Prep: | Cook: 480mins |Ready in:

Ingredients

- 1/2 c flour
- 2 tsp salt
- prepared mustard
- 1/2 tsp garlic powder
- 6 pork chops
- 2 tbsps olive oil

- 1 can cream of chicken or cream of celery soup
- 1/3 c water

Direction

- Mix up the flour, salt and garlic powder. Smear mustard on each side of the chops, just enough to cover lightly and then dredge in the dry ingredients. Heat a skillet and add the olive oil. Brown the chops on both sides. This step add the bits of goodness that you'll want in your gravy when it's all done. Put the chops in the crock pot. Mix the soup and water and pour over chops. Cover the crock pot and cook for 4 hours on high or 8 hours on low. Serve with mashed potatoes or rice or noodles. Add the crock pot juice as gravy. Thicken with some flour if needed, but usually it's not required for a nice gravy consistency.

56. Chicken Fried Steak Recipe

Serving: 2 | Prep: | Cook: 30mins |Ready in:

Ingredients

- 1 2lb. round steak 1/2- 3/4 inches thick
- flour
- chicken Fried steak Batter:
- 2 tbp. sugar
- 1/2 tsp. salt
- 2 eggs
- 1 tbs. baking powder
- 1 cup milk
- Gravy:
- 1 cup flour
- 1/2 stick butter
- 8 cups milk

Direction

- Prepare the Chicken Fried Steak batter: Mix the first 4 ingredients with 1/2 the milk and stir until smooth. Add remainder of milk and mix well

- Have the butcher tenderize the meat for you or thoroughly pound both sides with a tenderizing mallet
- Trim off fat and cut 2 pieces into 5-6 inches in diameter
- Flour each piece thoroughly and shake off excess
- Dip meat in the Chicken Fried Steak batter, drain
- Flour again
- Fill a large pan half way with a good vegetable oil 325 degrees
- Cook meat 7-10 minutes until golden brown
- To prepare the gravy:
- Use the pan used for cooking the meat
- Gradually add flour and the butter. Slowly add milk, stirring until desired thickness is achieved. Remove from heat
- Salt and pepper to taste

57. Chicken Fried Steak With Gravy Recipe

Serving: 4 | Prep: | Cook: 40mins | Ready in:

Ingredients

- 1 pound pork steak or cube steak
- 1 cup flour
- salt (to taste)
- pepper (to taste)
- paprika (to taste)
- garlic powder (to taste)
- dash of white pepper
- 2 eggs lightly beaten
- 1/4 cup milk
- oil for pan about 1/4 inch to 1/2 inch
- Gravy:
- 2 cups milk
- 1/2 cup flour
- dash of white pepper
- salt and pepper to taste

Direction

- Add oil to large pan and heat.
- Mix the milk and eggs together.
- Mix flour with salt, pepper, garlic powder, dash of white pepper-mix well.
- Salt and pepper each side of your meat, dip first into flour mixture then into egg and milk mixture, and once again into flour mixture-place in hot oil-cook until brown on both sides and juices are clear when pierced with fork.
- Repeat process for all your meat.
- Gravy:
- Drain off excess grease in pan except for about 3 tablespoons.
- Place your flour in grease, mix the flour and grease together to form a roux.* (roux is very important for a smooth gravy) keep stirring your roux for about 2 minutes-be careful not to burn.
- Carefully pour your milk into the roux and keep stirring constantly. Stir until gravy reaches desired thickness.
- Check seasoning at this point, add more salt and pepper and a couple dashes of white pepper.

58. Chicken Fried Pork Chops With Andouille Milk Gravy Over Buttermilk Mashed Potatoes Recipe

Serving: 4 | Prep: | Cook: 30mins | Ready in:

Ingredients

- 22 saltine crackers, finely crushed (or bread crumbs)
- 3/4 cup plus 2 tablespoons flour
- 1 teaspoon salt, divided, plus more for seasoning
- 3/4 teaspoon freshly ground black pepper, divided, plus more for seasoning
- 3/4 teaspoon Emeril's Original Essence, recipe follows
- 3/4 teaspoon baking powder

- 2 large eggs
- 3 cups plus 1/3 cup whole milk
- 8 boneless breakfast pork chops (small, thin cuts, about 1/4-inch thick each)
- 2 to 2 1/2 cups vegetable oil
- 8 ounces cooked and crumbled andouille sausage
- buttermilk mashed potatoes, recipe follows
- Emeril's ESSENCE creole seasoning (also referred to as Bayou Blast):
- 2 1/2 tablespoons paprika
- 2 tablespoons salt
- 2 tablespoons garlic powder
- 1 tablespoon black pepper
- 1 tablespoon onion powder
- 1 tablespoon cayenne pepper
- 1 tablespoon dried oregano
- 1 tablespoon dried thyme
- Combine all ingredients thoroughly.
- Yield: 2/3 cup
- Recipe from "New New Orleans Cooking", by Emeril Lagasse and Jessie Tirsch, published by William and Morrow, 1993.
- buttermilk Mashed Potatoes:
- 2 pounds idaho potatoes, peeled and cut into 1-inch pieces
- 1 1/4 cups buttermilk
- 4 tablespoons unsalted butter
- 1 teaspoon salt
- 1/4 teaspoon ground black pepper

Direction

- In a shallow bowl combine the crushed crackers, 3/4 cup of flour, 1/2 teaspoon salt, 1/4 teaspoon freshly ground black pepper, Essence, and baking powder.
- In a separate small bowl, whisk together the eggs and 1/3 cup of milk.
- Season pork chops lightly with salt and freshly ground pepper on both sides. Dust pork chops, one at a time, with the cracker-flour mixture and then dip in the egg mixture. Dredge pork chops with the cracker-flour mixture a second time, pressing to coat, and shaking off any excess flour.

- Heat the oil to 375 degrees F in a large skillet with 2-inch deep sides. (The oil should be about 1/4-inch deep.) Add the pork chops to the preheated oil, being careful not to over-crowd the pan. Pan-fry the chops for 2 minutes, or until golden brown. Turn the pork chops and cook an additional 2 to 3 minutes, or until golden brown and cooked through. Place the pork chops on a paper towel-lined plate and keep warm while you make the gravy.
- Carefully discard most of the oil from the pork chops, reserving 2 tablespoons plus any browned bits in the bottom of the skillet. Heat the oil over medium-low and add the Andouille sausage, stirring until warmed through and fragrant. Add the remaining 2 tablespoons of the flour to the oil-sausage mixture, stirring constantly to keep from burning, about 2 minutes. In a slow, steady stream, add the remaining 3 cups of milk, 1/2 cup at a time, whisking continuously. Bring the gravy mixture to a simmer, and cook 8 to 10 minutes, or until slightly thickened. Season the gravy with the remaining 1/2 teaspoon of salt and remaining 1/2 teaspoon freshly ground black pepper. Serve immediately over chicken fried pork chops and buttermilk mashed potatoes.
- Buttermilk Mashed Potatoes:
- Place the potatoes in a medium pot and cover with cold water by 1-inch. Bring to a boil, and reduce heat to medium-low. Simmer, uncovered, until the potatoes are fork tender, 15 to 20 minutes. Drain potatoes in a colander.
- Return the potatoes to the cooking pot and add the buttermilk, butter, salt, and black pepper. Mash with a potato masher or heavy fork until fluffy, about 4 minutes. Adjust seasonings with salt and pepper, to taste. Place potatoes in an ovenproof dish and cover with aluminum foil. Place mashed potatoes in a low (275 degree F) oven to keep warm until ready to serve with the pork chops.

59. Chili Recipe

Serving: 7 | Prep: | Cook: 140mins | Ready in:

Ingredients

- 1 lb of lean ground beef
- 3/4 lb of cubed beef sirloin
- 1 (14 1/2 oz) can of diced tomatoes
- 1 can of dark beer
- 1 cup of strong coffee
- 2 (6 oz) cans of tomato paste
- 4 (15 oz) cans of kidney beans
- 4 chopped chili pepper
- 2 tsp. of oil
- 2 chopped onions
- 1 can of of beef broth
- 1/2 c. of brown sugar
- 3 1/2 tbsp. of chili sauce
- 1 tbsp. of cumin
- 1 tbsp. of cocoa
- 1 tsp. of oregano
- 1 tsp. of cayenne
- 1 tsp. of coriander
- 1 tsp. of salt

Direction

- First take some olive oil in a medium pan over medium flame.
- Then add in the onions, garlic, and meat and cook until brown.
- Then add in the tomatoes, beer, coffee, tomato paste, and the beef broth.
- Now stir in the spices, plus the 2 cans of kidney beans and peppers.
- Let this simmer over a low flame for approx. 90 min.
- Then add in the last 2 cans of beans and simmer approx. 30 more min.
- Serve!

60. Chili Verde Recipe

Serving: 8 | Prep: | Cook: 180mins | Ready in:

Ingredients

- 1 teaspoon dried oregano, crumbled
- 1 tablespoon ground cumin
- 3 tablespoons green chile powder
- 19 oz can green enchilada sauce
- 32 ounces canned tomatillos with their liquid
- 7 oz can hat salsa verde
- 3 1/2 pounds pork sirloin, cubed
- lard or oil as needed to brown
- 2 cups onions, finely minced
- 1 1/2 tablespoons fresh garlic, pressed
- 2 pounds diced green chiles, fresh or frozen
- 2 cups mixed fresh green peppers, very finely minced
- 1 teaspoon lime juice
- 1/2 cup finely chopped cilantro leaves

Direction

- Combine powders. Combine enchilada sauce, tomatillos and salsa verde in a chili pot. Press tomatillos against the side of the pot to crush. Add powders to the liquids. Heat to boiling. Reduce heat and simmer, stirring frequently.
- Brown meat in lard or oil in batches with onions and pressed garlic. Drain meat and add to chili pot. Add diced green chiles. Return pot to simmer.
- After 2 hours, add half of finely minced green peppers. Add salt as desired. Taste and adjust, adding additional minced peppers as desired - simmer for 30 min. Thicken or thin as needed - simmer another 15 min. Adjust salt and other seasonings as needed, add lime juice and cilantro and just before serving.

61. Chipotle Beef Recipe

Serving: 6 | Prep: | Cook: 480mins | Ready in:

Ingredients

- 1 1/2 Lb boneless beef round steak or a small roast
- 1 14oz. can of diced tomatoes
- 1 med. red onion, diced
- 2 canned chipotle peppers in adobo sauce, chopped
- 1-2 tsp oregano
- 1 clove minced garlic
- dash of salt
- dash of cumin

Direction

- Trim fat from meat and set in your crock pot with all ingredients.
- Cook on low for 8-10 hours or high for 4-5 hours.
- Remove meat and shred with 2 forks.
- Stir in reserved juices - enough to moisten or make saucy.

62. Chorizo Pumpkin Pasta

Serving: 0 | Prep: | Cook: | Ready in:

Ingredients

- 3 cups uncooked gemelli or spiral pasta (about 12 ounces)
- 1 package (12 ounces) fully cooked chorizo chicken sausage links or flavor of choice, sliced
- 1 cup canned pumpkin
- 1 cup half-and-half cream
- 3/4 teaspoon salt
- 1/4 teaspoon pepper
- 1-1/2 cups shredded Manchego or Monterey Jack cheese
- Minced fresh cilantro, optional

Direction

- Cook pasta according to package directions. Drain, reserving 3/4 cup pasta water.

- Meanwhile, in a large skillet, saute sausage over medium heat until lightly browned; reduce heat to medium-low. Add pumpkin, cream, salt and pepper; cook and stir until heated through. Toss with pasta and enough pasta water to moisten; stir in cheese. If desired, sprinkle with cilantro.
- Nutrition Facts
- 1-1/3 cups: 471 calories, 20g fat (11g saturated fat), 92mg cholesterol, 847mg sodium, 48g carbohydrate (7g sugars, 3g fiber), 26g protein.

63. Cincinnati Bengal Chili Recipe

Serving: 10 | Prep: | Cook: 60mins | Ready in:

Ingredients

- 2 T butter
- 2 med. onions, finely chopped
- 6 cloves garlic, finely chopped
- 2 lbs. ground sirloin
- 1/4 c chili powder
- 1 t unsweetened cocoa powder
- 1 t ground cinnamon
- 1 t ground allspice
- 1 t ground cumin
- 2 c water
- 4 bay leaves
- 2 T cider vinegar
- 2 T honey
- 1 can red kidney beans, drained
- 1 lb elbow macaroni
- 2 T EVOO
- 1 T butter
- 2 c grated sharp cheddar cheese
- 1 c diced red onion

Direction

- Place large pot over medium heat.
- Melt butter.
- Add 2 med. onions (finely chopped) and cook until soft, about 5 min, stir often.
- Add garlic, cook 2 min.

- Increase heat to high and add meat.
- Cook until all pink disappears, stirring frequently and breaking meat up with spatula or back of spoon.
- Add chili powder, cocoa, cinnamon, allspice and cumin; cook 2 minutes stirring frequently.
- Add water, bay leaves, vinegar, and honey.
- Bring to a boil, reduce heat to low and simmer, covered, 45 minutes, stirring occasionally to keep bottom from scorching.
- Add beans and cook 15 minutes more.
- While chili is cooking, fill med. stovetop pot with water and salt generously with kosher salt.
- Bring to a boil.
- Add macaroni, EVOO and butter.
- Cook until al dente.
- Drain and rinse.
- Serve in bowls with pasta on bottom, chili, then cheddar cheese and diced red onion on top.
- *I like to add chopped tomato, black olives and sour cream.

64. Cinnamon Sirloin Chops With Peach Sauce Recipe

Serving: 4 | Prep: | Cook: 12mins | Ready in:

Ingredients

- 4 boneless pork sirloin chops, 1/2-inch thick
- 1 teaspoon vegetable oil
- 1/2 teaspoon paprika
- 1/2 teaspoon all-purpose flour
- 1/2 teaspoon salt
- 1/4 teaspoon ground cinnamon
- 1/4 teaspoon ground allspice
- 1/8 teaspoon ground cloves
- 1 teaspoon prepared mustard
- 1 (1-pound) can sliced peaches, drained

Direction

- Combine paprika, flour, salt, cinnamon, allspice and cloves.
- Sprinkle mixture on both sides of chops.
- Heat oil in a non-stick skillet over medium-high heat.
- Brown chops about 3 minutes per side, remove from skillet.
- Add peaches and mustard to pan, cook and stir, de-glazing by scraping up any brown bits from surface of pan.
- Return chops to pan, cover and simmer 5 minutes.
- Serves 4.

65. Classic Chicken Fried Steak And Gravy Ci Recipe

Serving: 4 | Prep: | Cook: 20mins | Ready in:

Ingredients

- 2lb round steak, trimmed, cut into serving size patties and thoroughly tenderized
- 1 1/2 cups flour
- 3-4 eggs(depending on size)
- salt(or your favorite seasoning salt blend with onion, garlic, etc)
- 1t cayenne pepper
- fresh ground black pepper
- 3T vegetable oil(olive or canola)
- 3T butter
- 3 cups chicken stock
- 1 cup milk or half and half
- 2T fresh parsley, chopped

Direction

- Season both sides of all steaks with salt (or blend) and black pepper.
- Beat eggs in large shallow pan or pie plate
- In another pie plate, combine flour with cayenne and more salt and pepper
- In large cast iron or other skillet, cover bottom with oil and bring to a medium-medium high heat

- Dredge steaks in egg, then flour mixture, then egg, then flour, again
- Let rest while oil comes to temperature.
- Fry steaks, 2 at a time on each side 4-5 minutes until golden brown.
- Drain on paper bags or over wire rack and keep warm while finishing all steaks and while making gravy.
- Once steaks are all browned and warming, add 3T of butter to pan and stir to combine. Add about 1/4 cup of left over flour from dredging to pan and whisk together.
- Add chicken stock SLOWLY to pan whisking entire time.
- Whisk over medium heat for about 5 minutes while flavours combine and gravy thickens.
- Add milk, slowly, then fresh ground black pepper and parsley and continue to stir to combine.
- Serve steaks topped with gravy.
- *this amount of gravy is assuming mashed taters will be served with steaks...if you don't, for some reason, you may want to cut the gravy ingredients in half.....or, just make the taters ;)

66. Coffee Glazed Lamb Chops Recipe

Serving: 8 | Prep: | Cook: 12mins | Ready in:

Ingredients

- For the glaze.
- 1/4 cup strong brewed coffee
- 2 Tbsp. molasses
- 2 Tbsp. apple cider vinegar
- 1 Tbsp. white or dark rum
- 1 tsp. garlic minced
- 1 tsp. instant espresso
- 1/2 tsp. ground cinnamon
- 1/4 tsp. ground allspice
- 1/4 tsp. red pepper flakes
- For the Lamb chops:

- 8 lamb rib or loin chops trimmed, seasoned with salt and pepper

Direction

- Boil glaze in a small skillet, reducing until syrupy, 1 to 2 minutes.
- Preheat the grill pan over high, when hot, reduce the heat to medium and coat with non-stick cooking spray.
- Brush lamb chops with glaze on one side, and then grill in batches or 4 chops, glazed side down, 4 to 5 minutes per side for medium. Glaze again, flip and grill the other side.
- Let chops rest for 5 minutes before serving.

67. Complete Pork Chop Dinner Recipe

Serving: 4 | Prep: | Cook: 35mins | Ready in:

Ingredients

- 4 pork loin chops (1/2 inch thick)
- 1 (10 3/4 oz) can of condensed cream of mushroom soup, undiluted
- 3 chopped medium red potatoes
- 2 c. of baby carrots
- 1 quartered onion
- 1 tbsp. of butter
- 1/4 c. of water

Direction

- First take a skillet over medium flame.
- Now melt the butter.
- Now add in the chops for 3 minutes on each side. Brown.
- Then add the potatoes, carrots and onion.
- In a small bowl add the soup and water; pour over chops.
- Put on a lid and cook for approx. 15 to 20 minutes letting veggies get tender.

68. Country Fried Steak Recipe

Serving: 4 | Prep: | Cook: 10mins | Ready in:

Ingredients

- Total preparation and cooking time: 20 minutes
- Servings: 4
- beef cubed steaks (about 1 pound)
- 2 egg whites, well beaten
- 2 tablespoons milk
- 2 tablespoons vegetable oil
- Prepared salsa, plain yogurt
- Coating:
- 1/2 cup unseasoned dry bread crumbs
- 1 tablespoon cornmeal
- 1/4 teaspoon salt
- 1/4 teaspoon pepper
- 1/2 teaspoon Spicy seasoning Mix (recipe follows):
- Spicy seasoning Mix: Combine 3 Tbs chili powder, 2 tsp ground cumin, 1-1/2 tsp garlic powder, 3/4 tsp dried oregano, 1/2 tsp ground red pepper in an airtight container. Shake before using.

Direction

- Combine egg whites and milk in shallow dish. Combine coating ingredients in second shallow dish. Dip beef steaks into egg white mixture, then into coating mixture, to coat both sides.
- Heat oil in large non-stick skillet over medium to medium high heat until hot. Place steaks in skillet; cook 5 to 6 minutes, turning once. Serve with salsa and yogurt.

69. Country Pork Chops With Sage Smashed Potatoes Recipe

Serving: 4 | Prep: | Cook: 20mins | Ready in:

Ingredients

- 4 medium potatoes cut into 1" chunks
- 1 tablespoon olive oil
- 1 large garlic clove pressed
- 4 pork chops
- 1-1/2 tablespoons butter
- 1/2 cup milk
- 1 teaspoon dried sage
- 1 teaspoon salt
- 1 teaspoon freshly ground black pepper

Direction

- In 2-quart saucepan over medium heat cook potatoes covered in 2 inches of boiling water until tender.
- While potatoes cook mix olive oil with garlic and rub on both sides of chops.
- Coat a large non-stick skillet with vegetable cooking spray and heat to medium.
- Fry chops until lightly browned on both sides.
- Season with salt and pepper.
- Drain potatoes and mash potatoes with fork leaving them lumpy.
- Mix in butter then milk and sage.
- Mix over low heat for 2 minutes.
- Season with salt and pepper.
- Serve chops with potatoes.

70. Cranberry Pork Chops Recipe

Serving: 4 | Prep: | Cook: 20mins | Ready in:

Ingredients

- 4 boneless pork chops
- 16 ounce can whole berry cranberry sauce
- 2 fresh jalapeno peppers seeded and chopped
- 1 green onion sliced
- 1 tablespoon fresh cilantro chopped
- 1 teaspoon ground cumin
- 1 teaspoon lime juice

Direction

- In a large non-stick skillet brown chops on one side over medium high heat.
- In a medium bowl stir together remaining ingredients.
- Turn chops and pour cranberry mixture over chops in skillet and bring to a boil.
- Lower heat then cover and simmer for 10 minutes.

71. Crock Pot Pork Chops Recipe

Serving: 4 | Prep: | Cook: 480mins | Ready in:

Ingredients

- 4 pork chops, 1/2" thick
- 2 medium onions, chopped
- 2 celery ribs, chopped
- 1 large green pepper, sliced
- 1 (14.5 ounce) can stewed tomatoes
- 1/2 cup ketchup
- 2 tablespoons cider vinegar
- 2 tablespoons brown sugar
- 2 tablespoons worcestershire sauce
- 1 tablespoon lemon juice
- 1 beef bouillon cube
- 2 tablespoons cornstarch
- 2 tablespoons water

Direction

- Salt and pepper chops, if desired.
- Add all ingredients except water and cornstarch to the crock pot.
- Cook on low setting for 5 1/2 hours.
- Mix cornstarch and water together and stir into crock pot.
- Cook 30 minutes more.
- Serve over rice.

72. Crock Pot Round Steak Recipe

Serving: 4 | Prep: | Cook: 380mins | Ready in:

Ingredients

- 1 large round steak
- 4 large carrots, sliced
- 4 large potatoes, sliced
- 1 can cream of mushroom soup
- 1/2 cup water
- 1 teaspoon lemon pepper
- salt and pepper to taste

Direction

- Cut round steak into serving slices.
- Sprinkle with lemon pepper on both sides.
- Put in crock pot and add other ingredients.
- Let simmer on low for 5 hours.

73. Crockpot Creole Steak Strips Recipe

Serving: 6 | Prep: | Cook: 8mins | Ready in:

Ingredients

- 1 1/2 lbs. boneless round steak
- salt and pepper
- 1/2 cup chopped onion
- 1 cup sliced celery
- 1 cup V-8 juice
- 2 tsp worcestershire sauce
- 1/8 tsp garlic powder (can use fresh)
- 1 medium green bell pepper chopped
- 1 10 oz. package frozen okra (about 1 1/2 cup)
- 1 4 oz can sliced mushrooms drained
- *can add diced tomato*
- cooked rice

Direction

- Cut steak into strips 1/2 inch wide and 2 inches long.

- Sprinkle with salt and pepper.
- Put meat in crockpot with onion, celery, juice, Worcestershire sauce and garlic.
- Cover and cook on low for 6 to 8 hours.
- Turn to high.
- Add peppers, partially thawed okra and mushrooms.
- Cover and cook for 30 minutes or until okra is done.
- Serve over hot cooked rice.

74. Crockpot Sour Cream Pork Chops Recipe

Serving: 6 | Prep: | Cook: 15mins | Ready in:

Ingredients

- 6 pork chops
- salt and pepper, to taste
- garlic powder, to taste
- 1/2 cup flour
- 1 large onion, sliced 1/4" thick
- 8 ozs. fresh mushrooms, sliced
- 1 chicken bouillon cube
- 1 cup boiling water
- 1 can cream of mushroom soup
- 1 8 oz. carton of sour cream

Direction

- Season pork chops with salt, pepper and garlic powder, and then dredge in flour. In a skillet over medium heat, lightly brown chops in a small amount of oil.
- In the bottom of a crockpot, place the onion and mushroom slices, topped with the pork chops.
- In a medium bowl, dissolve bouillon cube; stir in cream of mushroom soup. Pour over pork chop. Cover, and cook on LOW 7-8 hours.
- Preheat oven to 200*.
- After the chops have cooked, transfer the pork chops to the oven to keep warm. Be careful, the chops are so tender that will fall apart.

Add the sour cream to the contents inside the crockpot. Stir well. Turn crockpot on HIGH for 20 minutes to warm sauce. Serve the sauce over the pork chops, and noodles or rice.

75. Cube Steak Parmesan Recipe

Serving: 4 | Prep: | Cook: 45mins | Ready in:

Ingredients

- 3Tbs flour
- 1/2tsp salt
- 1/4tsp ground black pepper
- 2 eggs
- 2Tbs water1/3c crushed saltine crackers(I like panko crumbs)
- 1/3c grated parmesan cheese
- 1/2tsp dried basil
- 3Tbs veg oil
- 4(4oz) beef cube steaks
- 11/4c canned tomato sauce(I like the sauce with seasonings)
- 21/4tsp white sugar
- 1/2tsp dried oregano
- 1/4tsp garlic powder
- 4 slices mozzarella cheese
- 1/3c grated parmesan cheese

Direction

- Preheat oven to 350. In a shallow dish, stir together the flour, salt and pepper. In a separate bowl, whisk together the eggs and water with a fork. In a third bowl, mix together cracker crumbs or panko, 1/3c parmesan cheese and basil.
- Heat the oil in a large skillet over med heat. Dredge steaks in flour, dip in egg mixture, and coat with the cracker crumbs or panko mixture. Place in skillet and fry till just browned on each side. Arrange steaks in single layer in greased casserole dish.
- Bake for 25 mins. in preheated oven. Meanwhile, in a medium bowl, stir together

the tomato sauce, sugar, 1/4tsp oregano and garlic powder. Spoon over the steaks when 25 mins. are up. Top each with mozzarella cheese and remaining parmesan cheese; sprinkle remaining oregano over the top. Bake 5 mins more or until cheese is melted and sauce is hot!

- Combine the tomato sauce, sugar, 1/4 teaspoon oregano and garlic powder; spoon over steaks. Bake 10 minutes longer.
- Top each steak with mozzarella cheese; sprinkle with shredded Parmesan cheese and remaining oregano.
- Bake 2-3 minutes longer or until cheese is melted.

76. Cube Steaks Parmigiana Recipe

Serving: 4 | Prep: | Cook: 40mins | Ready in:

Ingredients

- 3 tablespoons all-purpose flour
- 1/2 teaspoon salt
- 1/4 teaspoon pepper
- 2 eggs
- 3 tablespoons water
- 1/3 cup finely crushed saltines
- 1/3 cup grated parmesan cheese
- 1/2 teaspoon dried basil
- 4 beef cube steaks (1 pound)
- 3 tablespoons vegetable oil
- 1 1/4 cups tomato sauce
- 2 1/4 teaspoons sugar
- 1/2 teaspoon dried oregano, divided
- 1/4 teaspoon garlic powder
- 4 slices mozzarella cheese
- 1/3 cup shredded parmesan cheese

Direction

- In a shallow bowl, combine the flour, salt and pepper.
- In another bowl, beat eggs and water.
- Place cracker crumbs, grated Parmesan cheese and basil in a third bowl.
- Coat steaks with flour mixture, then dip in egg mixture and coat with crumb mixture.
- In a large skillet, brown steaks in oil for 2-3 minutes on each side or until golden brown.
- Arrange steaks in a greased 13-in. x 9-in. x 2-in. baking dish. Bake, uncovered, at 375° for 25 minutes.

77. Cube Steaks In Gravy Recipe

Serving: 4 | Prep: | Cook: 90mins | Ready in:

Ingredients

- 4 cube steaks
- flour, all purpose
- salt and pepper, to taste
- additional seasoning of your choice (optional) (don't over-salt)
- 2 tablespoons butter, divided
- 1 small onion, chopped
- 8 ounces fresh mushrooms, sliced
- 1 (10-oz. can) condensed cream of mushroom soup
- 1 (10-oz. can) condensed golden mushroom soup
- 2 cloves garlic, minced
- 1 teaspoon Kitchen Bouquet
- 1 teaspoon worcestershire sauce
- mashed potatoes (optional)

Direction

- Sprinkle cube steaks with a little salt, pepper and additional seasonings, if desired.
- Place some flour in a paper lunch bag then add a cube steak and shake it up to coat it in flour.
- Remove steak from bag and repeat with remaining cube steaks, setting them to the side for about 15 minutes to allow the flour to "set" to the meat.
- In a large skillet, brown steaks in 1 tablespoon butter until browned on both sides.

- Transfer them to a covered casserole dish.
- Sauté the onions and mushrooms in remaining tablespoon butter until softened, about 6 minutes.
- Place the onion/mushroom mixture over the browned cube steaks in the casserole dish.
- Mix the soups together until well combined.
- Add the minced garlic, Worcestershire sauce, Kitchen Bouquet, and stir until well combined.
- Pour soup mixture over cube steak and mushroom/onion mixture.
- Place in preheated 350*F. oven and bake for 1 1/2 hours.
- Serve with mashed potatoes.

78. Cumin Rubbed Skirt Steak Fajitas Recipe

Serving: 23 | Prep: | Cook: 50mins | Ready in:

Ingredients

- 1/2 teaspoon cumin seeds
- 1/2 teaspoon fresh coarse ground black pepper
- 1 large garlic clove, quartered
- 2 teaspoons olive oil
- 1 lb skirt steaks (or flat iron steak)
- 4 poblano chiles
- 1/3 cup sour cream
- salt
- 6 (8 inch) flour tortillas
- 1 small onion, thinly sliced
- 1 cup tomatoes, finely chopped red and yellow
- 1 avocado, peeled and cut into 1/2-inch chunks

Direction

- Light a grill or preheat a cast-iron grill pan over low heat for about 10 minutes. In a small skillet, toast the cumin seeds over moderately high heat until lightly browned and fragrant, about 30 seconds.

- Transfer to a mortar to cool; then, using a pestle, coarsely grind. Add the black pepper and garlic and pound to a paste. (Alternatively, using a chef's knife, chop the cumin seeds as fine as you can and put them in a small bowl along with the black pepper. Mince the garlic and add it to the spices.) Stir in the olive oil. Rub the cumin oil on the skirt steak and marinate for at least 10 minutes or refrigerate overnight.
- Roast the poblano chiles directly on the grill or over a gas flame, turning often, until blistered all over; do not overcook or the flesh will burn.
- Transfer the chiles to a paper bag and let steam for about 5 minutes.
- Using a small knife, remove the skin, stems, and seeds. Cut the chiles into thin strips.
- In a small bowl, mix the chiles and sour cream. Season with salt.
- Season the skirt steak with salt and grill over a very hot fire or in the grill pan over high heat for about 2 1/2 minutes per side for medium-rare.
- Transfer to a carving board to rest for about 5 minutes. Using a very sharp knife, thinly slice the steak lengthwise against the grain.
- Warm the tortillas on the grill for a few seconds until pliable.
- Place the sour cream, onion, tomatoes, and avocado in bowls. Serve alongside the steak and tortillas and let each person assemble his own fajita.

79. Delicious Country Chicken Fried Steak Recipe

Serving: 4 | Prep: | Cook: 20mins | Ready in:

Ingredients

- chicken-Fried steak
- 3/4 cup all-purpose flour
- 3/4 teaspoon salt
- 1/4 teaspoon pepper

- 1/2 cup buttermilk
- 3/4 teaspoon hot sauce
- 1 pound beef cube steaks
- 1/4 cup plus 2 tablespoons vegetable oil, divided
- 2 tablespoons all-purpose flour
- 1 cup milk
- 1/4 teaspoon salt
- 1/4 teaspoon pepper

Direction

- Stir together first 3 ingredients in a shallow dish.
- Combine buttermilk and hot sauce in a bowl.
- Dredge steaks in flour mixture; dip into buttermilk mixture, and dip again in flour mixture.
- Heat 1/4 cup oil in a large skillet over medium-high heat.
- Add steaks, and cook 5 minutes on each side. Remove from skillet. Drain steaks on paper towels.
- Heat remaining 2 tablespoons oil in skillet; whisk in 2 tablespoons flour, and cook, whisking constantly, 5 minutes or until light golden brown.
- Gradually whisk in milk; cook, whisking constantly, over medium heat until thickened and bubbly (about 10 minutes).
- Stir in 1/4 teaspoon salt and 1/4 teaspoon pepper.
- Serve over steaks.

80. Diet Steak Recipe

Serving: 2 | Prep: | Cook: 20mins | Ready in:

Ingredients

- for the steak : 1 portion of rib eye or sirloin (TRIM THE FAT ! ! !)
- salt and pepper
- for the sallad: your favorite salad green,
- bell pepper,

- tear drop tomatoes
- for the dressing: 2 tbs of mustard
- 1/2 cup of lime juice
- 3 tbs of honey

Direction

- Cut steak into bite size pieces, marinade with salt and pepper
- On a very hot griddle, grill both sides very quickly
- Prepare salad dressing, toss salad with the dressing
- Serve with the steak

81. Dijon Sirloin Tips Recipe

Serving: 46 | Prep: | Cook: 2mins | Ready in:

Ingredients

- 1 1/4 pound sirloin tips, cubed
- 2 tbsp butter
- 1 tbsp cooking oil
- 3 cups sliced fresh mushrooms
- 1 garlic clove, minced
- 1/2 cup beef broth
- 1/4 cup white wine vinegar
- 1 1/2 tsp soy sauce
- 2 tsp Dijon mustard
- 2 tsp cornstarch
- 1/2 cup whipping cream
- Hot cooked noodles

Direction

- In a large skillet, brown the meat in butter and oil; transfer to an ungreased 2 qt. baking dish.
- In the same skillet, sauté mushrooms and garlic until mushrooms are tender, about 3 minutes.
- Pour mushrooms, garlic and drippings over meat.
- Cover and bake at 300* for 2 hours or until meat is tender.

- In a skillet, combine the broth, vinegar, and soy sauce; bring to boil.
- Boil for 2 minutes; set aside.
- Combine mustard, cornstarch, and cream; stir into broth mixture.
- Bring to a boil; boil for 2 minutes, stirring constantly.
- Drain juices from baking dish into broth mixture.
- Cook over medium heat, stirring constantly, until thickened and bubbly.
- Add beef mixture.
- Serve over noodles.

82. Dr Pepper Flank Steak Recipe

Serving: 4 | Prep: | Cook: 8mins | Ready in:

Ingredients

- 1-1/2 to 2 pounds flank steak
- 16 ounce bottle Dr. Pepper® soda
- 4 cloves garlic, peeled
- 2 cinnamon sticks
- 2 tablespoons grill seasoning:
- 4 tablespoons kosher salt
- 3 tablespoons chili powder
- 2 tablespoons dried granulated garlic
- 2 tablespoons sugar
- 2 tablespoons ground cumin
- 2 tablespoons ground black pepper
- 1 tablespoon ground thyme

Direction

- In a large bowl, combine Dr. Pepper®, garlic cloves and cinnamon sticks.
- Place flank steak in shallow dish and pour Dr. Pepper® mixture over top.
- Cover tightly with foil and refrigerate 12 hours turning once during marinating time.
- Mix all ingredients for grill seasoning and store in tightly sealed container.
- When steak is done marinating, remove from refrigerator and pat dry with paper towels.

- Prepare grill to medium-high heat.
- Season both sides with grill seasoning.
- Grill 3-4 minutes per side. Never cook flank steak past the medium-rare stage or it will end up being very tough.
- Remove from grill, cover loosely with foil, and let rest for 5 minutes.
- Cut across the grain into 1" slices.
- To use as fajita filling, warm tortillas and fill with steak and choice of toppings.
- Try with avocado sour cream; guess what...the recipe is posted :)

83. EASY CROCK CHOPS Recipe

Serving: 6 | Prep: | Cook: 360mins | Ready in:

Ingredients

- 6 boneless pork chops
- 1/4 C. brown sugar
- 1/2 tsp. cinnamon
- 1/4 tsp. ground cloves
- 1-8 oz. can tomato sauce
- 1-29 oz. can peach halves
- 1/4 C. vinegar
- salt and pepper to taste

Direction

- Lightly brown chops on both sides in skillet.
- Pour off excess fat.
- Combine brown sugar, cinnamon, cloves, tomato sauce, vinegar and 1/4 cup of syrup from peaches.
- Sprinkle chops with salt and pepper.
- Arrange chops in crock.
- Place drained peaches on top.
- Pour tomato mixture over all.
- Cover and cook on low for 6 hours.

84. EASY CROCK POT PORK CHOPS Recipe

Serving: 6 | Prep: | Cook: 360mins | Ready in:

Ingredients

- 6 pork chops of your choice
- 2 Tbs. or more flour
- 1 can chicken Rice soup

Direction

- Dredge the pork chops in the flour and brown in a skillet with oil.
- Place pork chops into Crock pot and pour the can of soup over the pork chops.
- DO NOT ADD WATER!
- Cook on High for 2-3 hours or low for about 5 hours.
- You can also pour in a box of stuffing mix and add 1/4 cup of water and have pork chops and stuffing.

85. East Meets West Vietnamese Pork Burgers Recipe

Serving: 4 | Prep: | Cook: 10mins | Ready in:

Ingredients

- 1 lb. lean ground pork
- 3 garlic cloves, chopped
- 2 green onions, chopped
- 2 teaspoon soy sauce
- 2 teaspoon peanut or other mild vegetable oil
- pinch of sugar
- a few drops Tabasco sauce, or a pinch of cayenne pepper
- hoisin sauce
- large whole green lettuce leaves – romaine works well
- ½ cup or so of roasted peanuts, coarsely ground
- a handful of cilantro, coarsely chopped

Direction

- Mix meat with garlic, onions, soy sauce, peanut oil, sugar and Tabasco or cayenne.
- Form into patties and grill until cooked through.
- Serve each grilled patty spread with hoisin sauce, wrapped in a leaf of lettuce, sprinkled with peanuts and cilantro.
- These are delicious exactly as described, however, you could spread the hoisin sauce inside a pita bread and insert the patties into it along with the lettuce for a more conventional burger experience.

86. Easy Beef Skillet Stew Dinner Recipe

Serving: 6 | Prep: | Cook: 30mins | Ready in:

Ingredients

- 1 1-1/2 - 2 lb. package of sirloin strip steak or stew beef cut in small pieces
- 5 lbs. red potatoes or any potato that produces good mashed potatoes
- 1 bag carrots (I used the peeled baby carrots)peeled and sliced in coin sizes
- 1 onion cut in slices and then quarters
- 1 Tablespoon minced garlic
- flour
- salt & pepper
- vegetable oil
- 1 Tablespoon Watkins beef soup and gravy mix

Direction

- Boil potatoes until done, drain and mash with butter and milk if desired. Set aside and keep hot.
- Dredge the beef in enough flour to coat well then brown in large, heavy skillet with enough oil to keep from sticking. Once browned, add enough water to cover. Add peeled carrots,

onion and garlic. Cover and simmer until done.

- Put 2 Tablespoons of the dredging flour, 1 tablespoon Watkins beef soup and gravy mix and enough water in a shaker cup to fill cup. Shake well and then add to the Beef and Carrot mixture. Stir until gravy is smooth adding more water as needed and desired gravy thickness is reached. Simmer for a few minutes to cook the gravy then serve the Beef and Carrot gravy over large servings of mashed potatoes. My kids loved making a big dip in their mashed potatoes for the beef, carrots and gravy. Never had to fight with them to eat their carrots either. Hope you enjoy as much as my family does.

87. Easy Beef And Noodles Recipe

Serving: 8 | Prep: | Cook: 20mins | Ready in:

Ingredients

- 1 package of petite sirloin (as much or as little as you like)
- 1 package of egg noodles
- 2 packets of Knorr Parma Rosa sauce mix
- 1 yellow onion
- 1 package of button mushrooms
- 1 tablespoon of butter or margarine
- coarse salt
- ground black pepper

Direction

- Cook sauce according to directions on package. (Requires milk and butter or margarine.) I always add extra milk, about two tablespoons, because I prefer thinner sauce.
- Cook egg noodles.
- Mix egg noodles and sauce and set aside on low heat, stirring occasionally.
- Dice yellow onion and slice mushrooms and sauté in one tablespoon of butter.

- Add to noodles, butter and all, still stirring occasionally.
- Place sirloin on broiler pan and salt and pepper each side. Place in broiler, about 2 to 3 minutes on each side for medium rare. (This time will vary, I have an electric broiler and it sucks!)
- Slice the sirloin when finished and place over noodles and serve.

88. Easy Crockpot Beef Stroganoff Recipe

Serving: 6 | Prep: | Cook: 8mins | Ready in:

Ingredients

- 2 lbs sirloin tips
- extra virgin olive oil
- Seasoned salt
- garlic pepper
- Unseasoned meat tenderizer
- worcestershire sauce
- Montreal steak seasoning
- 1/2 pkg dry beefy onion soup mix (or onion)
- 2 T minced onion
- 1 can sliced musrooms, drained
- 1 can mushroom soup
- 2 soup cans water (or, one soup can beef stock and one soup can water)
- 4 T sour cream
- 2 T cornstarch
- 2 T water
- Minute Rice or egg noodles, (cooked according to directions, for six servings)

Direction

- Lightly drizzle a little extra virgin olive oil over beef tips, and season well with seasonings
- Place in slow cooker
- Stir together Mushrooms, onion, soup, water/beef stock, dry soup mix and pour over meat

- Cook on low 6-8 hours
- ** If my meat is frozen, I leave it that way. It will be nice and brown and tender when you get home from work. Just cut back a little on the water **
- Remove slow cooker from base and place on stovetop, OR Transfer beef and sauce to stove top pot just before serving and bring to low boil
- Mix together the cornstarch and 2 T water
- Pour into pot and stir to thicken gravy
- Remove from heat and stir in sour cream
- Serve over rice or noodles

89. Easy Crockpot Beef Tips And Gravy Recipe

Serving: 6 | Prep: | Cook: 480mins | Ready in:

Ingredients

- 1 1/2 pounds beef stew meat, sirloin tips or chuck steak chunks
- 2 T. olive or other oil for browning
- 1 packet au jus mix, low sodium if available!
- 2 packets brown gravy mix, low sodium if available!
- Your favorite seasonings (no salt)
- 2 cups water, divided
- wide egg noodles or other choice of starch to serve

Direction

- Heat medium skillet to med-high heat, and brown tips lightly in oil.
- Transfer to crockpot.
- Mix "au jus" packet mix with 1 1/2 cups water, stir well and pour over beef tips.
- Add seasonings of your choice, such as black pepper, garlic, or herbs. Do not use salt---the packets are salty enough!
- Place lid on crock pot and cook on slow for 7 hours, or high for 5 hours.

- Mix the two brown gravy packets with another 1/2 cup COOL water, stirring well.
- Add gravy mix to crockpot, and let heat on high for about 30-40 minutes more.
- Remove lid, stir and cool down slightly before serving over noodles, mashed potatoes, or rice.
- Enjoy!

90. Easy Egg Foo Yung Recipe

Serving: 6 | Prep: | Cook: | Ready in:

Ingredients

- 1/3 cup cooked and crumbled ground beef
- 1/3 cup chopped cooked chicken breast
- 1/3 cup chopped cooked pork
- 8 beaten eggs
- 1 cup sliced celery
- 1/2 cup diced mushrooms
- 1 cup bean sprouts
- 1 cup finely chopped onion
- 1 tsp salt
- 2 cubes chicken bouillon
- 1/4 tsp ground black pepper
- 1 1/2 tbspns cornstarch
- Foo Yung sauce
- 1 1/2 cups hot water
- 1 1/2 tsps white sugar
- 6 tbspns cold water
- 2 tbspns soy sauce

Direction

- Beat the eggs in a good sized bowl. Add the onion, celery, sprouts, chicken, mushrooms, pork, beef, salt and pepper. Mix all together.
- Heat a little oil in a medium-sized frying-pan (preferably wok) and then brown the egg mix 1/2 cup at a time. When all of the mix is brown, set it aside for later.
- Now to create the finishing sauce. Dissolve the bouillon cubes in hot water in a small saucepan. Then add sugar and some soy sauce and blend it all over medium heat. Add (cold)

water and the cornstarch and stir it until it gets thick and smooth. Serve this with your delicious Egg Foo Yung!

91. Easy Mexican Pork Chop Dinner Recipe

Serving: 4 | Prep: | Cook: 50mins | Ready in:

Ingredients

- 1 tablespoon vegetable oil
- 4 boneless pork chops
- 1 t cumin
- 1 dash cayenne pepper
- 1 t seasoned salt
- 1 t pepper
- 1/2 med. onion, diced
- 2 (14.5 ounce) cans chopped stewed tomatoes, with juice
- 1 (8.75 ounce) can whole kernel corn, drained
- 1 (8 ounce) can black beans, drained
- 1/2 cup uncooked long grain white rice
- 1 (4 ounce) can diced green chilies, drained

Direction

- Preheat oven to 350 degrees
- Mix seasonings together and lightly rub over chops
- Heat the oil in a skillet over medium heat.
- Brown the pork chops with onions about 5 minutes on each side. Remove chops from skillet and drain oil.
- Mix the tomatoes, corn, kidney beans, rice, and chilies in same skillet and bring to a boil.
- Cook and stir for 1 minute, until heated through.
- Transfer the tomato mixture to a baking dish. Arrange the browned pork chops over the mixture.
- Bake covered 30 minutes in the preheated oven.

- Uncover, and continue baking 10 minutes, until rice is tender and pork has reached an internal temperature of 160 degrees

92. Easy Pork Chop Fajitas Recipe

Serving: 8 | Prep: | Cook: 30mins | Ready in:

Ingredients

- 1 medium yellow pepper, cut into strips
- 1 medium red pepper, cut into strips
- 1 medium onion, sliced
- 2 roma tomatoes, sliced lengthwise into strips
- 2 Tbsp. oil
- 2 Tbsp. fresh lime juice
- 1/2 tsp. ground cumin
- 8 boneless pork chops, 1/2 inch thick
- 1 packet SHAKE "N BAKE Hot &Spicy seasoned Coating Mix for chicken or pork
- 8 flour tortillas

Direction

- Mix peppers, onions, tomatoes, oil, lime juice and cumin in 13x9-inch baking pan.
- Coat chops as directed on package.
- Discard any remaining coating mix.
- Cut chops into strips and place chops on onion mixture.
- Bake at 425°F for 20 minutes or until chops are cooked through.
- Top tortillas with sliced pork and onion mixture; roll up.
- Serve with guacamole, Salsa, Sour Cream and Guacamole

93. Easy Smothered Pork Chops Recipe

Serving: 6 | Prep: | Cook: 20mins | Ready in:

Ingredients

- 6 3/4 inch thick pork chops (bone in or out)
- 1 cup flour
- 1/2 tsp. dried thyme
- 1/2 tsp. ground sage
- salt and pepper to taste
- 4 onions, thinly sliced
- 1 pkg. country gravy mix
- 1 pkg. pork gravy mix
- 2 cups water
- olive oil

Direction

- In plastic zip bag, add flour, thyme, sage, and salt and pepper
- Dredge chops in flour mixture.
- Place chops in fridge
- Preheat oven to 400.
- In sauté pan, add olive oil and onions and cook until tender. I usually let them start to caramelize.
- Remove onions and add a little olive oil to pan.
- Cook pork chops over medium high heat until seared on both sides.
- Remove from pan and put onto baking dish.
- Top chops with half of the cooked onions.
- Bake until done
- In saucepan add water and prepare both gravies together.
- Add other 1/2 of onions to gravy.
- Serve pork chops covered in gravy.

94. Elaines Shishkebabs Recipe

Serving: 8 | Prep: | Cook: 40mins | Ready in:

Ingredients

- Have 6 to eight large metal skewers ready... and the BBQ lit. A low flame is all that's needed to cook these. If you're using charcoal, have it burned down to fine glow to prevent a lot of flaming.
- 1 to ½ lbs steak, 1" thickness, cut into large cubes
- 1 to ½ lbs butterfly-cut pork chops, 1" thickness, cut into large cubes
- 1 to ½ lbs chicken breast , boneless, cut into large cubes
- 2-3 large onions quartered
- 2 green sweet peppers, cut into large chunks
- 2 red sweet peppers, cut into large chunks
- 2 yellow sweet pepper, cut into large chunks
- 2 medium potatoes, sliced about ½ inch thickness.
- 2 -3 medium-sized carrots, sliced into medium-sized, skewerable chunks.

Direction

- Slip the pieces onto the skewers in whatever fashion you prefer, although I make sure no potato pieces are on the outside ends -- the reason being that they'll dry out rather than cook. If the potato pieces are placed between the other layers, they cook just beautifully, and retain the moistness.
- BBQ, turning frequently, until done to your taste.
- Take a fork, and on the end of the skewer closest to you, push the food off the skewer onto the plate.
- Add salt, pepper or whatever spices you like, and enjoy!
- Hint:
- For those who prefer unsalted foods, McCormick's has a great substitute called "No Added Salt Citrus and Pepper Seasoning". It's terrific. I use it all the time in place of salt, and as a result, never miss using salt!
- Another hint:
- You might want to do these in the convection oven in the winter too--- using the broiler, they turn out great this way!

95. Entrecote Macbeth Ribeye Steaks That Macbeth Might Eat Were He Not A Work Of Fiction Recipe

Serving: 4 | Prep: | Cook: 20mins | Ready in:

Ingredients

- 4 rib-eye steaks about half a pound each
- fresh garlic
- butter
- salt, coarsely cracked black pepper
- -
- 1 super large, sufficiently sweet red onion (or two smaller)
- 2 tbls. of honey
- About ¾ cup of olive oil
- --- SAUCE---
- 1 ½ cups of demi-glace
- 2 cups of sickeningly sweet port wine
- 4 large shallots
- 5-6 fresh sage leaves
- 1 tsp. of fine Dijon mustard
- More butter (softened)
- More salt and pepper (if it be needed)

Direction

- FOR THE STEAKS: Mince the garlic and stud those steaks with it and season them with salt and black pepper. Let them wait in anticipation while you deal with the onions in this fashion:
- Cut the onion into eight slices which are half an inch thick – Mix the honey into the olive oil (you could heat it a little to make this easier) and slather the onions copiously with this. Bake them in a hot oven (450) until they soften and are slightly caramelized.
- Heat the butter in an iron skillet and sear the steaks on both sides. Set two of the onion slices on top of each steak and finish them beneath a broiler.
- **I strongly suggest that you do not cook them beyond med-rare if you can stand it. It will taste better, and when the blood seeps out

after you first stab it will add to the whole Macbeth motif.
- FOR THE SAUCE: Purge the skillet of all the left over butter and return it to the heat with a little fresh butter. Have the shallots, finely minced and ready, then toss them in. Cook them for a minute or so and then pour in the port.
- Lower the heat, add the sage leaves and cook it until the port has been halfway reduced. Add the demi-glace and the mustard and cook further for 4-5 minutes.
- Finish the sauce with a few tbsp. of the softened butter which should be 'swished' in off the heat. Season with salt and pepper if needed.
- This sauce is to be ladled over the steaks when served, it is not a dipping sauce or a Duncan sauce.
- Serve with some sautéed kale or other pretty Celtic green vegetable and also with OUT OUT DAMN SPUDS (see recipe) use three of these per serving.

96. Father In Laws Beef Stroganoff Recipe

Serving: 8 | Prep: | Cook: 20mins | Ready in:

Ingredients

- wide egg noodles (I use 1 1/2 packages)
- round steak (sliced into small thin pieces)
- 1 onion diced
- fresh mushrooms (canned mushrooms will work as well)
- 2 Tablespoons butter
- 2 Teaspoons of worcestershire sauce
- 3 Tablespoons of ketchup
- 2 Big cans of cream of mushroom soup
- 16 oz sour cream

Direction

- Boil water for noodles-be sure to salt the water to flavor your noodles.
- Cook noodles according to package directions.
- Melt butter in saucepan.
- Place sliced up round steak, onions, and mushrooms to sauté till onions are transparent and meat is browned evenly-let simmer for a few extra minutes.
- Drain off excess liquid.
- Pour in Cream of Mushroom Soup
- Put in your two teaspoons of Worcestershire sauce and Ketchup-let simmer for about 5 minutes.
- Put in the sour cream and heat thoroughly but do not let come to a boil!
- Serve with Sauce on top of noodles with bread!

97. Filet Mignon Recipe

Serving: 2 | Prep: | Cook: 20mins |Ready in:

Ingredients

- 1 tablespoon butter
- 2 6 oz beef steaks; 1-inch thick
- 2/3 cup beef broth
- 1/4 cup brandy
- 1/2 teaspoon rosemary
- 1/2 cup feta; crumbled

Direction

- Melt butter in heavy medium skillet over medium high heat.
- Season steaks with salt & pepper.
- Add steaks to skillet and sauté until cooked to desired doneness, about 4 minutes per side for medium rare.
- Transfer steaks to plate.
- Add broth, brandy & rosemary to skillet & boil until sauce is reduced to 1/3 cup.
- Scraping up browned bits, spoon sauce over steaks.
- Top each steak with 1/2 the cheese.

98. Filet Mignon Wild Mushrooms And Herbed Goat Cheese Fingerlings With Balsamic Reduction Recipe

Serving: 4 | Prep: | Cook: 20mins |Ready in:

Ingredients

- 4 prime beef filet mignon steaks
- kosher salt
- ~~~~~~~~~~~~~~~~~~~~~~~~~~~~~~~~~~~~~
- 1 pound fingerling potatoes
- kosher salt & freshly cracked pepper to taste
- 8 oz garlic and herb goat cheese log (you could use Boursin instead)
- 1/4 of a fresh french baguette, made into bread crumbs
- 1/4 cup melted butter
- a few leaves of fresh parsely, finely chopped
- ~~~~~~~~~~~~~~~~~~~~~~~~~~~~~~~~~~~~~
- 2 cups mixed fresh wild mushrooms (I use "mycopia" chef sampler which includes Trumpet Royale, Alba Clamshell, Brown Clamshell, Forest Nameko but any mix of mushrooms you like is fine)
- 4 tablespoons unsalted butter
- 1 shallot, sliced
- a few sprigs of fresh thyme, leaves removed & chopped
- kosher salt & white pepper to taste
- 1/2 cup aged balsamic vinegar

Direction

- To make sure the potatoes cook in the same length of time, I cut the largest ones in half width-wise. Place potatoes in large saucepan, cover with water and add kosher salt. Bring to boil and cook for 15 minutes. Drain and let cool. (I peel my fingerling potatoes after they are cooked because I don't like skin on potatoes but of course it perfectly fine if you leave the skins on). Butter the bottom of a baking dish. Arrange potatoes on bottom of dish and sprinkle with kosher salt and pepper. Crumble goat cheese over the potatoes. Mix breadcrumbs with parsley and melted butter then sprinkle over goat cheese layer. Bake at 350 degrees for 25 minutes.

- While potatoes are baking, season both sides of filets with kosher salt. Grill steaks to desired doneness over charcoal grill. Tent lightly with foil and let rest at least 10 minutes.
- Sauté shallots and mushrooms in butter until caramelized. Add thyme and season with salt and pepper. Remove to a bowl and keep warm. To the same pan, add the balsamic and reduce by half.
- To plate: place a steak and side of the potatoes on each plate. Top each steak with the mushroom mixture and drizzle with balsamic reduction.

---

99. Filet Mignon With Bearnaise Sauce And Roasted Asparagus Recipe

Serving: 4 | Prep: | Cook: 16mins | Ready in:

Ingredients

- For Béarnaise:
- 1/4 cup dry white wine
- 1/4 cup white-wine vinegar
- 1/4 cup finely chopped shallots
- 2 tablespoons chopped fresh tarragon, divided
- 3 large egg yolks
- 1 stick unsalted butter, cut into 8 pieces
- 1/2 teaspoon fresh lemon juice, or to taste
- kosher salt & black pepper to taste
- ~~~~~~~~~~~~~~~~~~~~~~~~~~~~~~~~~~~~~~~ ~~~~~~~~~~~~~~~~~~~~
- For Asparagus:
- 1 pound asparagus, trimmed

- 1-2 tablespoons olive oil
- kosher salt and freshly ground black pepper
- ~~~~~~~~~~~~~~~~~~~~~~~~~~~~~~~~~~~~~~~ ~~~~~~~~~~~~~~~~~~~~
- 4 (8-10 oz) beef filet mignons (if on a budget, TJ's Black Angus are pretty damn good!)
- minced parsley, for garnish

Direction

- For Béarnaise:
- Boil wine, vinegar, shallots, and 1 tablespoon tarragon in a small heavy saucepan until liquid is reduced to 2 tablespoons, then strain through a fine-mesh sieve set into a medium metal bowl, pressing on and then discarding solids.
- Whisk yolks into vinegar mixture, then set bowl over a pan of barely simmering water and cook, whisking constantly, until yolks have thickened slightly (do not scramble). Whisk in butter 1 piece at a time, adding each piece before previous one has melted completely. (Note: have your butter ready next to you so you don't accidentally overcook the eggs).
- Remove from heat and whisk in lemon juice, remaining tablespoon tarragon, about 1/2 teaspoon kosher salt, and 1/2 teaspoon pepper (or to taste).
- Transfer sauce to a smaller glass bowl and place it into a saucepan that has boiling hot water in it and cover with lid. This keeps the sauce warm while you grill or roast the filet mignon and roast the asparagus.
- For filet mignon:
- Season each steak with kosher salt.
- To ROAST the filets: In a roasting pan or ovenproof frying pan, heat 1 tablespoon of the olive oil and when hot, sear the filets on all sides until golden brown. Transfer the pan to the oven and roast for 7 to 8 minutes, turning the filets over after 3 to 4 minutes.
- To GRILL the filets: Grill the steaks over hot coals for about 8 minutes per side (5 minutes per side for rare).
- For Asparagus:

- Preheat the oven to 400 degrees F.
- Snap or cut the dry stem ends off each asparagus and place on a heavy baking sheet. Drizzle with olive oil, sprinkle with salt and pepper, and toss. Roast until the asparagus is tender, about 8-10 minutes, depending on how thick your asparagus is. Cool slightly and serve warm or at room temperature.
- To plate:
- Remove béarnaise from pan and smear sauce in the middle of plate. Line 4 asparagus spears in top of sauce, then top with grilled/roasted filet mignon. Garnish with parsley. I also served mine with pan roasted fingerlings with garlic, butter and smoked paprika.

100. Filet Mignon With Blackberries Recipe

Serving: 4 | Prep: | Cook: 12mins | Ready in:

Ingredients

- 4 (6-ounce) filet mignon steaks
- salt and freshly ground black pepper
- 2 tablespoons olive oil
- 1/4 cup finely chopped shallots
- 1/2 cup dry red wine (recommended: Cabernet Sauvignon)
- 1 cup low-sodium beef broth
- 3 tablespoons blackberry preserves
- 2 tablespoons unsalted butter
- Compound butter, for garnish, recipe follows
- blackberries, for garnish

Direction

- Pat the steaks dry with paper towels and season generously with salt and pepper. In a heavy skillet, heat the oil over medium-high heat until almost smoking. Sear the steaks in the hot oil for 3 minutes per side for medium-rare. Transfer the steaks to a serving plate, tent with foil, and let stand.

- Using the same skillet, sauté the shallots for 1 minute. Add the red wine, scraping up any browned bits on the bottom of the pan. Let wine boil until reduced by half. Add broth and blackberry preserves, return to a boil and reduce by half. (The sauce should coat the back of a spoon.) Whisk in the 2 tablespoons butter. Season sauce with additional salt and pepper, to taste.
- To serve, drizzle the sauce over the steaks. Place a pat of compound butter and scatter a few blackberries on the plate.
- Compound Butter:
- 1 stick unsalted butter, room temperature
- 1/4 cup fresh blackberries
- In a bowl, combine butter and blackberries and mix well.
- Place on plastic wrap to mold into a log shape. Wrap and refrigerate until ready to serve.

101. Filet Mignon With Mushroom Wine Sauce Recipe

Serving: 4 | Prep: | Cook: 25mins | Ready in:

Ingredients

- 1T butter, divided
- 1/3c shallots, finely chopped
- 8oz fresh shiitake mushroms, stems removed
- 1 1/2c Cabernet Sauvignon, divided
- 1 (10 1/2oz) can beef consomme, undiluted and divided
- cracked black pepper
- 4 (4oz) filet mignon steaks, about 1" thick
- 1T soy sauce, low-sodium
- 2t cornstarch
- 1t dried thyme
- thyme sprigs (optional)

Direction

- Melt 1 1/2 teaspoons butter in a non-stick skillet over medium heat. Add shallots and mushrooms; sauté 4 minutes. Add 1 cup wine and 3/4 cup consommé; cook 5 minutes, stirring frequently. Remove mushrooms with a slotted spoon; place in a bowl. Increase heat to high; cook wine mixture until reduced to 1/2 cup (about 5 minutes). Add to mushrooms in bowl; set aside. Wipe pan with a paper towel.

- Sprinkle pepper over steaks. Melt 1 1/2 teaspoons butter in pan over medium heat. Add steaks; cook 3 minutes on each side. Reduce heat to medium-low; cook 1 1/2 minutes on each side or until desired degree of doneness. Place on a platter; keep warm.
- Combine soy sauce and cornstarch. Add 1/2 cup wine and remaining consommé to skillet; scrape skillet to loosen browned bits. Bring to a boil; cook 1 minute. Add mushroom mixture, cornstarch mixture, and dried thyme; bring to a boil, and cook 1 minute, stirring constantly. Serve sauce with steaks. Garnish with thyme sprigs, if desired.
- Serving size: 1 steak and 1/2 cup sauce; 250 calories; 39% from fat.

102. Filet Mignon Coated With 3 Peppers And Wine Sauce Recipe

Serving: 4 | Prep: | Cook: 20mins | Ready in:

Ingredients

- 4 filet-mignon steaks, about 1/2 lb each
- 2 tsps white pepper, crushed
- 2 tsps black pepper, crushed
- 2 pink pepper, whole
- 1 tbsp butter
- 2 tbsp olive oil
- 1 shot glass of good quality red wine
- 1 cup single cream
- sea salt to taste

Direction

- Season the filet-mignon with salt to taste.

- Sear both sides in a hot frying pan with a drizzle of olive oil.
- In a pan, melt butter, add olive oil and the 3 types of pepper.
- Stir for 2 minutes over low heat.
- Add wine and let the alcohol evaporate.
- Add single cream and after 2 minutes the sauce will thicken.
- Serve immediately over the steaks.

103. Filipino Bistek Recipe

Serving: 4 | Prep: | Cook: 20mins | Ready in:

Ingredients

- 2 lbs beef (filet mignon is best, but a nice sirloin works well too).
- ½ cup fresh lime or lemon juice
- ¼ cup soy sauce
- Freshly ground black pepper
- 1 Medium size onion, cut into rings
- 3-4 garlic cloves (crushed)
- cooking oil

Direction

- Cut beef into thin strips and marinade in lime/lemon juice, soy sauce, pepper, and garlic for at least an hour before cooking. Heat skillet on high, add cooling oil and sauté onions until transparent. Remove onions and place in serving dish. Add beef (minus marinade) to remaining hot oil and cook until done. Add the remaining marinade and cooked onions to the beef and simmer for 10-15 minutes. Serve with steamed white rice and steamed vegetables

104. Finger Licking Good Beef Steak Recipe

Serving: 4 | Prep: | Cook: 180mins | Ready in:

Ingredients

- 2 pounds round steak
- 3 tablespoons vegetable oil
- 4 lemon slices
- 3 medium sliced white onions
- 2 cloves minced garlic
- 1/2 cup flour
- 1 can beef bouillon
- 1 can beer
- 3 tablespoons brown sugar
- 1 tablespoon parsley flakes
- 2 teaspoons thyme
- 1/2 teaspoon salt
- 1 teaspoon freshly ground black pepper
- 8 ounces cooked egg noodles
- green pepper slices for garnish
- cherry tomatoes for garnish

Direction

- Add lemon slices to oil.
- Cut steak into serving size pieces then brown on all sides in a frying pan with a little vegetable oil.
- Remove steak to a baking dish large enough to bake it.
- Layer onions and garlic over meat then sprinkle flour over top.
- Combine bouillon, beer, sugar, parsley flakes, thyme, salt and pepper.
- Pour over steak and bake uncovered at 325 for 3 hours.
- Serve over cooked noodles then garnish with pepper slices, parsley and cherry tomatoes.

105. Fried Pork Chops Recipe

Serving: 6 | Prep: | Cook: 20mins | Ready in:

Ingredients

- 6 boneless pork chops (about 1/2 inch thick)
- 1/2 C flour
- 1/8 C. corn meal
- 1/2 tsp. garlic salt
- 1/4 tsp. sugar
- small bowl of water
- cooking oil (I use canola)

Direction

- Put about 1/2 inch of oil in a large heavy skillet over medium high heat.
- Put all the dry ingredients into a large zip lock baggy and shake well to combine.
- Dip each pork chop into the bowl of water then drop into the bag of dry ingredients and shake well to coat.
- Take pork chop out of bag and put into medium hot oil.
- Fry for about 10 minutes on each side or until golden brown.
- When done drain on a paper towel and serve.

106. Garlic And Thyme Roast Beef With Port Jus Recipe

Serving: 6 | Prep: | Cook: 60mins | Ready in:

Ingredients

- 8 cloves of garlic, peeled
- 2 T olive oil
- 1 T fresh thyme leaves, coarsely chopped or 1 tsp dried
- 2 sweet potatoes (about 2 lbs) peeled and cut into 1 1/2 inch cubes
- 2 medium onions, peeled and cut into 8 wedges
- 1 tsp kosher salt, divided
- 3/4 tsp ground pepper, divided
- 1 top sirloin beef roast (about 3 lbs) with some fat intact, tied
- 3/4 C low sodium chicken broth

- 1/4 C tawny port

Direction

- Adjust oven rack to center position and preheat oven to 500.
- Combine garlic and olive oil in a small microwave safe bowl and cover with plastic wrap.
- Microwave for 1 minute or until garlic is soft; let stand 5 minutes.
- Strain out oil into a large bowl and mash garlic with a fork to form a paste; stir in thyme and 2 tsp of the strained oil.
- Place a heavy bottomed roasting pan in oven to preheat for 5 minutes.
- Meanwhile, add sweet potatoes, onions, 1/4 tsp of salt and 1/4 tsp pepper to the bowl with the remaining oil and toss to coat well.
- Dry roast beef with paper towels and season with remaining salt and pepper.
- Place the roast in the preheated pan fat side down and roast for 5 minutes, turn roast over and roast 5 more minutes.
- Remove roasting pan from oven and using a heat proof spatula or large spoon, spread garlic-thyme paste over top of roast.
- Scatter vegetables around the roast in the pan.
- Return pan to oven and roast until internal temperature reaches 125 for medium rare, or until desired doneness.
- Stir vegetables once or twice during cooking.
- Transfer to roast to a platter and tent with foil, let rest for at least 15 minutes.
- Transfer vegetables to a serving platter and cover.
- Place roasting pan on top of stove, add broth and bring to a boil over medium high, using a wooden spoon deglaze the pan of any bits stuck to the bottom.
- Simmer, stirring occasionally until reduced by half, about 3 minutes.
- Add port and continue to boil mixture until thick and glossy, another 2 minutes.
- Pour in any accumulated juices from platter and simmer another 30 seconds.

- To serve, slice roast and transfer to the platter with the vegetables and serve with sauce.

107. Garlic Steak With Asparagus Recipe

Serving: 2 | Prep: | Cook: 5mins | Ready in:

Ingredients

- 2 10 - 12 oz. boneless beef top loin (strip) steak, 3/4 inch thick
- 1 or 2 large cloves garlic, coarsely chopped
- 1/2 tsp. cracked or coarsely ground black pepper
- 1/4 tsp. salt
- 8 to 10 thin asparagus spears, trimmed (6 oz.)
- 2 tsp. garlic-flavored olive oil or olive oil
- 1/2 cup beef broth
- 1 Tbsp. dry white wine
- 1/4 tsp. dijon-style mustard

Direction

- Rub the steak on both sides with a mixture of the garlic, pepper, and salt, pressing in the mixture with your fingers. Place the asparagus in a shallow dish and drizzle with the oil.
- For sauce, in a medium skillet stir together the broth and wine. Cook over high heat for 4 to 5 minutes or until mixture is reduced to 1/4 cup. Whisk in mustard; keep warm.
- Preheat grill on high setting. Place steak on the grill rack, close lid. Grill until steak is desired doneness. (3 to 4 minutes for medium rare or 5 to 7 minutes for medium, turning steak once.) Add asparagus to grill for the last 4 to 5 minutes of grilling. Cook asparagus until crisp-tender.*
- Spoon sauce on serving plate. Cut steak in half crosswise. Serve steak halves atop sauce with asparagus on top.
- *Note: The asparagus cooking time will vary with the size of asparagus. Also, if there is no

room on the grill, the asparagus can be grilled after the steak.

108. Garlic Studded Pot Roast Recipe

Serving: 810 | Prep: | Cook: 240mins | Ready in:

Ingredients

- 1 (4 to 5-pound) sirloin tip roast, netted or tied at 1-inch intervals
- 10 cloves garlic, peeled and halved lengthwise, plus 4 to 6 garlic cloves, peeled
- 1 tablespoon Essence, plus 1 1/2 teaspoons
- 1 1/4 teaspoons freshly ground black pepper
- 1 1/4 teaspoons salt
- 1 cup dry red wine
- 3 tablespoons tomato paste
- 4 large carrots, scrubbed
- 2 stalks celery, trimmed and cut in half crosswise
- 2 medium yellow onions, peeled and quartered
- 1 pound small new potatoes
- 2 tablespoons vegetable oil
- 1 cup beef stock, or canned low-sodium beef broth
- 2 bay leaves
- Essence (Emeril's creole seasoning):
- 2 1/2 tablespoons paprika
- 2 tablespoons salt
- 2 tablespoons garlic powder
- 1 tablespoon black pepper
- 1 tablespoon onion powder
- 1 tablespoon cayenne pepper
- 1 tablespoon dried leaf oregano
- 1 tablespoon dried thyme
- Combine all ingredients thoroughly and store in an airtight jar or container.
- Yield: about 2/3 cup
- Recipe from "New New Orleans Cooking", by Emeril Lagasse and Jessie Tirsch. Published by William and Morrow, 1993.

Direction

- With a small, sharp knife, make 30 (1 1/2-inch deep) slits around the outside of the roast. Insert the half cloves of garlic into the slits. Rub the roast with 1 tablespoon of the Essence, 1 teaspoon of the black pepper, and 1 teaspoon of the salt.
- Preheat the oven to 400 degrees F.
- Heat the oil in a large, heavy skillet over medium-high heat. Add the roast and sear on all sides, about 4 minutes per side. Remove from the pan. Deglaze the pan with the red wine, scraping up any brown bits on the bottom of the pan with a wooden spoon. In a mixing bowl, whisk together the tomato paste and 1 cup of water. Add the tomato paste mixture to the red wine and cook for 2 minutes.
- Meanwhile, in a large roasting pan or Dutch oven, alternate the carrots and celery flat on the bottom of the pot. Place the bay leaves on the vegetables. Scatter the onions, potatoes, and garlic over the bottom. (The vegetables will form a "nest" on which the roast will be placed.) Place the roast on top of the vegetables. Add the red wine mixture and the stock. Cover the roasting pan tightly with aluminum foil and bake for 1 1/2 hours.
- Uncover the pot roast, baste with the pan juices, and lower the heat to 350 degrees F. Cover the roast and continue cooking until the meat is completely tender and begins to fall apart, 2 to 2 1/2 hours, uncovering and basting each hour. Remove from the oven, uncover, and baste. Let rest for 15 minutes before carving. Serve each portion of the carved roast with onion quarters, new potatoes, 1 carrot, and 1 piece of celery. Spoon the pan juices over the meat and vegetables, and serve.

109. Garlicked Sirloin Pot Roast Recipe

Serving: 8 | Prep: | Cook: 360mins | Ready in:

Ingredients

- 1 teaspoon salt
- 1 teaspoon freshly ground black pepper
- 1 teaspoon paprika
- 3 pound top sirloin roast
- 6 cloves garlic, slivered
- 6 yukon gold potatoes, peeled and quartered
- 4 carrots, cut into 2" pieces
- 2 large sweet onions, peeled and chopped
- 1/2 cup water
- 1/2 cup beef broth
- 3 beef bouillon cubes
- 1 bay leaf
- 2 large green bell peppers, cut into 2" pieces

Direction

- Rub meat with paprika, salt and pepper.
- Make slits in roast with a small knife.
- Insert garlic slivers into meat.
- Place the potatoes, carrots and onions in slow cooker.
- Place roast on top of the vegetables.
- Pour in water and beef broth; add bouillon cubes and bay leaf.
- Place lid on slow cooker and cook on High for 6 hours OR on Low for 8 hours.
- Add green peppers during last half hour of cooking.

110. Garlicky Steak And Asparagus Recipe

Serving: 2 | Prep: | Cook: 10mins | Ready in:

Ingredients

- 1 12- to 14-oz. boneless beef top loin (strip) steak, cut about 3/4 inch thick
- 1 or 2 large cloves garlic, coarsely chopped
- 1/2 tsp. cracked or coarsely ground black pepper
- 1/4 tsp. salt
- 8 to 10 thin asparagus spears, trimmed (6 oz.)
- 2 tsp. garlic-flavored olive oil or olive oil
- 1/2 cup beef broth
- 1 Tbsp. dry white wine
- 1/4 tsp. dijon-style mustard

Direction

- Rub the steak on both sides with a mixture of the garlic, pepper, and salt, pressing in the mixture with your fingers.
- Place the asparagus in a shallow dish and drizzle with the oil.
- For sauce, in a medium skillet stir together the broth and wine.
- Cook over high heat for 4 to 5 minutes or until mixture is reduced to 1/4 cup.
- Whisk in mustard; keep warm.
- Preheat an indoor electric grill on high setting, if available.
- Place steak on the grill rack. If using a covered grill, close lid. Grill until steak is desired doneness. (For a covered grill, allow 3 to 4 minutes for medium rare or 5 to 7 minutes for medium
- . For an uncovered grill, allow 6 to 8 minutes for medium rare or 8 to 10 minutes for medium, turning steak once.)
- If space allows, add asparagus to covered grill for the last 2 to 3 minutes or for uncovered grill the last 4 to 5 minutes of grilling.
- Cook asparagus until crisp-tender.*
- Spoon sauce on serving plate.
- Cut steak in half crosswise. Serve steak halves atop sauce with asparagus on top.
- *Note: The asparagus cooking time will vary with the size of asparagus. Also, if there is no room on the grill, the asparagus can be grilled after the steak.

111. German Beef Rouladen Recipe

Serving: 4 | Prep: | Cook: 120mins | Ready in:

Ingredients

- 8 round boiling potatoes
- a little salt
- 12 thin filets 1/4" thick about 2" wide and 5" long, length and wide can vary, beef can be round steak, flank steak, etc. (approximately 1.25 lbs of beef)
- 6 slices of bacon
- 2 dill pickles
- 1 dry onion, cut into 12 sections
- olive oil
- toothpicks
- 2 beef bullion cubes or equivalent
- 3 carrots
- 3 stalks celery
- A little flour
- Kitchen Bouquet (optional)

Direction

- Scrub the potatoes and boil in lightly salted water.
- When tender (~45 minutes), remove potatoes to a colander, rinse to arrest cooking, and reserve 2 cups of the water the potatoes were boiled in.
- Assemble the rouladen as follows:
- - Lay out a fillet.
- - Place 1/2 slice bacon on the fillet.
- - Place a small slice of pickle and a section of onion on the bacon.
- - Roll up the beef tightly and secure the roll with one or two toothpicks.
- Put a little olive oil in a heavy pot and over high heat, brown the rouladen (it may be easier to do this in two batches); toss in any remaining onion.
- Make two cups of beef bouillon, using the reserved potato water, and add to the pot, which now contains all of the rouladen.
- Reduce heat, cover, and simmer until tender, about 1.5 to 2 hours.
- Peel the carrots and chop the carrots and celery into 2-inch pieces.
- Add the carrots and celery to the rouladen when about 30 minutes of cooking remain.
- Remove the rouladen and vegetables to a plate when they are done.
- Reduce the liquid on high heat and make a gravy using the flour and Kitchen Bouquet.
- Serve the gravy over the rouladen and the potatoes.
- This is simple and delicious. Some recipes recommend including mustard, salt, and pepper when assembling the rouladen. I find it unnecessary as the bouillon provides enough salt and the added mustard flavor is rooted in the European habit of eating mustard on steaks.

112. German Pork Chops Recipe

Serving: 4 | Prep: | Cook: 60mins | Ready in:

Ingredients

- 28 ounces canned sauerkraut drained and rinsed
- 2 teaspoons caraway seeds
- 4 pork loin chops
- 1 teaspoon freshly ground black pepper
- 2 cooking apples peeled cored and sliced
- 2 tablespoons raisins
- 4 teaspoons firmly packed brown sugar
- 4 tablespoons apple juice or water

Direction

- Preheat oven to 375.
- Grease shiny side of four sheets of heavy duty aluminum foil.
- Place sauerkraut into a colander then press out excess liquid.

- Place 1/4 of sauerkraut onto centre of each sheet of foil and sprinkle caraway seed over the top.
- Place pork chops onto top of sauerkraut and season with pepper.
- Arrange apple slices and raisins evenly over pork chops.
- Sprinkle each portion with 1 teaspoon brown sugar.
- Over each portion spoon 1 tablespoon apple juice or water.
- To wrap bring two opposite ends of foil up and over making a double fold to seal tightly.
- Close both ends and seal tightly.
- Place packets onto a baking sheet and bake 1 hour then remove from oven.
- Carefully open packets and transfer pork mixture onto individual serving plates.

113.   German Pork And Kraut Recipe

Serving: 6 | Prep: | Cook: 40mins | Ready in:

Ingredients

- 6 bone in center pork chops cut 1/2 thick
- 3 cans of sauerkraut drained (each can about 14 oz each)
- 4 small red apples finely chopped
- 2 medium onion finely chopped
- 2 carrots fine chopped
- salt and pepper to taste
- 1/4 tsp celery seed
- 1/4 cup water

Direction

- Cook chops in skillet until browned on both sides.
- In a very large bowl stir together remaining ingredients except water.
- Pour this over chops in skillet.
- Add the water
- Bring to a boil

- Then reduce heat to a simmer and cover and cook about 30 to 40 minutes until chops are fully cooked and flavours blended.

114.   Ginger Beef Recipe

Serving: 4 | Prep: | Cook: 20mins | Ready in:

Ingredients

- 1 pound sirloin
- 1 celery stalk
- 1 carrot
- 3 hot chili peppers
- 2 tablespoons fresh ginger minced
- 2 cloves garlic minced
- 1 teaspoon sesame oil
- Marinade:
- 2 tablespoons dark soy sauce
- 1 tablespoon cooking wine
- 1 teaspoon sugar
- 2 tablespoons ginger juice
- 1 egg white lightly beaten
- 1/4 cup water
- 1/4 cup flour
- 1/4 cup cornstarch
- 1 tablespoon hot chili oil
- Sauce:
- 1 tablespoon wine
- 2 tablespoons soy sauce
- 1 tablespoon vinegar
- 4 tablespoons honey
- 1/2 teaspoon sesame oil
- 2 tablespoons water
- 1 teaspoon chili powder
- 5 cups oil for deep-frying
- 1 Tbsp oil for stir-frying

Direction

- Cut beef into matchstick strips cutting along the grain. Peel and grate ginger then squeeze out juice. Mix four marinade ingredients. Add to beef and marinate 30 minutes. Cut carrots, celery and pepper into thin strips. Mince garlic. For ginger use the leftover minced ginger from the preparation of ginger juice. Mix sauce ingredients and set aside.

- Beat egg white and add water then add flour and cornstarch. Mix batter thoroughly and drop into marinated meat. Heat wok. When heated add 5 cups oil. When oil is ready add about 1/4 of the meat batter mixture. Deep fry beef until golden brown. Remove and set aside. Let oil come back to original temperature and add more meat. When meat is cooked clean the wok. Heat and add 1 tablespoon oil. When oil is ready, add vegetables and begin stir frying. Pour in the sauce and let come to a boil. Add the deep fried beef then toss quickly and remove. Sprinkle with sesame oil and serve hot.

115.   Ginger Beef With Cabbage Recipe

Serving: 4 | Prep: | Cook: 10mins | Ready in:

Ingredients

- - 1.5 tsp sugar
- - 2 tbsp sake
- - 1/3 C Japanese soy sauce
- - 1 tsp grated fresh ginger
- - 2 lbs. beef rump steak/strips
- - 8 leaves of green cabbage
- - vegetable oil
- - 3 tsp fresh ginger juice
- - Optional: black & white sesame seeds

Direction

- Combine sugar, sake, sauce and grated ginger in a medium bowl. Stir until the sugar dissolves.
- Cut the beef into thin strips.
- Add it to the marinade, let stand for 10 minutes. (But no longer, otherwise the meat will get tough.)

- Drain over a small bowl, and reserve the marinade.
- Cut the cabbage leaves into one inch squares, removing the thick ribs.
- Heat some oil in a large skillet or wok, add the meat and stir-fry for 3 minutes.
- Add the cabbage, the reserved marinade and the ginger juice, and stir-fry a little longer until everything is heated through.
- Add sesame seeds to garnish.
- Serve in bowls over steamed rice and eat with chopsticks.

116.   Ginger Flank Steak With Sake Glazed Vegetables Recipe

Serving: 6 | Prep: | Cook: 30mins | Ready in:

Ingredients

- 1/2 cup soy sauce
- 1/2 cup sake
- 1/4 cup (packed) dark brown sugar
- 3 tablespoons minced peeled fresh ginger
- 1 tablespoon balsamic vinegar
- 4 garlic cloves, crushed
- 1 2-pound flank steak
- 1 pound asparagus, trimmed, cut into 1 1/2-inch lengths
- 3 tablespoons peanut oil
- 2 red bell peppers, cut into 1-inch-wide strips
- 1 1/2 pounds crimini mushrooms, halved, each half cut crosswise into 1/4-inch-thick slices
- 4 green onions, cut into 1-inch lengths
- 2 teaspoons cornstarch

Direction

- Combine first 6 ingredients in 13x9x2-inch glass baking dish. Add meat. Cover and refrigerate at least 2 hours and up to 1 day.
- Let stand at room temperature 1 hour before continuing.
- ~~

- Cook asparagus in large pot of boiling salted water until crisp-tender, about 4 minutes. Drain. Rinse under cold water to cool. Drain again.
- Heat 2 tablespoons peanut oil in heavy large skillet over medium-high heat.
- Add red bell pepper strips and sauté 3 minutes.
- Add cremini mushrooms and sauté until mushrooms are soft, about 5 minutes.
- Add green onions and asparagus and sauté until vegetables are tender, about 2 minutes longer.
- Transfer vegetables to serving platter. Tent with foil to keep warm.
- Heat remaining 1 tablespoon peanut oil in same skillet over high heat.
- Remove steak from marinade; reserve marinade.
- Add steak to skillet and cook to desired doneness, about 4 minutes per side for medium-rare. Transfer to cutting board. Tent with foil and let stand 5 minutes.
- Meanwhile, place reserved marinade in small saucepan. Whisk in cornstarch. Whisk over high heat until sauce thickens and boils, about 3 minutes. Remove sauce from heat. Season sauce to taste with salt and pepper.
- Cut steak across grain on diagonal into 1/2-inch-thick slices. Arrange steak slices atop vegetables on platter.
- Spoon some of sauce over meat and vegetables. Serve, passing remaining sauce separately.

117. Gorgonzola Stuffed Pork Chops Recipe

Serving: 4 | Prep: | Cook: 60mins | Ready in:

Ingredients

- 2 tablespoon butter
- 1 tablespoon dried thyme
- 1 cup chopped granny smith apples
- ground black pepper to taste
- 1/2 cup gorgonzola cheese at room temperature, crumbled
- 4 thick cut pork chops
- 1 teaspoon olive oil
- 2 cloves garlic
- 1/4 cup gorgonzola cheese
- 4 tablespoons dry sherry
- 1/4 cup heavy cream
- 1/2 cup chicken broth - divided
- salt and pepper to taste

Direction

- Preheat oven to 375 degrees F
- Apple stuffing: In a sauté pan or skillet on medium heat, melt the butter and sauté thyme, chopped apples, salt and pepper together until the apples are completely softened; about 15 to 20 minutes.
- Place the apple mixture in a bowl and mix in 1/2 cup Gorgonzola cheese. The cheese should liquefy into the stuffing within a couple of minutes.
- Pork chops: Butterfly the pork chops by slicing them parallel to the plane of the chop from the fat side to the bone. Stuff each one with about 2 to 3 tablespoons of the apple mixture.
- Place the chops on a rack with the two stuffing sides pressed together to hold the stuffing inside the chops. Bake the chops for about 1 hour.
- Sauce: Heat the oil in a sauté pan or skillet on medium heat, then sauté the garlic until transparent then add the sherry, let cook for a minute until combined, then add the cream and 1/4 cup of the chicken stock, salt and pepper. Stir until well blended. Stir occasionally and reduce the liquid on medium high heat until the sauce begins to caramelize and turn darker brown. Add the remaining 1/4 cup chicken stock and the cheese and continue reducing until there is just 1/4 to 1/2 cup of thick liquid remaining.

118. Gorgonzola Stuffed Steak With Prosciutto Recipe

Serving: 2 | Prep: | Cook: 60mins |Ready in:

Ingredients

- 2 NY Strip or sirloin steaks, 1½ to 2-inches thick
- 6 large fresh sage leaves
- 6 large fresh basil leaves
- 2 sprigs oregano, leaves removed
- 2 cloves garlic
- 2 tablespoons olive oil
- 2 tablespoons pine nuts
- Freshly ground black pepper
- ½ cup gorgonzola cheese, crumbled
- 4 slices prosciutto or pancetta

Direction

- Preheat oven to 425°F.
- Place the sage, basil and oregano leaves, the garlic cloves and olive oil into a food processor, and pulse several times until finely minced. Add the pine nuts and pulse again until smooth. Add the black pepper and gorgonzola cheese, and process again for a few seconds until it reaches a smooth consistency. Set aside.
- Trim the steaks of excess fat. Cut a slit through the middle of each steak, horizontally, about three-quarters of the way to the other side. Be careful not to cut all the way through the steaks. You want to create a pocket leaving the two sides and back of the steak intact.
- Open the pocket of the steak and stuff with the gorgonzola filling. Do not overfill, as the gorgonzola will melt and ooze out of the steak.
- Wrap each steak with 2 pieces of prosciutto or pancetta, covering the opening to seal the gorgonzola in.
- Heat the cast-iron skillet over medium-high heat until very hot. Brush the wrapped steaks with oil and place in the pan, searing each side for about 3 minutes.
- Carefully remove the skillet from the stove and place in the preheated oven to finish cooking the steaks to your desired doneness.
- Remove the steaks from the oven, place on serving platter and cover with foil.
- Let the steaks rest for 5 minutes before serving.

119. Grandmas Porkchop Scalloped Potatoes Recipe

Serving: 6 | Prep: | Cook: 70mins |Ready in:

Ingredients

- 1 onion, chopped
- 1 clove garlic, minced
- 2 tbsp. butter
- 1 tbsp. all-purpose flour
- pepper and salt to taste
- 1 cup milk
- 1/3 cup dry white wine (the kind you would normally drink)
- 3/4 cup heavy cream
- 6 medium red potatoes
- 1 lb. pork chops
- 1 tsp. chipotle cinnamon spice (optional)
- 1/2 cup shredded cheddar cheese
- 1/2 cup shredded monterey jack cheese

Direction

- Grease 9x13 inch casserole dish and set aside.
- For sauce, in a skillet cook onion and garlic in butter until tender. Stir in flour, pepper and a pinch of salt. Whisk in milk. Cook and stir till thickened. Add wine and heavy cream. Cook and stir another 5 minutes.
- Wash potatoes. Do not peel skins off. THINLY slice potatoes. Place half the sliced potatoes in the prepared casserole. Sprinkle lightly with salt and pepper. Cover with half the sauce.
- Mix together cheddar and Monterey jack cheeses. Sprinkle half of the cheese mixture over potatoes.

- Season the pork chops with chipotle cinnamon spice. (Can be subbed with just salt and pepper, or pork rub spice). Place seasoned pork chops over potatoes. Leave the pork chops whole for easy portioning (one per person).
- Place the other half of sliced potatoes over the pork chops. Sprinkle lightly with salt and pepper. Cover with remaining sauce and sprinkle with the rest of the shredded cheese.
- Bake, covered, in a 350F oven for 40 min. Uncover and bake 30 min. more, or till potatoes are tender and the cheese is lightly browned.
- *Hint: potatoes will cook through better if they are sliced real thin.

120.   Gravy Baked Pork Chops Recipe

Serving: 4 | Prep: | Cook: 45mins | Ready in:

Ingredients

- 4 (1 1/4 inch thick) pork chops
- 2 to 4 oz. fresh mushrooms or can of sliced mushrooms
- 1 ts minced garlic
- salt and pepper to taste
- 1 ts oil of choice (I use EVOO)
- 1 Tbls EVOO or butter
- 3/4 cup milk
- 1/4 cup water
- 1 can cream of mushroom soup

Direction

- Preheat oven to 350°F.
- If using fresh mushrooms, slice them and place them in skillet with a teaspoon of oil on med heat and sauté for 5 minutes or so.
- I also add a teaspoon of minced garlic to the cooking mushrooms in the last 3 minutes of cooking mushrooms but you can just add it to the soup mixture.

- Season pork chops with salt and pepper to taste.
- Melt the butter in a large skillet over medium high heat.
- Sauté the pork chops in the butter for about 5 minutes per side.
- In a separate medium bowl, combine the milk, water and soup mushrooms and garlic.
- Place the pork chops in a 9X113 inch baking dish and pour the soup mixture over the chops.
- Bake at 350°F for 45 minutes
- Enjoy

121.   Grecian Goddess Pork Chops Recipe

Serving: 4 | Prep: | Cook: 15mins | Ready in:

Ingredients

- 1/4 cup olive oil
- 1/4 cup lemon juice
- 1/2 tsp dry rosemary, crumbled
- 2 cloves garlic, crushed
- 4 thick boneless chops (about 1 1/2 inches, may use bone-in)

Direction

- Combine first 4 ingredients in a bowl, mix well. Place chops in a heavy plastic bag (freezer) and pour marinade over top. Expel air and seal bag. Turn bag around several times to evenly distribute marinade. Place in fridge for 4-24 hours.
- Remove chops and place on broiling pan, reserving marinade. Broil for 12-15 minutes, turning once and basting occasionally with reserved marinade.

122. Greek Style Pork Chops Recipe

Serving: 4 | Prep: | Cook: 30mins | Ready in:

Ingredients

- 2 Tbs red wine vinegar,divided
- 1 tsp dried oregano
- 2 tsp olive oil,divided
- 2 garlic cloves,minced
- 4 (4oz) boneless,center-cut loin chops
- 3/4 c plain fat-free Greek style yogurt
- 1 Tbs chopped fresh dill
- 1/2 tsp salt,divided
- 1-1/2 c diced plum tomatoes(about 2 medium)
- 1 c diced seeded cucumber
- 1/2 c diced red onion
- cooking spray

Direction

- Combine 1 Tbsp. red wine vinegar, oregano, tsp. olive oil and garlic in Ziploc bag. Add pork to bag, and seal. Marinate 20 mins at room temperature, turning after 10 mins.
- Combine remaining 1 Tbsp. vinegar, remaining 1 tsp. oil, yogurt, 1 Tbsp. dill and 1/8 tsp. salt, stirring well with whisk. Cover and chill
- Combine tomatoes, cucumber and onion. Sprinkle tomato mixture with 1/8 tsp. salt; toss to combine.
- Heat grill or grill pan to med-high. Coat with spray. Remove pork from bag and discard marinade.
- Sprinkle both sides of pork evenly with remaining 1/4 tsp. salt. Add pork to grill and cook 4 mins a side or till desired doneness. Remove pork and let stand 2 mins.
- Place 3/4 c tomato mixture on each of 4 plates and top each serving with 1 pork chop and about 3 Tbsp. yogurt mixture.

123. Grillades Recipe

Serving: 4 | Prep: | Cook: 120mins | Ready in:

Ingredients

- 2 lbs round steak
- 2 teaspoons kosher salt
- 1/4 teaspoon cayenne pepper
- 1/2 Cup flour seasoned
- 2 Tablespoons creole seasoning
- 3 Tablespoons vegetable oil
- 3 Tablespoons unsalted butter
- 2 Medium onions, Julienned
- 1 red bell pepper, Julienned
- 2 Ribs celery, Julienned
- 3 cloves garlic, Chopped
- 2 Cups beef stock
- 3 Tbsp worcestershire sauce
- 2 Cups tomatoes, Chopped
- 2 fresh bay leaves
- 1 Tablespoons red wine vinegar
- Crystal hot sauce to taste
- 1 Tablespoon corn Starch (whisked together with 1 Tablespoon water)
- 1/4 cup flat leaf parsley, chopped
- 1/2 cup green onions, thinly sliced on the bias
- salt & pepper to taste

Direction

- Pound the round steak on both sides to about ½ inch thickness, then cut into 4 inch squares. Season the grillades with the salt & cayenne pepper. Combine the flour and Creole Seasoning, dip the Grillades one at a time into the seasoned flour and shake off any excess. In a cast iron Dutch oven, heat the vegetable oil over medium heat until very hot, but not smoking. Brown the Grillades well on both sides without burning. Transfer the Grillades to a plate. Drain off the vegetable oil and melt the butter over medium heat. Add the Onions, Bell Pepper, Celery, and Garlic and, stirring frequently, cook until the vegetables are soft but not brown. Stir in the Beef Stock, Worcestershire, Tomatoes, and Bay Leaves;

bring the mixture to a boil. Reduce the heat to medium-low. Return the Grillades and the accumulated juice from the plate back to the pot. Submerge the Grillades in the sauce and simmer for about 1 ½ hours or until they're very tender. When the Grillades are tender remove them to a plate and bring the sauce to a boil. Add the corn starch mixture and whisk until the sauce is slightly thickened. Stir in the parsley, 1/4 cup of the green onions, red wine vinegar, hot sauce, and salt & pepper. Mound grits on 4 heated plates and divide the steaks on top of grits. Pour the sauce over the Grillades & Grits, top with the remaining Green Onions and serve immediately. This can also be served with rice.

---

124. Grilled Apple Stuffed Pork Chops Recipe

Serving: 4 | Prep: | Cook: 35mins | Ready in:

Ingredients

- 3 cups apple wood chips
- 1/4 teaspoon freshly ground black pepper
- 1/8 teaspoon onion salt or garlic salt
- 1/8 teaspoon ground cloves
- 1/8 teaspoon ground red pepper (optional)
- 1/4 pound bulk Italian pork sausage or bulk turkey sausage
- 1 apple, cored and finely chopped
- 1/4 cup chopped onion
- 1/2 cup corn bread stuffing mix
- 2 tablespoons snipped fresh parsley
- 1 to 2 tablespoons apple juice
- 4 pork loin rib chops, cut 1-1/2 inches thick (about 3 lb. total)
- Purchased apple butter
- Grilled sliced apples (optional)

Direction

- At least 1 hour before cooking, soak wood chips in enough water to cover. Drain.

- For the rub, stir together the black pepper; onion or garlic salt; cloves; and, if desired, red pepper.
- For stuffing, in a saucepan cook the sausage, apple, and onion for 5 minutes or until sausage is cooked through. Drain fat. Stir in stuffing mix and parsley; add enough of the apple juice to moisten. Remove from heat; set aside until cool.
- Trim fat from chops. Cut a pocket in each chop by cutting a slit in the meat and working the knife inside to cut almost to bone, keeping original slit small. Spoon stuffing into pockets. If necessary, secure with wooden toothpicks. Sprinkle the rub evenly over both sides of the pork chops; rub into meat.
- Drain wood chips. Prepare grill for indirect grilling; test for medium heat above the drip pan. Place chops on the lightly oiled grill rack directly over the drip pan.
- Cover and grill chops for 35 to 40 minutes or until an instant-read thermometer inserted into centre reads 165 degree F, turning chops once. Add more wood chips every 15 minutes. Brush with apple butter every few minutes during last half of grilling. If using wooden toothpicks, remove them before serving. Serve with grilled sliced apples, if desired.

---

125. Grilled Beef Fajitas With Green Yogurt Sauce Recipe

Serving: 6 | Prep: | Cook: 8mins | Ready in:

Ingredients

- 1 1/2 cups plain yogurt
- juice of 2 limes (1/3 cup)
- 2 tablespoons extra-virgin olive oil plus 1/4 cup for brushing vegetables
- 1 tablespoon hot pepper sauce
- 2 tablespoons chopped fresh thyme leaves, a few sprigs
- 1 (1 1/2 pound) sirloin steak or flank steak

- 2 red or green bell peppers, halved and seeds removed
- 1 large sweet onion, such as Vidalia, Maui or Texas Sweet
- salt and pepper, to taste
- 1 jalapeno pepper, seeded and coarsely chopped
- 1/2 cup cilantro leaves, loosely packed
- 1 teaspoon salt
- 8 to 12 large flour tortillas
- 2 yellow, orange or red vine-ripe tomatoes, chopped

Direction

- Heat a grill pan or electric grill to high heat, or prepare outdoor grill.
- In a shallow dish, combine the juice of 1 1/2 limes (reserving 1/2 lime) with 2 tablespoons olive oil, hot pepper sauce and chopped thyme leaves. Coat beef in the lime-oil. Grill beef 6 or 7 minutes on each side.
- Baste pepper halves with a little oil, and set on grill alongside beef. Cut onion into 4 or 5 thick slices, cutting across the onion. Remove outer ring of the sliced onion, discarding the skin. Baste onion with oil and place on grill. Season beef and vegetables with salt and pepper. Peppers and onions will grill in about 10 minutes. They should be charred at edges, but still have a bite to them.
- In a food processor, combine yogurt, the juice of reserved 1/2 lime, the jalapeno pepper, cilantro leaves and salt. Process the ingredients into a smooth, green sauce.
- Once you remove beef and vegetables from the grill, char and warm tortillas. Slice cooked beef on an angle and transfer to a serving plate. Slice peppers into strips and cut onion rings in half. Transfer cut veggies to platter alongside beef.
- To assemble, pile beef, pepper strips and onions into tortillas and top with chopped tomatoes and lots of yogurt green sauce.
- Makes 4 to 6 servings.

Serving: 4 | Prep: | Cook: 15mins | Ready in:

Ingredients

- 1 clove garlic, large, chopped
- 1 tablespoon onion, finely chopped
- 1 tablespoon lime juice, fresh
- 1 teaspoon chili powder, chipotle, kind
- 1 teaspoon chili powder, ancho, kind
- 2 teaspoons salt
- 1 teaspoon ground cumin
- 1 tablespoon olive oil
- 1 1/2 pounds flank steak, scored on both sides
- 10 lime wedges
- 3 1/2 ounces monterey jack cheese, shredded
- 12 6-inch corn tortillas, warmed

Direction

- In food processor, pulse garlic with onion, lime juice, chili powder, salt and cumin. With the machine on, slowly drizzle in the olive oil until a paste forms. Rub the paste all over the steak and let marinate at least an hour.
- Grill the steak over a medium-high fire for 10 minutes, turning once, until an instant-read thermometer inserted in the thickest part registers 130-135 degrees for medium-rare. Transfer to cutting board and let rest for 5 minutes.
- Cut the steak across the grain into 1/4" slices. Squeeze the juice from 2 lime wedges over the steak slices, then top with the shredded cheese. Serve with warm tortillas and the remaining lime wedges.

127. Grilled Chipotle Flank Steak Recipe

Serving: 4 | Prep: | Cook: 10mins | Ready in:

Ingredients

- 1small onion, quartered
- 1 clove garlic
- 1/2 cup chili sauce
- 1-2 chipotle chiles in adobo sauce
- 1 tbls. olive oil
- 1 tbls. lime juice
- 1 tbls. brown sugar
- 1 1/2 tsp. cumin
- salt to taste
- 1 1/2 lbs. flank steak

Direction

- Cook time does not include marinade time
- In processor, chop onion and garlic
- Add chili sauce, chipotles, 1 tbsp. oil, lime juice, sugar, cumin, and salt
- Process until smooth
- Marinate beef in mixture at least 3 hours but overnight is better
- Grill steak over medium heat on grill 3-4 minutes a side

128. Grilled Flank Steak With Provencal Spices Recipe

Serving: 4 | Prep: | Cook: 20mins | Ready in:

Ingredients

- 3 tablespoons extra virgin olive oil
- 1 teaspoon salt
- 2 garlic cloves peeled
- 2 teaspoons fresh rosemary leaves
- 2 teaspoons fresh lavender leaves
- 1 teaspoon fennel seeds
- 2 teaspoons fresh thyme leaves
- 1 teaspoon cracked black pepper
- 2 pounds flank steak

Direction

- Start a charcoal or wood fire or heat a gas grill or broiler.
- Combine all ingredients except steak in food processor and blend until minced but do not puree.
- Cover meat with spice mixture and when fire is hot grill meat 6 minutes per side turning once.
- Remove from fire and let rest 5 minutes before slicing thin and serving.

129. Grilled Kurobuta Pork Loin Chops With A Nicoise Olive And Red Wine Sauce Recipe

Serving: 4 | Prep: | Cook: 45mins | Ready in:

Ingredients

- For the Pork:
- 4 ea., 8-10 oz. Kurobuta pork loin chops
- ½ cup extra virgin olive oil
- 3-4 cloves garlic, smashed
- 2 sprigs Fresh rosemary
- 3 sprigs Fresh thyme
- kosher salt to taste
- fresh cracked pepper to taste
- For the Sauce:
- 2 cups Madeira
- 2 cups merlot
- 1 cups veal stock
- 1 spring Fresh rosemary
- 2 ea., bay leaves
- 4 shallots, finely chopped
- ½ cup leeks, white part only, chopped
- ½ cup mushroom scraps, chopped
- ½ cup carrot, chopped
- 1 Tbsp. black peppercorns
- 8 oz. unsalted butter
- ½ cup nicoise olives, seeds removed and halved
- kosher salt to taste

Direction

- In a marinating dish or Ziploc bag, combine all of the ingredients for the pork except the salt and pepper. Marinate the pork for at least 4 hours or overnight. Let the pork stand at room temperature for at least 30 minutes before cooking.
- In a sauce pan, sauté the shallots, carrots, leeks, and mushrooms in 3-4 Tbsp. butter until lightly browned. Add the Madeira, merlot, rosemary, bay leaves, and peppercorns, and reduce until approximately 1 cup of liquid remains. In a separate sauce pan, reduce the veal stock by half. Combine the reduced veal stock to the reduced wine mixture, then strain into a sauce pan and return to the stove. Add the olives to the sauce, then off the heat, whisk in the butter until emulsified. Season to taste with kosher salt and fresh cracked pepper, and keep warm.
- Pre-heat grill to medium. Remove the pork from the marinade and shake off any excess oil. Season both sides with kosher salt and pepper, and cook until the pork reaches an internal temperature of 140 degrees. Serve immediately with the olive and red wine sauce.

130.   Grilled Lamb Chops With Ladolmono Sauce(Olive Oil And Lemon Dressing) Recipe

Serving: 4 | Prep: | Cook: 20mins | Ready in:

Ingredients

- Lamb;
- 12 lamb rib chops(about 3 lbs)
- 2 TB chopped parsley
- 2 TB chopped mint
- Ladolemono Sauce:
- 1/2 c olive oil
- 1/4 c fresh lemon juice

- 1 tsp dried oregano
- 1 pinch salt
- 1 pinch pepper
- Chopped garlic ,to taste,if desired

Direction

- Drizzle lamb chops with olive oil and season with salt and pepper. Grill over high heat till nicely charred outside and med-rare within, 2 to 3 mins per side. Transfer chops to platter and drizzle with Ladolemono. Sprinkle with parsley and mint and serve. Great with stuffed tomatoes
- Ladolemono: In a small jar with tight lid, combine olive oil, lemon juice, oregano, salt and pepper and garlic, if desired. Seal and shake till well blended. Use to brush on meats, chicken, fish, vegetables or as a salad dressing. Shake or stir before using.

131.   Grilled Lamb Chops With Tabouli Beef Tenderloin Kabob With Hummus And Minted Yoghurt Recipe

Serving: 2 | Prep: | Cook: 8mins | Ready in:

Ingredients

- Hummus:
- 1/2 can organic chickpeas, drained and washed
- 1 lemon, juice and zest
- 1/4 cup olive oil
- 2 T fresh parsley, chopped
- 1 garlic clove
- pinch of cayenne
- kosher salt, to taste
- ~~~~~~~~~~~~~~~~~~~~~~~~~~~~~ ~~~~~~~~~~~~~~~~~~~
- Middle Eastern Yoghurt:
- 3 T english cucumber, brunoise
- 6 T yoghurt (I like Greek style)

- 1/4 T fresh oregano
- kosher salt and freshly ground pepper
- 1 T red onion, brunoise
- ~~~~~~
- parsley couscous Salad:
- 4 T each parsley & mint leaves, minced
- 1 cup plain couscous, cooked
- 1 tsp sesame oil
- kosher salt and freshly ground pepper
- 1 T chardonnay vinegar
- 2 T olive oil
- 2 T toasted pine nuts
- 1 lemon, juice and zest
- ~~~~~~
- Lamb Chops:
- 4 lamb rib chops, frenched (just ask your butcher to do this)
- 1/4 tsp fennel seed
- 1/4 tsp cumin
- 1/4 tsp cinnamon
- 1/4 tsp coriander
- 3 T olive oil
- 2 garlic cloves
- kosher salt and freshly ground pepper
- ~~~~~~
- beef Kabob:
- 8 1/2-inch cubes of beef tenderloin
- 8 baby cipollini onions, pre-roasted (or pearl onions)
- 4 skewers
- kosher salt and freshly ground pepper
- 1/4 tsp cumin
- 2 T olive oil
- ~~~~~~
- mint Oil:
- 2 T mint, julienne
- 1 T oregano julienne
- 4 T olive oil
- kosher salt and freshly ground pepper
- zest and juice of 1 lemon

Direction

- Hummus: Blend all ingredients in food processor until smooth (add a little water if too thick). Place in fridge until ready to serve.
- Middle Eastern Yoghurt: Mix all items together and place in fridge until ready to serve.
- Parsley Couscous Salad: Mix all items together and place in fridge until ready to serve.
- Lamb Chops: Marinade lamb with all spices and oil. Sear on a hot charcoal grill 2-4 minutes, each side.
- Beef kabob: Skewer meat and onions and marinade with all the spices and the oil. Sear on a hot charcoal grill 2-4 minutes, each side.
- Mint Oil: Mix together and set aside until ready to serve.
- To assemble: On a rectangle/square large serving platter, place a dollop of hummus on one side and a dollop of the yoghurt on the other. Fill a small ramekin with the couscous, pack down and invert in the center (between the hummus and the yoghurt). On the side with the hummus, place 2 lamb chops and garnish with parsley. On the side with the yoghurt, place 2 beef kabobs and garnish with mint oil.

---

132. Grilled Ny Steak California Chanterelles And Corn Saute Garlic Rosemary Broken Vinaigrette Recipe

Serving: 4 | Prep: | Cook: 30mins | Ready in:

Ingredients

- 4 prime NY strip steaks, 8 oz each
- kosher salt
- For corn:
- 4 tablespoons unsalted butter
- 4 ears of fresh white corn, cut off the cob
- 1 cup chanterelle mushrooms, cut in peices if they are really big
- 1 small shallot, chopped

- 4 sprigs of fresh thyme, leaves only
- white pepper & kosher salt to taste
- For "broken" vinaigrette:
- 1/2 cup extra virgin olive oil (I used one from Spain, very fruity)
- 1 clove garlic, smashed
- 1 sprig rosemary
- 1/4 cup aged balsamic vinegar

Direction

- For "broken" vinaigrette: Place garlic, rosemary and olive oil in saucepan over medium heat until you can smell the aromas and the oil is warm. Take off heat and allow to sit for one hour so oil becomes infused.
- Strain oil into small bowl. Add balsamic and VERY LIGHTLY stir with a small spoon. What you want is to keep the vinegar and oil separate so you get these cool looking beads of vinegar floating in the oil.
- For corn: Melt butter in large non-stick pan. Add remaining ingredients and sauté over med-high until mushrooms are cooked and corn is slightly caramelized.
- For steaks: Remove the steaks from the refrigerator about 30 to 40 minutes before cooking. Cover loosely with plastic wrap and allow the steaks to come to room temperature. Before grilling, shape the steaks by gently pushing the sides into the center to create height. Season both side with kosher salt
- Place the meat on the hottest part of your charcoal grill. If at any time the grill flares up, move the steaks to the outside edge, returning them to the center when the flame dies down. Do not slide the steaks across the grill; gently pick them up with tongs. The key is not to flip them around. Ultimately you want to turn a New York strip steak only three times, cooking each side twice for 3 minutes at a time (for a total cooking time of 12 minutes), to get a rare steak with adequate char. Tent with foil and let rest for 10-15 minutes.
- To plate: Place mound of corn in center of serving plate. Slightly overlap the steak on the corn. With a teaspoon, drizzle the vinaigrette

in a swirl pattern around the plate. Garnish with fresh rosemary sprig.

---

133. Grilled Pork Chops With Onion Marmalade And Cauliflower Puree Recipe

Serving: 4 | Prep: | Cook: 16mins |Ready in:

Ingredients

- For the pork chops:
- 4 thick cut boneless natural pork chops (Niman Ranch)
- 1/4 cup olive oil
- 1 cup of red wine (Zinfandel)
- 1 cinnamon stick
- 3 cloves of garlic, minced
- 1 sprig of rosemary, bruised
- juice of 1/2 a lemon
- kosher salt & fresh ground black pepper
- ~~~~~~~~~~~~~~~~~~~~~~~~~~~~~~~~~~~~ ~~~~~~~~~~~~~~~~~~

- onion Marmalade:
- 2 Tbsp. butter, divided
- reserved pork chop marinade
- 1 medium red onion, sliced
- 1/3 cup honey
- 1/4 cup aged balsamic vinegar
- fresh thyme leaves, chopped
- kosher salt and pepper to taste
- ~~~~~~~~~~~~~~~~~~~~~~~~~~~~~~~~~~~~~ ~~~~~~~~~~~~~~~~~~~

- cauliflower Puree:
- 1 large head of cauliflower
- few sprigs of fresh thyme
- 2 tablespoon cream cheese
- 1/4 cup grated parmigiano-reggiano
- 3 cloves garlic , roasted
- lemon juice to taste
- 3 tablespoons unsalted butter
- kosher salt and white pepper to taste

Direction

- For Pork Chops:
- Make one or two slits into the fat that hugs that hugs the round part of your chops. Season each side with salt and pepper.
- In a large bowl or zip-lock bag, add all your marinade ingredients and mix well. Reserve 3 tablespoons of marinade. Add your pork chops to the marinade in bag and ensure the chops are covered well by the marinade. Seal/cover and refrigerate for 3 hours. Bring back to room temperature before grilling.
- Take pork chops out of marinade, pat dry with paper towels. Drizzle a little olive oil on the chops to coat and re-season with salt and pepper (keep the rosemary to throw into your hot coals for a great aroma and flavour).
- Get your charcoal grill heated up to medium-high heat (no more than 400F).
- Grill your chops for about 6 minutes per side (depending on thickness) over medium-high heat.
- When your chops are done. Let them rest for 5 minutes before serving.
- ~~~~~~
- For onion marmalade:
- In a medium pot, add 1 tablespoon butter over medium heat and slowly sauté your onions for about 5 minutes. Cover and reduce the heat to low and simmer for another 15 minutes.
- Add the reserved marinade, honey and balsamic vinegar and reduce until you get the consistency of a jam or marmalade. Adjust seasoning with salt and pepper, finish with remaining 1 tbsp. butter and reserve.
- ~~~~~~
- For Cauliflower:
- Bring a large pot of water to boil. Meanwhile, cut off the stems of the cauliflower and break into florets. Put florets, topped with fresh thyme and a few squirts of lemon juice, in a steamer basket atop the boiling water and steam for about 15 minutes or until totally tender.
- In a food processor, puree the hot cauliflower with the cream cheese, Parmesan, roasted

garlic, salt and pepper until smooth. Transfer to saucepan and add butter, 1 tbsp. at a time until melted. Keep warm.
- ~~~~~~
~~~~~~~~~~~~~~~~~~~~~
- To plate:
- Smear a dollop of cauliflower puree in centre of plate. Top with pork chop and a dollop of onion marmalade on top. Garnish with fresh thyme leaves.

134. Grilled Pork Tortilla Wraps And Pineapple Salsa Recipe

Serving: 8 | Prep: | Cook: 30mins | Ready in:

Ingredients

- 1/2 teaspoon garlic powder
- 1/4 teaspoon salt
- 1/4 teaspoon freshly ground pepper
- ground red pepper to taste
- pork rub to taste
- 6 boneless pork loin chops, trimmed
- cooking spray (preferably olive oil)
- 8 inch flour tortillas, warmed
- pineapple salsa
- 1/4 cup orange juice
- 2 tablespoons lemon juice
- 1 tablespoon honey
- 1/4 teaspoon salt
- 1/4 teaspoon ground pepper
- 2 cups chopped fresh pineapple
- 2-3 tablespoons chopped fresh cilantro
- 1/4 cup small red onion, chopped

Direction

- Combine first 5 ingredients in bowl
- Sprinkle over pork chops
- Coat the pork chops evenly with cooking spray

- GRILL, covered with the lid of grill over medium heat...350-400 degrees, about 3-4 minutes on each side
- Check for doneness
- Let stand about 10 minutes
- Coarsely chop pork
- PINEAPPLE SALSA
- Whisk together 1/4 cup orange juice and next four ingredients
- Stir in pineapple, cilantro and onion
- WARM TORTILLAS COVERED IN OVEN....THEY ARE MOISTER WARMED IN OVEN
- Fill warmed tortilla with chopped pork and pineapple salsa
- *NOTE: SLICED AVOCADO MAY BE ADDED TO THE TORTILLA

135. Grilled Ribeye Steak With Onion Blue Cheese Sauce Recipe

Serving: 2 | Prep: | Cook: 15mins | Ready in:

Ingredients

- 2 ribeye steaks
- 2 tablespoons butter
- salt
- pepper
- 4 tablespoons butter
- 1 very large yellow onion
- 3/4 to 1 cup heavy cream
- 1/2 cup crumbled blue cheese

Direction

- Sauté onions in 4 tablespoons butter over high heat. Cook for 5 to 7 minutes, or until dark and caramelized.
- Reduce heat to simmer and pour in cream. Cook for 3 to 5 minutes, or until reduced by half.
- Stir in blue cheese until melted.

- Serve steaks on generous portion of sauce. Faint.

136. Grilled Rosemary Flank Steak Recipe

Serving: 6 | Prep: | Cook: 16mins | Ready in:

Ingredients

- 1/4 cup of olive oil
- 2 tablespoon balsamic vinegar
- 2 cloves garlic, crushed
- 1 rosemary sprig, chopped
- kosher salt to taste
- freshly ground black pepper
- 2 pounds flank steak

Direction

- Put peeled garlic cloves in zip lock bag and crush (I use the end of a marble rolling pin!) Add the oil, vinegar and rosemary to the bag. Salt and pepper the flank steak to taste, add to bag, seal and "Smoosh around" so marinade gets all over the meat.
- Refrigerate for at least 30 minutes or overnight.
- Preheat the grill.
- Grill the flank steak for 4 to 8 minutes on each side, depending on the desired doneness.
- Let the steak rest on a carving plate for 1 or 2 minutes.
- Slice the steak on the bias. Garnish with fresh rosemary and minced parsley, if desired.

137. Grilled Skirt Steak Recipe

Serving: 6 | Prep: | Cook: 6mins | Ready in:

Ingredients

- 1-1/2 lb. skirt steak, flank steak can be substituted
- MARINATE steak IN:
- 3 Tbsp. olive oil
- 3 Tbsp. fresh lime juice
- 2 Tbsp. brown sugar
- 1/2 tsp. crushed red pepper flakes
- 3 cloves garlic crushed

Direction

- Trim off as much fat as possible from both sides of skirt steak. Some of it is loosely attached and can be removed by hand. Otherwise, use a knife on places where it's firmly attached.
- Trim as much silver skin as you can.
- Marinate steak in olive oil, lime juice, brown sugar, crushed red pepper flakes and garlic for 30 minutes.
- Preheat the grill, when hot remove steak from marinate and season with salt and pepper.
- Place steak on grill. Cover and cook until seared, about 3 minutes.
- Flip steak over cook another 3 minutes.
- Transfer meat to a cutting board, tent with foil and let steak rest 8 minutes before slicing thin.

---

138.   Grilled Skirt Steak Sandwich With California Avocado And Blue Cheese Recipe

Serving: 4 | Prep: | Cook: 15mins | Ready in:

Ingredients

- 2 (8 to 10 oz.) skirt steaks
- 1 medium, sweet yellow onion cut in 1/4-inch slices
- 2 small tomatoes cut in 1/4-inch slices
- 2 tablespoons canola oil
- salt and freshly ground black pepper
- 2 tablespoons extra virgin olive oil

- 2 tablespoons balsamic vinegar
- 2 teaspoons chopped fresh thyme leaves
- 4 (6-inch) pieces of baguette sliced in half lengthwise and lightly toasted
- 1/2 ripe Fresh California avocado thinly sliced, for garnish
- 4 fresh thyme sprigs for garnish
- cracked black pepper
- --- California avocado Blue cheese spread
- 4 ounces Roquefort cheese (or similar blue cheese) at room temp.
- 2 tablespoons Freshly squeezed lemon juice
- 4 dashes hot sauce (I like Frank's Xtra Hot)
- 1 teaspoon Freshly ground black pepper
- salt to taste

Direction

- -- California Avocado Blue Cheese Spread:
- In a large bowl, combine avocados with blue cheese, lemon juice, hot sauce, and pepper. Mash with a fork until mixture is thoroughly combined. Taste and season lightly with salt (Note: careful here, blue cheese can be salty)
- -- Grilled Steak:
- About 30 minutes before cooking, remove skirt steaks from refrigerator. Trim any outer pieces of fat or silver skin, but marbling within beef should remain.
- Preheat grill or sauté pan to very hot. Pat skirt steaks dry. Brush steaks and onion and tomato slices with canola oil and season generously with salt and pepper. Grill or sauté steaks, 2 minutes per side for rare. Allow steak to rest several minutes on a cutting board.
- Meanwhile, on the grill or in the same sauté pan, char the onion slices until just tender, separating into rings. Grill or sauté the tomato slices briefly, until lightly charred and warmed through.
- In a small bowl, combine olive oil, vinegar and thyme. Add grilled onion and tomato slices to vinaigrette mixture and toss gently.
- Spread toasted top halves of baguettes with California Avocado Blue Cheese Spread. Place on the upper level of the grill with the top

closed, or under a broiler, until warmed, about 1 to 2 minutes.

- Arrange the charred onion and tomato slices on the bottom halves of the baguettes. Slice the steak thinly, at an angle across the grain, and place over the vegetables. Drizzle steak with any leftover balsamic vinaigrette.
- Serve sandwiches open-faced, side-by-side on a plate, with thin slices of avocado, thyme sprigs and cracked black pepper for garnish.
- Large avocados are recommended for this recipe. A large avocado averages about 8 ounces. If using smaller or larger size avocados adjust the quantity accordingly.

139. Grilled Skirt Steak And Potatoes With Herb Sauce Recipe

Serving: 4 | Prep: | Cook: 30mins | Ready in:

Ingredients

- 2 cups fresh flat-leaf parsley
- ¼ cup fresh oregano
- 2 cloves garlic
- 1 teaspoon red wine vinegar
- ½ cup extra-virgin olive oil
- ¼ teaspoon cayenne pepper
- ¾ teaspoon kosher salt
- 1 ½ pounds skirt steak
- ½ teaspoon black pepper
- 1 ½ pounds potatoes, cut on the diagonal into ¼-inch-thick slices

Direction

- Heat grill to medium.
- Place the parsley, oregano and garlic in the bowl of a food processor and pulse until roughly chopped. Add the vinegar, oil, cayenne and ½ teaspoon of salt and pulse to combine. Set aside.
- Season the steak with the remaining salt and the pepper. Grill to desired doneness, about 4

minutes per side for medium-rare. Transfer to a cutting board and let rest for 5 minutes before slicing.

- Meanwhile, as the steak cooks, toss the potatoes in a large bowl with 1/3 cup of the herb sauce. Place them on the grill in a single layer. Cook, turning once, until tender, about 4 minutes each side.
- Divide the steak and potatoes among individual plates and serve with the remaining sauce on the side.

140. Gyro Loaf And What To Do With It Recipe

Serving: 4 | Prep: | Cook: 120mins | Ready in:

Ingredients

- 5 lbs. of fatty lamb meat (leg and sirloin)
- Half a lb of salt pork
- 1 plump onion
- 8 cloves of garlic
- 1 bunch of flat leaf parsley
- 1 cup of fine bread crumbs
- 1 large egg
- 1 oz. of fresh oregano
- 1/4 an oz. of fresh rosemary
- Half a cup of sweet red wine
- 1 tbls. of black peppercorns
- 1 tbls. of cumin
- 1 tsp. of allspice
- Half a tsp of ground clove
- 1/4 tsp. of ground bay leaf
- 1/4 cup of tomato paste
- 2 oranges or lemons (optional)

Direction

- Cut the lamb into large chunks – keep some of the solid fat on it but trim away the stringy skin-like fat. Cut the pork into similarly sized pieces. Chop up the onion. Pluck the leaves from the oregano and rosemary and chop them as finely as possible.   Remove the outermost rind from the orange or lemons.

- Run the lamb and salt pork through a meat grinder fitted with a blade and screen that will produce a medium grind.
- Run the meat through again but this time fitted with a blade and screen to produce a fine grind. While doing this add the onion, peppercorns, and the citrus peeling along with the meat. Put this into a large mixing bowl.
- Thoroughly mix in the breadcrumbs, eggs, wine, tomato paste, herbs and the seasonings. Let it chill for 3-4 hours.
- Grease a shallow rectangular pan, and pack the meat mixture as tightly as possible (the meat layer should be 1 ½ inches thick) Set a heavy pan of the same size on top of it and press down firmly and fill the top pan with water .
- Now set these two pans into yet another larger and like-shaped pan halfway filled with water.
- Bake at 300° for 2 hours. Let it cool slightly and then pour off the grease. Let it chill until required.
- FOR THE EATING: Cut the resulting product made from the above described procedure into fairly long and 3/4 of an inch thick strips. Re-heat them atop a charcoal grille along with some bell peppers, onions and thickly sliced tomatoes.
- Wrap in thin Middle Eastern style flat bread, also lightly grilled and as a change from the usual tzatziki (yoghurt sauce), try an avocado-tahini sauce flavored strongly with lemon.

141.   HEARTY PORK CHOPS AND NOODLES Recipe

Serving: 4 | Prep: | Cook: 15mins |Ready in:

Ingredients

- 4 boneless pork chops, 3/4" thick
- 1 can cream of celery soup
- 1/4 C. apple juice
- 2 Tbs. Dijon mustard
- 1 Tbs. honey
- 1/8 tsp. pepper
- 4 C. cooked egg noodles

Direction

- Spray non-stick skillet with cooking spray and heat 1 min.
- Add chops and cook until browned.
- Add soup, apple juice, mustard, honey and pepper.
- Heat to a boil.
- Cover and cook over low heat 10 min. or until done.
- Serve over noodles.

142.   Harissa Crusted Tri Tip Roast Recipe

Serving: 6 | Prep: | Cook: 15mins |Ready in:

Ingredients

- 1 3/4 teaspoons caraway seeds
- 1/4 cup extra-virgin olive oil
- 6 garlic cloves
- 1/4 cup chili paste (such as sambal oelek)*
- 2 tablespoons tomato sauce
- 1 1/2 teaspoons ground cumin
- 1 1/4 teaspoons chili powder
- 1 1 3/4- to 2-pound tri-tip beef roast, most of fat layer trimmed

Direction

- Preheat oven to 400°F.
- Toast caraway seeds in small non-stick skillet over medium heat until seeds darken and begin to smoke, stirring often, about 5 minutes.
- Add olive oil and garlic cloves to caraway seeds in skillet. Cover; remove from heat. Let stand 1 minute.

- Pour caraway mixture into processor. Add chili paste, tomato sauce, cumin, and chili powder and blend until garlic cloves are pureed. Season harissa to taste with salt.
- Sprinkle beef all over with salt and pepper; place beef, fat side down, on rack on rimmed baking sheet. Spread with half of harissa.
- Turn beef over; spread remaining harissa over top and sides.
- Roast beef until thermometer inserted into center registers 125°F to 130°F for medium-rare, about 35 minutes. Let rest 10 minutes. Slice and serve.
- *Available in the Asian foods section of my supermarket and at my local Asian markets.

143.   Harvest Round Steak Recipe

Serving: 6 | Prep: | Cook: 20mins | Ready in:

Ingredients

- 2 lbs. beef round steak, cut 3/4 inch thick
- 3 tbs flour
- 1 tsp salt
- 1/8 tps. pepper
- 3 tbs cooking oil
- 3 medium sweet potatoes, peeled and halved
- 3 small onions, quartered
- 3/4 cup water
- 1 1/2 inch stick of cinnamon
- 3 medium cooking apples, peeled and quartered

Direction

- Cut steak into six pieces.
- Pound mixture of flour, salt and pepper into steak until steak is 1/4 in. thick.
- In 12 in. skillet with and ovenproof handle, brown steak on both sides in hot oil.
- Add sweet potatoes, onion, water and cinnamon; cover and bake in a 350° oven for 1 hour.

- Add apples and bake covered, 15 minutes more.
- Remove meat, potatoes, onion and apples to platter.
- Measure pan juices; add water to make 1 3/4 cups.
- Combine 1/4 cup cold water to 2 tbsp. flour and 1/4 tsp salt; add to pan juices.
- Cook and stir until bubbly.
- Drizzle over meat dish!

144.   Hearty Beef Braciole With Simple Tomato Sauce Recipe

Serving: 4 | Prep: | Cook: 105mins | Ready in:

Ingredients

- 1/2 cup dried Italian-style bread crumbs
- 1 garlic clove, minced
- 2/3 cup grated Pecorino Romano
- 1/3 cup grated provolone
- 2 tablespoons chopped fresh Italian parsley leaves
- 4 tablespoons olive oil
- salt and freshly ground black pepper
- 1 (1 1/2-pound) flank steak (can use round steak in a pinch)
- 1 cup dry white wine
- *
- 3 1/4 cups Simple tomato sauce, recipe follows, or store-bought marinara sauce
- ****
- Simple Tomato Sauce:
- 1/2 cup extra-virgin olive oil
- 1 small onion, chopped
- 2 cloves garlic, chopped
- 1 stalk celery, chopped
- 1 carrot, chopped
- 2 (32-ounce) cans crushed tomatoes
- 4 to 6 basil leaves
- 2 dried bay leaves
- sea salt and freshly ground black pepper

- 4 tablespoons unsalted butter, optional

Direction

- For the Braciole:
- Stir the first 5 ingredients in a medium bowl to blend. Stir in 2 tablespoons of the oil. Season mixture with salt and pepper and set aside.
- Lay the flank steak flat on the work surface. Sprinkle the bread crumb mixture evenly over the steak to cover the top evenly. Starting at 1 short end, roll up the steak as for a jelly roll to enclose the filling completely.
- Using butcher's twine, tie the steak roll to secure. Sprinkle the braciole with salt and pepper.
- Preheat the oven to 350 degrees F.
- Heat the remaining 2 tablespoons of oil in a heavy large ovenproof skillet over medium heat. Add the braciole and cook until browned on all sides, about 8 minutes.
- Add the wine to the pan and bring to a boil. Stir in the marinara sauce. Cover partially with foil and bake until the meat is almost tender, turning the braciole and basting with the sauce every 30 minutes.
- After 1 hour, uncover and continue baking until the meat is tender, about 30 minutes longer. The total cooking time should be about 1 1/2 hours.
- Remove the braciole from the sauce. Using a large sharp knife, cut the braciole crosswise and diagonally into 1/2-inch-thick slices. Transfer the slices to plates. Spoon the sauce over and serve.
- ****
- For the Simple Tomato Sauce:
- In a large casserole pot, heat oil over medium-high heat. Add onion and garlic and sauté until soft and translucent, about 2 minutes. Add celery and carrot and season with salt and pepper. Sauté until all the vegetables are soft, about 5 minutes.
- Add tomatoes, basil, and bay leaves and reduce the heat to low.
- Cover the pot and simmer for 1 hour or until thick. Remove bay leaves and taste for seasoning. If sauce tastes too acidic, add unsalted butter, 1 tablespoon at a time, to round out the flavor.
- Pour half the tomato sauce into the bowl of a food processor. Process until smooth. Continue with remaining tomato sauce.
- **NOTE: If not using all the sauce, allow it to cool completely and then pour 1 to 2 cup portions into plastic freezer bags. Freeze for up to 6 months.

---

145.   Herbed Pork Cutlets Or Chops With Onions And Figs Recipe

Serving: 4 | Prep: | Cook: 20mins | Ready in:

Ingredients

- 4 boneless center cut pork chops or cutlets
- 1 t. chili powder
- ½ t. garlic powder
- 1 t. sugar or Splenda
- 3 T. chopped fresh sage leaves. pineapple sage is great!
- olive oil
- 2 T. chopped fresh thyme leaves
- 2 medium sweet onions, chopped
- 2 T. sweet butter
- ½ t. turmeric
- 12 fresh figs, rinsed and halved.
- salt and pepper to tast

Direction

- Cover both sides of pork chops with chili powder, garlic powder, Splenda and chopped sage. Rub with olive oil. Cover with plastic wrap and let sit in refrigerator for 6-8 hours.
- Bring to room temperature before cooking.
- Bring a grill pan to high heat with a little olive oil. Cook pork on high for 4 minutes per. Turnover and cook over medium heat for 4

minutes. Let sit 5 minutes while you prepare the onions and figs

- In a separate pan, melt butter. Add thyme leaves and cook 30 seconds. Add turmeric and onions. Cook until onions are wilted. Add figs. Cook until figs are soft. Add salt and pepper to taste.
- Makes 4 servings.

146.   Herbed Skirt Steak Recipe

Serving: 4 | Prep: | Cook: 10mins | Ready in:

Ingredients

- 1 ½ lb skirt steak, aka flap meat
- ¼ c sharp or grainy mustard
- 2 c assorted fresh herbs — my friend used tarragon, thyme and parsley; I recently used chervil, basil and thyme. I would grab pretty much anything except mint — and maybe that would work too. If you are using rosemary, I would keep that to under ¼ c. of the mixture.
- 2 T butter
- 2 T peanut oil
- 1/3 c red wine (optional)
- 1 additional T butter (optional)

Direction

- Dry skirt steak on paper towels.
- Using a very sharp knife, cut the pieces of steak lightly across the grain. This cut varies in thickness, so you might like to divide the pieces up so that each half is mostly thick or mostly thin.
- Spread mustard lightly on the filament side of each piece. You may not need all the mustard.
- Mince herbs somewhere between fine and coarse. A mezzaluna is perfect for this. You do not want them puréed.
- Press the herbs into the mustard. Try to cover the entire steak in a thin, even layer.

- Melt butter in a non-stick sauté pan, and add oil. Set the flame/heat on high.
- Sauté the steak, non-herb side down, over high heat until a nice dark crust has formed. Turn and sauté on the other side. You might like to add a bit more butter or oil, because the herbs will tend to stick. This side will not brown as much. Look to see that the juices are still very red, or cut into the meat to make sure that it still looks no more than medium-rare, rare if possible. They will continue cooking on retained heat when you remove them from the pan. Place them on a serving platter.
- If you like, deglaze the pan with the red wine. Simmer and scrape until the wine is reduced and there is no more alcohol smell. Remove pan from heat, add 1 T butter, and swirl until the butter is incorporated. **Do not stir! **
- Pour this sauce over the steak and serve. Yummers.

147.   Hoisin Tri Tip Roast Recipe

Serving: 4 | Prep: | Cook: 20mins | Ready in:

Ingredients

- 1/4 cup hoisin sauce
- 2 teaspoons minced ginger
- 3 cloves garlic, minced
- 2 tablespoons rice vinegar
- 2 tablespoons soy sauce
- Heaping 1/4 teaspoon freshly ground black pepper
- 1 (2-pound) tri-tip roast
- 1 tablespoon olive oil

Direction

- Stir together hoisin, ginger, garlic, vinegar, soy sauce, and pepper until well blended. Rub marinade all over roast, coating it well. Place in a glass baking dish, cover, and allow to marinate in the refrigerator at least 8 hours, but preferably overnight.

- Remove tri-tip from the refrigerator and let it sit at room temperature for 30 minutes. Heat oven to 375°F. Blot roast dry with paper towels to remove some of the excess marinade.
- Heat olive oil in a large frying pan over medium-high heat. Sear roast for about 2 minutes per side or until nicely browned. Transfer roast to a small roasting pan or baking dish and place in the oven. Cook until roast reaches an internal temperature of 125°F for medium rare, about 20 to 22 minutes.
- Remove roast from the oven and cover loosely with foil. Let rest for 15 minutes before carving. Slice tri-tip across the grain and serve.

148. Hoisin Marinated Pork Chops Recipe

Serving: 6 | Prep: | Cook: 20mins | Ready in:

Ingredients

- 1 1/2 cups plus 2 tablespoons hoisin sauce
- 1 cup oyster sauce
- 1/4 cup black bean garlic sauce
- 3 garlic cloves, chopped
- 1 tablespoon chopped peeled fresh ginger
- 1 teaspoon red food coloring
- 6 12- to 14-ounce pork rib chops, each about 1 1/2 inches thick

Direction

- Mix first 6 ingredients in large bowl for marinade. Place chops in extra-large resealable plastic bag. Add marinade to bag. Seal top, releasing excess air. Turn bag to coat chops.
- **Refrigerate 3 to 5 days, turning bag occasionally.
- Preheat broiler, adjusting rack 8 inches below heat source. Line rimmed baking sheet with heavy-duty foil.

- Remove chops from marinade. Place chops on prepared pan with some marinade still clinging.
- Broil until chops are cooked through and thermometer inserted horizontally into centre registers 145°F, watching closely to prevent burning (chops may char slightly in spots), about 9 minutes per side.
- Transfer to plates and serve.
- **Good served with Asian slaw, your favourite Asian-inspired rice or noodles. - and a white wine with snappy acidity and lemon-lime notes, like dry Riesling or Grüner Veltliner.

149. Honey Garlic Chops Recipe

Serving: 4 | Prep: | Cook: 20mins | Ready in:

Ingredients

- 4 boneless center pork loin chops
- 1/4 cup lemon juice
- 1/4 cup honey
- 2 tablespoon soy sauce
- 1 tablespoon dry sherry
- 2 cloves garlic -- minced

Direction

- Combine all ingredients except pork; pour over chops in heavy plastic bag; seal. Refrigerate 4-24 hours.
- Prepare covered grill with drip pan in centre, banked by medium-hot coals.
- Remove chops from marinade; reserve marinade.
- Grill chops 16-18 minutes, turning once and basting occasionally with reserved marinade.
- Or broil chops 5 inches from heat source for 13-18 minutes, turning once.

150. Honey Glazed Grilled Chicken Or Porkchops Recipe

Serving: 6 | Prep: | Cook: 20mins | Ready in:

Ingredients

- 1/2 cup honey
- 2 tablespoons soy sauce
- 2 tablespoons dry white wine or dry sherry
- 2 tablespoons minced green onions
- 2 cloves garlic peeled and minced
- 2 tablespoons freshly squeezed lemon juice
- 1 tablespoon fresh ginger
- salt and freshly ground pepper to taste
- 2 1/2 to 3 pounds of chicken pieces or 6 pork chops

Direction

- Combine all ingredients in a large bowl and toss to coat chicken with marinade.
- Cover and refrigerate 20 minutes to 24 hours.
- Prepare hot coals.
- Place dark meat on grill skin side down.
- Cook 15 minutes and flip.
- Place white meat on grill, skin side down.
- Cook 15 minutes to 20 minutes flipping once.
- Juices should run clear when the chicken is pricked.

151. Hot And Sour Soup Recipe

Serving: 2 | Prep: | Cook: 10mins | Ready in:

Ingredients

- 7 ounces extra-firm tofu , drained (this is the tofu in a box, use the whole box)
- 6 tablespoons soy sauce
- 2 teaspoon toasted sesame oil
- 5 tablespoons cornstarch , plus an additional 2 1/2 teaspoons

- 2 boneless, center-cut, pork loin chop (1/2 inch thick, 1lb), trimmed of fat and cut into 2 inch by 1/8-inch matchsticks
- 3 tablespoons cold water , plus 1 additional teaspoon
- 1 large egg
- 6 cups low-sodium chicken broth
- 1 cup bamboo shoots (from one 5-ounce can), sliced lengthwise into 1/8-inch-thick strips
- 8 ounces fresh shiitake mushrooms , stems removed, caps sliced 1/4 inch thick (about 1 cup) or sliced baby portabellas.
- 5 tablespoons black Chinese vinegar or 1 tablespoon red wine vinegar plus 1 tablespoon balsamic vinegar (see note below)
- 2 teaspoons chili oil (see note below, I used one teaspoon and it was warm and you know it was there)
- 1 teaspoon ground white pepper
- 3 medium scallions , sliced thin

Direction

- Notes 1, 2 & 3:
- Note 1.This soup is very spicy. For a less spicy soup, omit the chili oil altogether or add only 1 teaspoon.
- Note 2.To make slicing the pork chop easier, freeze it for 15 minutes. Recipe call said they liked the distinctive flavour of Chinese black vinegar. If you can't find it, they said a combination of red wine vinegar and balsamic vinegar approximates its flavour. The substitution for the Chinese vinegar worked well. I got the Chinese black vinegar and didn't care for the flavour. Restaurant owner said he uses white vinegar! I have tried white and it works also.
- Note 3. I doubled the amount and mushrooms (found baby portables were just fine. I added the starch at the very end to thicken the soup. For vegetarians, remove the pork, not sure what to do about the chicken broth, and would add at least another box of tofu. Serves 6 to 8 as an appetizer or 2 people eating two bowls each for dinner and 1 cup each left over for lunch the next day.

- Cooking Directions:
- Place tofu in pie plate and set heavy plate on top. Weight with 2 heavy cans; let stand at least 15 minutes (tofu should release about 1/2 cup liquid). The tofu in the pic was just Firm and it crumbled when the box was opened and pressed. I liked the tofu in the final product with the broken up pieces. I poured the water off the plate and cut through any large pieces to get them to the 1/2 inch called out. I then poured the whole plate in, crumbled and all. For those who don't know, Tofu in the box has no smell or taste. The Tofu in the refrigerated section in the vegetable department in packages with water smells and tastes like cardboard, I can't eat it. Use the box, Mori-nu, it is good stuff. The box Tofu is what I put in my health shake I posted.
- Whisk 3 tablespoon soy sauce, sesame oil, and 2 teaspoon cornstarch in medium bowl; toss pork with marinade and set aside for at least 10 minutes (but no more than 30 minutes). The meat absorbs most of the marinade.
- Combine 3 tablespoons cornstarch with 3 tablespoons water in small bowl and mix thoroughly; set aside, leaving spoon in bowl. Mix 1/2 teaspoon cornstarch with remaining 1 teaspoon water in small bowl; add egg and beat with fork until combined, set aside. Mix 2 tablespoons corn starch with 2 tablespoons water in a small bowl. Set aside.
- Bring broth to boil in large saucepan set over medium-high heat. Reduce heat to medium-low; add bamboo shoots and mushrooms and simmer until mushrooms are just tender, about 5 minutes. Add tofu and pork, including marinade, to soup, stirring to separate any pieces of pork that stick together. Continue to simmer until pork is no longer pink, about 2 minutes.
- Stir 3 tablespoon cornstarch mixture to recombine. Add to soup and increase heat to medium-high; cook, stirring occasionally, until soup thickens and turns translucent, about 1 minute. Stir in vinegar, chili oil, pepper, and remaining 3 tablespoons soy sauce; turn off heat.

- Without stirring soup, slowly drizzle thin stream of egg mixture into pot in circular motion. Let soup sit 1 minute, then return saucepan to medium-high heat. Bring soup to gentle boil, add last bowl of corn starch, stir one minute, and then immediately remove from heat. Gently stir soup once to evenly distribute egg; ladle into bowls and top with scallions.

152. Hot Chili Cheese Express Recipe

Serving: 3 | Prep: | Cook: 40mins | Ready in:

Ingredients

- 1/4 pork
- 3 cloves of garlic
- 1 onion
- cheese (Either Cheddar or Powder)
- 1 tomato
- red chili (As many as you want)
- 6 Kikiam
- salt
- pepper
- soy sauce

Direction

- Sauté garlic, onion and tomato
- Add pork, kikiam, pepper and salt
- Apply a small amount of soy sauce
- Add water (not plenty)
- Let it simmer about 30 to 40 minutes
- Add cheese and chili
- Mix well
- Wait until it's cooked

153.   Hungarian Steak Casserole Recipe

Serving: 6 | Prep: | Cook: 120mins | Ready in:

Ingredients

- 2 lbs. round steak, cut into 1/2 inch cubes
- 3 tbls. olive oil
- 1 lg. onion diced
- 1 clove garlic, finely minced
- 2 tbls. flour
- 1 3 oz. can mushrooms with liquid
- 1/2 cup chopped celery
- 1 cup sour cream
- 1 8 oz. can tomato sauce
- 1 tsp. each of salt and pepper
- 1 tbls. worcestershire sauce

Direction

- In pan, brown meat in olive oil
- Add onion and garlic and cook until translucent
- Stir in flour then remaining ingredients
- Mix thoroughly and put into buttered casserole dish
- Bake at 350 for 1 1/2-2 hours.
- I've served with buttered noodles or rice.

154.   Hungarian Stir Fry Recipe

Serving: 6 | Prep: | Cook: 10mins | Ready in:

Ingredients

- 1 pound top round steak
- 1 tablespoon cornstarch
- 1/4 cup dry red wine
- 2 tablespoons oil divided
- 1 large sweet onion sliced and separated into rings
- 1 cup sliced fresh mushrooms
- 1 tablespoon Hungarian paprika

- 1/2 cup beef broth
- cooked rice

Direction

- Slice steak diagonally across the grain into thin strips.
- Combine cornstarch and wine then pour over steak.
- Pour 1 tablespoon oil around top of wok preheated to 375 degrees then add onion and mushrooms and stir-fry 3 minutes.
- Remove and set aside.
- Pour 1 tablespoon oil into wok.
- Drain steak reserving marinade and stir-fry 3 minutes.
- Return vegetables to wok.
- Combine reserved marinade, paprika and beef both then add to wok and cook until thickened.
- Serve over rice.

155.   Indian Curry From Scratch Recipe

Serving: 6 | Prep: | Cook: 60mins | Ready in:

Ingredients

- Whole spice Blend (Optional)
- 1 1/2 cinnamon sticks (3-inches)
- 4 whole cloves
- 4 green cardamom pods
- 8 black peppercorns
- 1 bay leaf
- curry
- 1/4 cup vegetable oil (or canola oil)
- 1 medium onion , sliced thin
- 4 large cloves garlic , pureed in a minichopper with 1 tablespoon water (about 2 tablespoons)
- 1 tablespoon fresh ginger , pureed in a minichopper with 1-2 teaspoons water
- 1 1/2 pounds top sirloin or boneless leg of lamb, trimmed and cut into 3/4-inch cubes, or

- 6 chicken thighs, skinned, or 1 1/2 pounds shrimp, peeled and deveined
- 2 teaspoons ground cumin
- 2 teaspoons ground coriander
- 1 teaspoon ground turmeric
- table salt
- 3 plum tomatoes (canned), chopped, plus 1 tablespoon juice, or 2/3 cup crushed tomato, or 1/2 cup plain low-fat yogurt
- 2 bunches spinach (1 1/2 pounds), stemmed, thoroughly washed, and chopped coarse (optional)
- 1 cup chopped fresh cilantro leaves (optional)
- 2 cups water
- 1 jalapeño chile , stemmed and cut in half through the stem end
- 1/2 cup Indian split peas (channa dal), or 4 medium boiling potatoes, peeled and cut into 3/4-inch cubes, or 4 medium zucchini, cut into 1/2-inch cubes, or 1 cup green peas
- 2 - 4 tablespoons chopped fresh cilantro leaves (use the lesser amount if you've already added the optional cilantro)

Direction

- 1. Heat oil in large deep skillet or soup kettle, preferably nonstick, over medium-high heat until hot, but not smoking. If using whole spice blend, add to oil and cook, stirring with wooden spoon until cinnamon stick unfurls and cloves pop, about 5 seconds. If omitting whole spice blend, simply add onion to skillet; sauté until softened, 3 to 4 minutes, or browned, 5 to 7 minutes.
- 2. Stir in garlic, ginger, selected meat (except shrimp), ground spices, 1/2 teaspoon of salt, and tomatoes or yogurt; cook, stirring almost constantly, until liquid evaporates, oil separates and turns orange, and spices begin to fry, 5 to 7 minutes, depending on skillet or kettle size. Continue to cook, stirring constantly, until spices smell cooked, about 30 seconds longer.
- 3. Stir in optional spinach and/or cilantro. Add the water and jalapeño and season with salt; bring to simmer. Reduce heat; cover and simmer until meat is tender, 20 to 30 minutes for chicken, 30 to 40 minutes for beef or lamb.
- 4. Add selected vegetable (except green peas); cook until tender, about 15 minutes. Stir in cilantro. Add shrimp and/or peas if using. Simmer 3 minutes longer and serve.

---

156. Intoxicated Fajitas Recipe

Serving: 4 | Prep: | Cook: 20mins | Ready in:

Ingredients

- 2 pounds flank steak or skirt steak
- 1/2 cup balsamic vinegar
- 1/3 cup olive oil
- 1/3 cup tequila
- juice of 1 lime
- 1 teaspoon garlic powder
- 1 teaspoon chipotle chili powder or chili powder
- 1 teaspoon onion powder
- 1 teaspoon salt
- flour tortillas (grilled if desired)
- grilled onions
- grilled peppers
- salsa or pico de gallo
- guacamole
- sour cream

Direction

- Place steak in a large resealable bag.
- In a bowl, mix vinegar, olive oil, tequila, lime juice, garlic powder, chipotle powder, onion powder and salt.
- Whisk well.
- Pour over steak.
- Refrigerate 8 hours or overnight.
- Preheat grill to a medium-high heat. If you have mesquite chips available, you can use them for a different flavor.
- Remove steaks from bag.

- Grill for 8-10 minutes per side, or until done.
- Remove meat and let it rest for a few minutes before slicing into strips.
- Serve in flour tortillas (I grilled those) and top with grilled onions, grilled peppers and salsa. Top with guacamole and/or sour cream if desired.

157. Irish Apple Maple Pork Chops Recipe

Serving: 4 | Prep: | Cook: 20mins | Ready in:

Ingredients

- 4 - 6 oz. boneless pork loin chops
- 1 Tbsp. olive oil
- 2 cloves garlic, minced
- 1/4 cup good Irish whiskey or bourbon
- 1/2 cup chicken broth
- 1/4 cup maple syrup
- 1 apple, washed, peeled, cored and chopped
- 1/4 tsp fresh thyme
- salt & pepper to taste

Direction

- Cook pork chops in a heavy skillet about 10 - 12 minutes on medium heat.
- Do not overcook the chops.
- Remove & keep warm.
- Add to the skillet the oil, garlic, bourbon & cover.
- Cook over high heat 1 minute.
- Add the chicken broth, maple syrup, apple, salt & pepper cooking until slightly thickened, about 5 minutes.
- Stir in the thyme & cook 1 minute.
- Serve sauce over the chops.
- Can be served with either spuds or noodles!

158. Iron Skillet Rib Eyes With Brandied Black Peppercorn Sauce Recipe

Serving: 4 | Prep: | Cook: 16mins | Ready in:

Ingredients

- steakS
- 4 (12-ounce) rib-eye steaks
- olive oil
- 1/2 teaspoon finely ground coffee
- 1/2 teaspoon cinnamon - (I Omit this)
- 1/2 teaspoon black pepper
- 1/2 teaspoon salt
- 1/2 teaspoon chili powder
- 1/2 teaspoon cayenne pepper
- 1/2 teaspoon sugar - (I Omit this)
- SAUCE
- 1/2 tablespoon olive oil
- 1 shallot, sliced thin
- 1 cup beef stock
- 1/4 cup brandy
- 1 tablespoon whole black peppercorns
- salt, to taste

Direction

- Preheat oven to 400 degrees.
- Coat steaks with olive oil.
- In a bowl, combine coffee, cinnamon, black pepper, salt, chili powder, cayenne and sugar.
- Dust steaks with the spice mixture.
- Heat a large, flat, cast-iron skillet or griddle over high heat, until smoking.
- Sear the steaks, in batches if necessary, until caramelized and brown; do the same to the other side.
- If using a skillet, transfer steaks to a baking pan and cook for 8 minutes.
- Turn steaks and cook for another 8 minutes, or until medium rare. Remove from oven and allow to rest while you make the sauce.
- SAUCE
- Using the same cast-iron pan, heat olive oil over medium-high heat. Add the shallots and sauté until light brown.

- Add beef stock to deglaze, then the brandy.
- Add peppercorns and simmer to reduce by one-third.
- Season with salt to taste.
- Put the steaks onto four plates and drizzle sauce on top.

159.	Italian Pork Chop Dinner

Serving: 4 | Prep: | Cook: 20mins | Ready in:

Ingredients

- 6 bacon strips, diced
- 1/2 pound fresh mushrooms, sliced
- 1 medium onion, finely chopped
- 1 garlic clove, minced
- 3/4 cup all-purpose flour
- 4 teaspoons Italian seasoning, divided
- 1/4 teaspoon salt
- 1/4 teaspoon garlic powder
- 1/8 teaspoon pepper
- Dash cayenne pepper
- 6 bone-in pork loin chops (1 inch thick)
- 1 can (14-1/2 ounces) diced tomatoes, undrained
- 1 can (14-1/2 ounces) chicken broth
- 1 can (6 ounces) tomato paste
- 1 package (10 ounces) frozen peas, thawed
- Hot cooked pasta

Direction

- In a large skillet, cook the bacon over medium heat until crisp. Using a slotted spoon, remove to paper towels. In the drippings, saute mushrooms, onion and garlic until tender. Transfer to a 5-qt. slow cooker with a slotted spoon. In a shallow bowl, combine the flour, 3 teaspoons Italian seasoning, salt, garlic powder, pepper and cayenne; coat pork chops with flour mixture.
- In the same skillet, brown the pork chops; transfer to the slow cooker. Top with tomatoes and bacon. Combine the broth, tomato paste

and remaining Italian seasoning; add to slow cooker.
- Cover and cook on low for 4-6 hours or until pork is tender; add peas during the last 30 minutes. Serve with pasta.
- Nutrition Facts
- 1 pork chop: 528 calories, 23g fat (8g saturated fat), 124mg cholesterol, 842mg sodium, 31g carbohydrate (8g sugars, 5g fiber), 48g protein.

160.	Italian Pork Chops And Olive Sauce Recipe

Serving: 4 | Prep: | Cook: 20mins | Ready in:

Ingredients

- 4 Center Cut pork chops
- all-purpose flour
- salt & pepper
- 3 Tablespoons olive oil
- 1 Cup dry white wine
- Either 6 Large kalamata olives, And 6 Large oil-cured green olives Pitted And Finely Chopped OR
- 1/4 Cup Olivada Spread
- fresh parsley To Garnish

Direction

- Cut away the extra fat from the chops.
- Season about 1/2 cup of flour with salt and pepper in a large plastic bag.
- Dry the chops well, and then drop each one into the bag separately, to lightly cover with flour.
- In a frying pan large enough to hold all four chops, melt the oil until hot.
- Add the chops and brown well on both sides.
- Pour 3/4 cup of the wine over the chops and cook until it has almost evaporated.
- Remove the chops to a heated platter while you prepare the sauce. Add the remaining wine, and the finely chopped olives, and cook

for a few minutes, scraping up the browned bits off the bottom of the pan.

- Pour the sauce over the chops, and serve immediately with a sprinkling of fresh parsley to garnish.

161.   Jack Daniels Flank Steak Recipe

Serving: 4 | Prep: | Cook: 15mins | Ready in:

Ingredients

- 1-1/2 pounds flank steak (1/2" thick)
- 1 clove garlic minced
- 2 teaspoons dry mustard
- 1/4 cup Jack Daniels Whiskey
- vegetable oil
- 2 tablespoons butter
- salt to taste
- black pepper to taste

Direction

- Score the flank steak with a sharp knife about 1/8-inch deep in a diamond pattern then set aside.
- Mash the garlic with the mustard.
- Stir in the whiskey.
- Pour mixture over steak and refrigerate covered overnight.
- Set out at room temperature for 2 hours before cooking.
- Grill using charcoal or gas grill.
- Cook over high heat 3 to 5 minutes per side dotting each side with butter while cooking.
- Slice the steak immediately by cutting across the grain into 1/4-inch thick slices.
- Sprinkle with salt and pepper.

162.   Jaegarschnitzel Recipe

Serving: 8 | Prep: | Cook: 30mins | Ready in:

Ingredients

- 3 lb pork loins cut into chops
- flour
- seasoned salt
- 3 eggs
- milk
- seasoned bread crumbs
- paprika
- oil
- 1/4 cup butter
- 1/2 lb. mushrooms
- 1 onion
- 2 packages brown gravy mix
- 3/4 cup red wine--not too sweet or too dry. I usually use Lambrusco
- 1/2 bag frozen sweet peas

Direction

- To make the schnitzel: Take the pork chops and
- Pound the pork with a meat mallet until it is about ¼".
- In one bowl put about 1½ cups flour mixed with a about a teaspoon of seasoned salt (I like Jane's Crazy Mixed-up Salt).
- In another bowl mix take 3 eggs and mix with about ¼ cup milk.
- In a third bowl take about 3 cups of seasoned bread crumbs, and add about 1 tsp. paprika.
- Put about ½" of oil in heavy frying pan. You want the grease hot, but not too hot.
- Dip the pork in the flour, then the egg, then the bread crumbs and fry. They fry up quickly, maybe only 3-4 minutes on each side.
- Put on rack over absorbent paper towels and keep warm in oven set at its lowest temperature.
- For the sauce: Clean the pan out. Add butter and let it melt, but don't let it burn.
- Take ½ lb. of sliced fresh mushrooms and an onion, sliced, and sauté lightly it in the pan.

- Add two packages of brown gravy mix and 1 1/4 cup water, 3/4 cup red wine, stir until it comes to a boil.
- Add ½ bag of sweet peas.
- Cover and simmer about 20 minutes.
- Serve the sauce over the schnitzel.

163. Jamacian Flank Steak Recipe

Serving: 4 | Prep: | Cook: 6mins | Ready in:

Ingredients

- • 2 lbs. beef flank steak
- • 1/4 cup packed brown sugar
- • 3 tablespoons orange juice
- • 3 tablespoons lime juice
- • 3 cloves garlic, minced
- • 1 piece (1 1/2 x 1 inches) fresh ginger, minced (use powdered ginger if fresh is not available, about teaspoon)
- • 2 teaspoons grated orange peel
- • 2 teaspoons lime peel
- • 1 teaspoon salt
- • 1 teaspoon black pepper
- • 1/4 teaspoon ground cinnamon
- • 1/8 teaspoon ground cloves
- • Shredded orange peel
- • Shredded lime peel

Direction

- 1. Score both sides of beef by cutting 1/4 inch deep diagonal lines about 1 inch apart in surface of steak to form diamond-shaped designs….. I would make the cuts 1/2 inch apart to more marinade into the meet.
- 2. Combine brown sugar, juices, garlic, ginger, grated peels, salt, pepper, cinnamon and cloves in 2-quart glass dish…..after grating the orange and lime, roll them on the counter to loosen up the juice. Then cut in half, squeeze as much as possible then use a spoon to break

the rest of the juice from each half. I didn't strain the juice of pulp, just took any seeds out.
- 3. Add beef; turn to coat. Cover and refrigerate steak at least 2 hours….. Mine marinated about 4 hours on the counter.
- 4. Remove beef from marinade; discard marinade.
- 5. Grill beef over medium-hot heat about 6 minutes per side until medium-rare or to desired doneness….. I grilled over an open high flame, 3 minutes per side.
- 6. Garnish with shredded orange and lime peels.
- 7. We all got talking and I forgot to take a pic of the grilled steak so all I had to post where the left over slices. Everyone like the flavour, the orange was the most pronounced flavour.
- 8. I usually do flank steak with a marinade of teriyaki marinade, a little soy sauce, ginger and sliced green onions.

164. Jamaican Style Beef Stew Recipe

Serving: 5 | Prep: | Cook: 90mins | Ready in:

Ingredients

- 1 Tbsp. canola oil
- 1 Tbsp. sugar
- 1-1/2 lb. boneless sirloin steak, cut into 3/4" cubes
- 5 grape tomatoes, finely chopped
- 3 large carrots cut into 1/2" slices
- 3 celery ribs, cut into 1/2" slices
- 4 green onions, chopped
- 3/4 cup beef broth
- 1/4 cup barbecue sauce (your choice)
- 1/4 cup soy sauce
- 2 Tbsp. steak sauce (your choice)
- 1 Tbsp. garlic powder
- 1 tsp. dried thyme, crushed
- 1/4 tsp. allspice
- 1/4 tsp. black pepper

- 1/8 tsp. hot sauce
- 1 Tbsp. cornstarch
- 2 Tbsp. cold water
- Hot cooked rice, noodles or mashed potatoes if desired

Direction

- In a Dutch oven heat oil over medium-high heat.
- Add sugar, cook and stir for 1 minute or until lightly browned.
- Add beef and brown on all sides.
- Stir in vegetables, broth, barbecue sauce, soy sauce, steak sauce and seasonings.
- Bring to a boil.
- Reduce heat.
- Cover and simmer for 1 to 1-1/4 hours or until vegetables and meat are tender.
- Combine cornstarch and water until smooth, stir into stew.
- Bring to a boil, cook and stir for 2 minutes or until thickened.

---

165.   Japanese Steak And Noodles Recipe

Serving: 2 | Prep: | Cook: 10mins | Ready in:

Ingredients

- 8 - 10 ounce rib-eye steak
- 2 tsp. dark sesame oil
- 1 cup green onions sliced diagonally in 1-inch pieces
- 2 cups packaged cole slaw with carrots
- 2 packages beef-flavoured ramen noodle soup (I use Ichiban)
- 1 1/2 cups water
- 1 tbsp. soya sauce

Direction

- Season steak liberally with salt and pepper. Heat 1 tsp. oil in skillet over medium-high

heat and brown the steak well on both sides. Remove the steak and keep warm.
- Add remaining 1 tsp. oil to skillet, add slaw, onions and soya sauce and a little salt and stir-fry 30 seconds.
- Remove slaw from skillet and keep warm.
- Heat water in the skillet with a little salt, add one of the ramen seasoning packets and bring to a boil.
- Break noodles from both ramen packages in half and add to skillet.
- Cook noodles for two minutes stirring frequently. Almost all water will be absorbed.
- Slice the steak into long, thin slices.
- In two bowls, layer noodles, then slaw, then steak.
- Serve immediately. If you split an 8 oz. steak, then one portion is 10 WW points.

---

166.   Jewish Cabbage Rolls Recipe

Serving: 6 | Prep: | Cook: 90mins | Ready in:

Ingredients

- 12 large cabbage leaves
- 1 pound ground sirloin
- 1 cup cooked rice
- 1 teaspoon parsley finely chopped
- 1 egg
- 2/3 cup milk
- 1/4 cup onion finely chopped
- 1 teaspoon salt
- 1/2 teaspoon pepper
- 2 tablespoons fat
- 2 tablespoons brown sugar
- 1 can condensed tomato soup
- 1/2 soup can water
- 1 bay leaf
- 4 cloves

Direction

- Remove outer leaves of a large head of cabbage then drop into boiling salted water.
- Parboil 5 minutes then drain well and trim out thick center vein.
- Combine meat, rice, parsley, egg, milk, 1/2 onion, salt, basil, thyme, oregano and pepper.
- Place large spoonful on each cabbage leaf and roll up and fasten with toothpicks.
- Melt fat in heavy iron skillet then brown cabbage rolls turning to brown evenly.
- Sprinkle with sugar then cover with soup and water.
- Add remaining onion, bay leaf and cloves.
- Cover and bake at 350 for 1-1/2 hours.

167. Johnny's Menudo Recipe

Serving: 4 | Prep: | Cook: |Ready in:

Ingredients

- 1 kg of pork
- 4 cloves of garlic
- onion
- 2 tomatoes
- salt
- oil
- tomato sauce
- potato cuts
- 2 chili peppers
- 2 hotdogs
- water

Direction

- Sauté garlic, onion and tomatoes in oil.
- Add pork, add salt.
- Stir-fry until pork lard comes out.
- Add water (not plenty)
- Leave and cover it for 30 mins. in a low fire
- Add tomato sauce. Mix well.
- Add potato cuts when pork is tender.
- Add hotdogs and chili peppers. Mix well.
- Wait until meat is cooked and ready to eat!

168. Juicy Marinated Skirt Steak Recipe

Serving: 4 | Prep: | Cook: 12mins |Ready in:

Ingredients

- 1/2 cup balsamic vinegar
- 2 tablespoons light-brown sugar
- 2 garlic cloves, minced
- 1 teaspoon crushed dried rosemary
- coarse salt and ground pepper
- 1 1/2 pounds skirt steak, cut crosswise into 4 equal pieces
- oil for grates

Direction

- In a resealable plastic bag or shallow dish, combine vinegar, sugar, garlic, rosemary, 1 teaspoon coarse salt, and 1/2 teaspoon pepper. Pierce meat all over with a fork; add to marinade, and turn to coat. Let marinate at room temperature at least 15 minutes, or cover and refrigerate up to 1 day.
- Heat grill to high; oil grates. Remove steaks from marinade, allowing excess to drip off. Grill steaks 2 to 4 minutes per side for medium-rare. Transfer to a plate; cover loosely with aluminum foil, and let rest 5 minutes. Serves 4. You can also broil these steaks, instead!
- Note: For a perfect meal, serve in a family-style dish with sautéed wild mushrooms and pea shoots (grilled with a soy/butter glaze) and Texas 1015 onion rings. Corn on the cob is also a nice side with this dish.

169. Killer London Broil Recipe

Serving: 5 | Prep: | Cook: 120mins |Ready in:

Ingredients

- 1 3-pound trimmed flank steak
- 2 tbsp dark brown sugar
- 1 tbsp beef base concentrate
- 1 tsp chopped garlic
- ½ cup vegetable oil
- 1 tbsp coarse ground black pepper
- 3 tbsp light soy sauce
- 1 tsp onion powder
- ½ cup warm water

Direction

- Mix warm water with beef base and brown sugar to dissolve. Add all other ingredients together and mix well. Place flank steak in glass baking dish and cover top and bottom with marinade. Cover with plastic wrap and place in refrigerator for 6 hours.
- Grill until done and slice against the grain. Serve on hot French bread with sautéed mushrooms and onions. Top with shredded Swiss cheese and place under broiler until melted.
- ***grill to your doneness

170.   Korean Barbecue Recipe

Serving: 4 | Prep: | Cook: 20mins | Ready in:

Ingredients

- for the meat:
- 1 lb rib eye beef, very thinly sliced (sirloin and other well-marbled cuts also work well)
- 2 Tbsp. sugar (approximate)
- 2 Tbsp. soy sauce
- 2 tsp. Asian sesame oil
- 2 cloves garlic, finely minced
- 1 Tbsp. rice vinegar
- 3 Tbsp. oil
- for the sauce:
- 2 Tbsp black bean sauce
- 2 Tbsp. sweet chili sauce

- 1 garlic clove, finely minced
- 1/2 tsp. rice vinegar
- for the rice:
- 1 C. short-grain rice
- 2 C. water
- for serving:
- 1 head green leaf lettuce, washed and separated into whole leaves

Direction

- Sprinkle the sugar evenly over both sides of all the slices of meat. Let sit for 10 minutes.
- In the meantime, prepare the marinade. In a small bowl, blend together the soy sauce, sesame oil, garlic, and rice vinegar.
- Pour the soy sauce mixture over the meat and mix well. Marinate for 10 minutes.
- While the meat is marinating, begin cooking the rice. Bring the rice and water to a boil in a medium covered saucepan. Reduce the heat to the lowest setting, cover the pot with a lid, and allow the rice to steam for 20 minutes.
- Once the rice is cooking, prepare the sauce. Mix the black bean sauce, sweet chili sauce, garlic, and rice vinegar in a small bowl. Set aside until serving time.
- Finally, cook the meat. In a skillet over high heat, heat the 3 Tbsp. oil until shimmering. Cook the meat in small batches until brown and caramelized; be careful not to overcrowd the pan. As the meat is cooked, remove to a platter. Each batch should take 2-3 minutes to cook.
- Serve the meat along with the sauce, rice, and lettuce leaves.
- To eat, place a large spoonful of rice down the center of a lettuce leaf, add a few slices of meat, and top with sauce. Roll the lettuce leaf around the filling, and eat like a wrap.

171.   Korean Beef Recipe

Serving: 4 | Prep: | Cook: 15mins | Ready in:

Ingredients

- 1 1/2lbs beef sirloin steak, cut 1/2 inch thick
- 1/4c soy sauce
- 2 green onions, finely chopped
- 2 cloves garlic, minced
- 2T sugar
- 2T sesame oil
- 2T dry sherry
- 1/8tsp pepper

Direction

- Cut meat into serving size pieces; score both sides of meat.
- Place meat in shallow pan.
- Mix soy sauce, onions, garlic, sugar, oil, sherry, and pepper.
- Pour over beef and let stand 1 hour at room temp; turning once.
- Drain.
- Preheat both sides of grill on HIGH for 10 minutes.
- Turn both sides to MEDIUM.
- Grill meat with hood closed about 15 minutes or till done, turning once.
- Makes 4 to 6 servings.

172. Korean Flank Steak Recipe

Serving: 23 | Prep: | Cook: 10mins | Ready in:

Ingredients

- ½ lb flank steak
- ⅛ C soy sauce
- 2 T sugar
- 1 lemon, juiced
- 1 teaspoon sesame oil
- 2 cloves garlic, minced
- ¼ teaspoon pepper

Direction

- Remove the silver skin, if any, from the flank steak with a boning knife. Pat steak dry and make gentle slices in the meat (1-2mm) against the grain.
- Mix together the rest of the ingredients and add them and the steak to a Ziploc or marinating container.
- Marinate for 4-8 hours or overnight.
- Bring the steak up to room temperature. Remove from the marinade and pat dry.
- Bring the marinade to a light simmer in a saucepan and preheat your grill to medium heat. Oil your grill.
- Grill the steak to no more than medium rare, about 3-4 minutes per side for your average flank steak.
- Allow to rest for 5-10 minutes then slice against the grain and serve with the sauce.

173. Korean Marinated Flank Steak Recipe

Serving: 6 | Prep: | Cook: 15mins | Ready in:

Ingredients

- 4 cloves garlic
- 1 teaspoon minced fresh ginger
- 1 onion, roughly chopped
- 2 1/2 cups low sodium soy sauce
- 1/4 cup toasted sesame oil
- 3 tablespoons worcestershire sauce
- 2 tablespoons unseasoned meat tenderizer
- 1 cup white sugar
- 2 pounds beef flank steak, trimmed of excess fat

Direction

- Place garlic, ginger, and onion in the bowl of a blender. Add soy sauce, sesame oil, Worcestershire sauce, meat tenderizer, and sugar. Puree until smooth.
- Pour the marinade into a resealable plastic bag or glass bowl. Score the flank steak and place

into the marinade. Marinate overnight in the refrigerator.

- Preheat a grill for medium-high heat.
- Grill steak on preheated grill to desired doneness, about 7 minutes per side for medium.

174. Korean Pork Chops Recipe

Serving: 6 | Prep: | Cook: | Ready in:

Ingredients

- 6 pork chops
- 1 tbsp Korean chile bean paste
- 3 garlic cloves, pressed
- 1/2 cup soy sauce
- 1/2 cup chicken broth
- salt and pepper, to taste

Direction

- In a slow cooker, combine together the bean paste, garlic, soy sauce, and chicken broth. Season the chops with salt and pepper, then place them in the slow cooker. Turn to coat completely with sauce, cover and cook for 5 hours on Low setting.

175. Lanas Country Fried Steak N Gravy Recipe

Serving: 4 | Prep: | Cook: 20mins | Ready in:

Ingredients

- Lanas Country Fried steak n gravy
- ==
- 1 1/2 lbs cubed steak
- 1 cup flour (ABOUT)

- salt
- fresh pepper, ground
- 2 tablespoons bacon grease (optional, but adds great taste)
- Extra oil as needed to have about 1/4" deep in the pan.
- 3 tablespoons flour
- 1 cup half-and-half
- 1 cup milk

Direction

- Mix flour, salt, and pepper in a shallow, wide bowl
- Dredge each piece of meat in it, coating well on both sides.
- ==
- Heat grease or oil until hot but not smoking in a heavy, wide skillet with a lid. (A well 'seasoned' iron skillet is superior!! :))
- Brown the meat pieces on both sides, turn heat down a bit, cover and let steak fry like
- Chicken for 15 to 20 minutes, until done. Remove cover and let steak crisp for about 5 minutes.
- Take steak from the pan and drain well.
- Leave about 3 Tbsp. of drippings and all the browned flecks of crust in the pan.
- ==
- (GRAVY)
- Turn the heat a bit lower, sprinkle flour into the drippings and stir to keep from lumping while it browns.
- Slowly add half and half, stirring. Then the milk (same)
- Let it cook until thick, about 3 to 5 minutes.
- Taste and add seasoning as needed.
- Return the steaks to the gravy and cook an additional 5 mins or so.
- (My husband likes his gravy and meat separate, so I leave some out :)
- ==

- Serve with mashed potatoes, or rice. Maybe some green beans or peas, dinner rolls and a fruit salad.

176.   Lasagna Slow Cooker Or Crock Pot Style Recipe

Serving: 6 | Prep: | Cook: 240mins | Ready in:

Ingredients

- 1-1/2 lb. ground beef
- Note: you can use ground turkey, or a combination of ground beef and pork
- 1 onion, chopped
- 3 cloves garlic, minced
- 1 large jar spaghetti sauce
- 1/4 tsp. oregano
- 8 oz. no-boil lasagna noodles
- 16 ounces mozzarella cheese, shredded
- 1 lb. ricotta cheese
- 1/4 cup milk
- 1 egg
- 1/4 cup parmesan cheese, shredded
- 1/4 cup romano cheese, shredded
- 1/4 tsp. salt
- 1/4 tsp. pepper

Direction

- In a large skillet- brown beef, onion & garlic. Drain any fat.
- Add spaghetti sauce and oregano into meat mixture & mix together.
- In a medium bowl blend ricotta cheese, milk & egg.
- Beat until smooth & mix or fold in the mozzarella, Parmesan & Romano cheeses.
- Spray the sides and bottom of your slow cooker or crock pot with a non-stick spray.
- Place 1/4 of the meat & sauce mix at bottom of crock pot.
- Put a layer of noodles on top.

- Put 1/3 of cheese mixture on top, then repeat with sauce, noodles & cheese for another 2 layers.
- Top with meat sauce.
- Cook on low for 4-6 hours or until noodles are tender

177.   Lebanese Donair Recipe

Serving: 7 | Prep: | Cook: 50mins | Ready in:

Ingredients

- 3 1/4 pounds boneless top round steak, sliced very thin
- 1/2 cup red wine vinegar
- 1/2 cup olive oil
- 1/4 cup fresh lemon juice
- 1 teaspoon allspice
- 1/2 teaspoon ground cinnamon
- 1/4 teaspoon cardamom
- 1/2 teaspoon ground black pepper
- salt, to taste
- 2 large tomatoes, coarsely chopped
- 1 clove garlic, minced
- parsley Sauce
- 1 bunch finely chopped fresh parsley
- 1 large sweet onion, finely chopped
- 1/3 cup olive oil
- 3 tablespoons fresh lemon juice
- 3 large tomatoes, coarsely chopped
- tahini Sauce
- 2 cloves garlic, minced
- 1 cup tahini (sesame-seed paste)
- 1/2 cup fresh lemon juice
- 1/2 cup water
- salt, to taste
- 7 (6 inch) pita bread rounds

Direction

- 1. Place the sliced beef into a flat, ovenproof dish. Stir the red wine vinegar, 1/2 cup olive oil, lemon juice, allspice, cinnamon, cardamom, black pepper, salt, tomatoes and garlic together in a bowl until well blended. Pour over the beef, turning slices to coat evenly. Cover, and refrigerate 4 hours.

- 2. Preheat oven to 425 degrees F (220 degrees C).
- 3. Remove the cover from the dish with the beef, and cook in preheated oven until the meat is no longer pink, about 50 minutes. Cool slightly.
- 4. Meanwhile, make the parsley sauce by mixing the parsley, sweet onion, and 1/2 cup olive oil together in a bowl. Place the tomatoes in a bowl, and set aside until needed.
- 5. Make the tahini sauce by mixing the garlic, tahini, lemon juice, and water together in a bowl. Season to taste with salt.
- 6. To serve, place the pita bread rounds on serving plates. Spoon some of the meat mixture down the center of each pita round. Top with the parsley mix, tomatoes, and tahini sauce. Roll up the sides of the pita bread around the filling, and serve.

---

178.   Lemon Feta Pork Chops Recipe

Serving: 4 | Prep: | Cook: 20mins | Ready in:

Ingredients

- 4 pork chops
- 1 tsp parsley
- 1 tsp basil
- 4-5 cloves garlic - minced
- 1/2 cup to 1 cup lemon juice
- 1/2 tsp pepper
- feta cheese (Sun dried tomato feta is good - use as much as you want and any flavor you desire!)

Direction

- Combine Parsley, Basil, minced garlic, pepper and lemon juice
- Pour mixture over pork chops

- Marinate for 30 mins to 1.5 hours
- Sear pork chops on both sides - about 5-7 minutes per side - until cooked through
- Sprinkle feta over pork chops, reduce heat to low, and cover for 3-5 minutes or until pork chops are done

---

179.   Lima Bean Casserole Recipe

Serving: 8 | Prep: | Cook: 45mins | Ready in:

Ingredients

- 1/2 lb. dried lima beans
- 1 lb. ground round or sirloin
- Boiling, salted water
- Sauce:
- 1 medium onion, sliced thinly
- 2 Tbl. sugar
- 2 Tbl. worchestershire sauce
- 2 tsp. salt (kosher)
- 1/2 tsp. chili powder
- 1 bottle chili sauce
- 3/4 cup water

Direction

- Simmer beans in salted water for 2 hrs. Drain.
- Brown ground beef
- Cook sauce in a medium sauce pan until onions are tender
- Layer beans, ground beef and sauce in a casserole dish.
- Cook in a 350 degree oven for 45 minutes.

---

180.   Lip Smacking Loin Chops Recipe

Serving: 4 | Prep: | Cook: 15mins | Ready in:

Ingredients

- 4 large pork chop, sliced 1" thick
- 4 slices large sweet onion, sliced 1/4-inch thick
- 4 slices lemon, sliced 1/4" thick
- 4 tablespoons barbecue sauce or ketchup
- 8 tablespoons brown sugar

Direction

- 1. Preheat oven to 350 degrees.
- 2. Coat baking dish, large enough to hold the chops in a single layer, with non-stick cooking spray.
- 3. Place chops in dish, top each in this order. Slice of onion, slice of lemon, tbsp. of barbeque sauce or ketchup, two tablespoons of brown sugar.
- 4. Cover with foil and bake at 350 degrees for an hour.
- 5. Remove from oven, carefully pick the lemon rind off of each chop. Serve immediately.

181.   Love Me Tender Recipe

Serving: 4 | Prep: | Cook: 30mins | Ready in:

Ingredients

- 1/2 cup real or light mayonnaise
- 1/3 cup soy sauce
- 1/4 cup lemon juice
- 2 tablespoon prepared mustard
- 1 clove garlic -- minced
- 1/2 teaspoon ground ginger
- 1/4 teaspoon pepper
- 1 beef top round steak -- (3 lb) 2-inches
- thick

Direction

- 1. In large shallow dish, combine mayonnaise, soy sauce, lemon juice, mustard, garlic, ginger and pepper. Add steak, turning to coat.
- 2. Cover; chill several hours or overnight.

- 3. Grill or broil about 6 inches from source of heat, turning once, 25 to 30 minutes or until desired doneness.
- 4. Slice diagonally across grain.

182.   Lovers Pork Chops Recipe

Serving: 2 | Prep: | Cook: 15mins | Ready in:

Ingredients

- 2 centre-cut pork chops
- 1 tablespoon brown sugar
- salt and pepper to taste
- 1/4 teaspoon ground cinnamon
- 1/4 teaspoon ground nutmeg
- 1 tablespoon unsalted butter
- 1 tart apple - peeled, cored and sliced

Direction

- Heat a large skillet over medium-high heat.
- Brush chops lightly with oil and place in hot pan.
- Cook for 5 to 6 minutes, turning occasionally, or until done.
- In a small bowl, combine brown sugar, salt and pepper, cinnamon and nutmeg.
- Add butter to skillet, and stir in brown sugar mixture and apples.
- Cover and cook until apples are tender.
- Score pork chops lightly, add to apple mixture in pan.
- Coat with apple mixture and cook 2-3 minutes, stirring occasionally.

183.   Low Carb Diabetic Bulgogi Recipe

Serving: 8 | Prep: | Cook: 5mins | Ready in:

Ingredients

- 2 pounds top sirloin steak, partially frozen and sliced thin
- 5 tablespoons lite soy sauce
- 1/4 cup granulated Splenda or equivalent liquid Splenda
- 1/2 teaspoon black pepper
- 1/4 cup green onion, chopped
- 2 tablespoons garlic, minced
- 2 teaspoons of fresh grated ginger
- 1 tablespoon sesame oil
- 1 tablespoon of rice wine vinegar
- 5 tablespoon water
- Boston or Bibb leaf lettuce, optional

Direction

- Partially freeze the beef about an hour or so to make it easier to slice.
- Slice the beef as thinly as possible against the grain. It should be in very thin slices, but not falling apart.
- Mix all the remaining ingredients except the lettuce. Pour over the meat and marinate at least 1 hour.
- I put the meat and marinade in a ziploc bag, set it in a baking pan, and turned it occasionally.
- Preheat an indoor nonstick grill and grill the meat in batches.
- Turn meat after a few seconds (it cooks very quickly) to brown the other side and remove to a serving plate; repeat with remaining meat.
- You can sauté the meat in a nonstick skillet as well. Serve beef rolled up in lettuce leaves if desired.

---

184. Marinated Flank Steak With Horseradish Sauce Recipe

Serving: 6 | Prep: | Cook: 15mins | Ready in:

Ingredients

- ½ c. soy sauce
- ½ c. dry white wine
- ½ onion, chopped
- 3 TB chopped fresh rosemary
- 2 TB olive oil
- 2 cloves garlic, chopped
- 2 lbs flank steak, trimmed
- pepper
- SAUCE:
- ½ c. sour cream
- 1 TB plus 1 tsp. prepared horseradish
- 2 green onions, chopped
- pepper
- romaine lettuce leaves

Direction

- For Steak: Combine the first 6 ingredients in a glass baking dish. Add steak and turn to coat. Cover and marinate overnight, turning occasionally.
- For Sauce: Mix the first 3 ingredients in a small bowl. Season with a generous amount of pepper. (If preparing a day ahead, cover and refrigerate)
- Prepare barbecue. (High heat). Drain steak. Pour marinade into a small saucepan and boil 1 minute. Season steak with generous amount of pepper. Grill to desired doneness, basting occasionally with marinade, about 6 minutes per side for rare. Transfer steak to plate and let stand at least 15 minutes. Cut steak across grain into thin diagonal strips. Line platter with romaine leaves. Top with steak. Serve warm or at room temperature with horseradish sauce.

---

185. Marinated Pork Tenderloin With Pink Peppercorns Recipe

Serving: 4 | Prep: | Cook: 30mins | Ready in:

Ingredients

- 1 kilo boneless pork tenderloin or pork ham
- 2 finely chopped garlic cloves
- 1 spoonful thyme honey
- ½ cup of orange juice
- ¼ cup balsamic vinegar
- ½ cup olive oil
- ¼ cup orange liqueur
- ½ teaspoon seasoning salt
- 1 teaspoon crushed pink peppercorns
- ¼ ground mixed peppers
- ¼ teaspoon ground allspice
- ¼ teaspoon ground cumin
- Extra olive oil for frying
- all-purpose flour for dredging
- ½ teaspoon salt
- For sauce
- All marinade
- 1spoonful flour
- ¼ cup of milk
- For decoration
- 1 orange
- 2 red bell peppers
- A few pink peppercorns

Direction

- Combine garlic, balsamic vinegar, honey, oil, liqueur and seasoning salt to make marinade. Cut the meat into thin slices 1cm thick and marinate for at least 2 - 3 hours in refrigerator.
- Place bell peppers in a small baking tin, wet with a teaspoon of olive oil, sprinkle with salt and place in preheated oven at 180 degrees centigrade for half an hour. Remove and place in a plastic bag for 10 minutes and then remove skin and seeds and set aside to cool.
- Orange Sauce
- Remove pork from marinade, reserving remaining marinade. Drain meat and then dredge pork slices into flour with salt and sauté on both sides. Remove to a platter and add marinade into skillet. Stir constantly, scraping the pan. Place meat in skillet again and simmer for 20 minutes. Remove to a platter and add the milk and if needed add a spoonful of flour to thicken the sauce.

- Decorate platter with the red roasted peppers and slices or orange.

186.	Meatloaf Patty Recipe

Serving: 2 | Prep: | Cook: 10mins | Ready in:

Ingredients

- 1 1/3 pounds ground sirloin, 90 percent lean ground beef
- 1 slice white bread, spread with softened butter, then cut into small cubes
- 1/8 cup (a splash) milk
- 1 egg
- 2 teaspoons grill seasoning blend, or coarse salt and black pepper combined
- 1/2 teaspoon ground allspice
- 1 rounded tablespoon tomato paste
- 1 medium onion, finely chopped, reserve 1/4 amount
- 3-Condiment Pan Gravy: (recipe to follow making of patties)

Direction

- Place meat in a large mixing bowl and create a well in the center of the meat. Fill the well with the bread cubes and dampen them with a splash of milk. Pour 1 beaten egg over bread and add seasoning or salt and pepper, allspice, tomato paste and onion to the bowl.
- Combine the meat, bread and grill seasoning or salt and pepper and form mixture into 4 large oval patties 3/4-inch thick. Pan fry meatloaf patties in a non-stick skillet over medium high heat 7 minutes on each side under a loose tin foil tent. The tent will reflect heat and allow the steam to escape the pan. Remove meat loaf patties to a platter and return pan to heat.
- **3-Condiment Pan Gravy: **
- 2 tablespoons butter
- 1/4 medium onion, finely chopped, reserved from meatloaf mixture

- 2 tablespoons (a handful) all-purpose flour
- 1 to 1 1/2 cups beef stock
- 1 tablespoon ketchup
- 1 rounded teaspoon spicy brown mustard
- 1 tablespoon steak sauce
- Reduce heat to medium and add butter and onion to your skillet. Cook the onion 2 minutes and sprinkle pan with flour. Cook flour 1 minute and whisk in 1 cup beef stock. Bring broth to a bubble. If gravy is too thick, thin with additional stock. Stir in condiments and remove gravy from heat.
- Slice meatloaf patties and drizzle with gravy. Pile smashed potatoes (see Vegetables for recipe) alongside and make a well in the center for sour cream or gravy. Serve meatloaf and smashed potatoes with baby carrots, or with a tossed salad dressed with oil and vinegar.

187.   Mediterrrean Pork Or Lamb Chops Recipe

Serving: 4 | Prep: | Cook: 10mins | Ready in:

Ingredients

- 4 small pork or lamb chops
- 1/4 cup olive oil
- 1/2 cup flour
- 1 tsp salt
- 1/2 tsp black pepper
- 2 garlic cloves minced
- 2 Tbs capers
- 1/2 cup chicken broth
- 4 anchovy fillets
- 2 or 3 fresh sage leaves
- grated zest of one lemon

Direction

- Heat olive oil in a heavy duty Dutch oven on medium heat.
- Combine flour, salt and pepper in a wide bowl.

- Coat chops in seasoned flour and cook in pan until golden brown on each side (several minutes on each side).
- Remove chops from pan. Add garlic and cook and stir to release flavour.
- Then add capers, broth, zest, anchovies and sage leaves.
- Stir and mash anchovies into sauce.
- Place the chops back in the pan and reheat them gently until fully cooked.
- Serve chops with sauce spoon over them.

188.   Melt In Your Mouth Swiss Steak Recipe

Serving: 6 | Prep: | Cook: 200mins | Ready in:

Ingredients

- 3-4 lbs Chuck or round steak
- 2 jars beef gravy
- 2 jars mushroom Gravy
- 1 can Chopped or stewed tomatoes
- 1 Tbs worcestershire sauce
- 1 Cup flour
- salt and pepper

Direction

- Cut the meat into palm sized pieces and pound them out just a little and salt & pepper them.
- Dredge the meat in flour and shake off excess and brown in a skillet in olive oil.
- Mix the gravy with Worcestershire sauce in a large bowl, add tomatoes, then spoon out 1/3 of the gravy into a large baking pan and place the meat evenly in pan and cover with remaining gravy.
- Cover the pan with a lid or foil and bake in a pre-heated 325 degree oven for 3 hours. Remove foil or lid and bake for another 1/2 hour and let sit for 20 minutes before serving.
- This is even better the next day. Enjoy!

189. Mexicali Round Steak Recipe

Serving: 6 | Prep: | Cook: 480mins | Ready in:

Ingredients

- 1 1/2 pounds beef boneless round steak
- 1 cup frozen whole kernel corn
- 1 cup chopped fresh cilantro
- 1/2 cup beef broth
- 3 medium stalks celery, thinly sliced, about 1 1/2 cups
- 1 large onion, sliced
- 1 jar salsa (20 ounce)
- 1 can black beans (15 ounce) rinse & drained, rinse & drain again.
- 1 cup shredded monterey jack cheese with jalapeno peppers (4 ounces)

Direction

- Trim excess fat from beef. Cut into 6 serving pieces. Place beef in 3 1/2 to 6 quart slow cooker.
- Mix remaining ingredients, except cheese. Pour over beef.
- Cover and cook on low 8 - 9 hours until beef is tender.
- Sprinkle cheese over beef mixture right before serving.

190. Mexican Manicotti In The Microwave Recipe

Serving: 6 | Prep: | Cook: 18mins | Ready in:

Ingredients

- ½ pound ground sirloin (don't use a fatty ground beef for this)
- 1 cup refried beans or black beans
- ½ cup diced onion
- 1 or 2 tablespoon taco seasoning
- 8 manicotti shells, uncooked
- 1¼ cups water
- 8 ounces salsa
- 8 ounces sour cream
- ¼ cup chopped onions
- ¼ cup sliced black olives
- ½ cup shredded mexican cheese blend, or cheddar cheese
- sliced jalapeno peppers

Direction

- Combine uncooked meat, beans, 1/2 cup diced onions and taco seasoning; fill uncooked manicotti shells with mixture. Arrange filled shells in a 10x7 glass baking dish. Combine water and salsa; pour over shells. Cover with plastic wrap, poking a couple holes in it to allow steam to escape as it cooks. Microwave on High for 5 minutes; let it stand for 5 minutes. Cook on High for another 5 minutes. Using tongs, remove saran (BE CAREFUL of steam!) and turn shells over. Cover again, venting as before. Microwave on Medium for 10 to 18 minutes, until pasta is done. If your microwave does not have a turntable, be sure to turn baking dish every 5 minutes during all cooking times. Combine sour cream, ¼ cup chopped onions and olives; spoon down center of baked casserole. Top with cheese. Microwave on High, with just a piece of waxed paper on top to prevent splattering, for 1 minute, or until cheese begins to melt. Serve with jalapeno pepper slices on the side for anyone who likes more "heat".

191. Mexican Pepper Steak Recipe

Serving: 4 | Prep: | Cook: 10mins | Ready in:

Ingredients

- 1 1/2 lbs. top sirloin or other tender steak

- 2 tablespoons oil or lard
- 4 cloves garlic, minced
- 2 cups coarsely cut onion
- 2 cups coarsely cut green pepper
- 1 can (4 oz) diced green chilies
- 1 1/2 teaspoon salt
- 1 teaspoon cumin
- 1/2 teaspoon dried oregano leaves
- 1/4 teaspoon pepper
- 2 tomatoes, peeled, seeded, chopped
- Hot cooked rice

Direction

- Tim fat from steak. Cut into bite-size cubes or into thin strips.
- Heat oil in large skillet over high heat. Add meat and garlic. Cook, tossing, until browned.
- Add onion, green pepper and chilies. Cook and stir over medium heat until vegetables are tender crisp, about 3 minutes.
- Add seasonings and tomato.
- Heat briefly until tomatoes warmed.
- Serve with rice.

192. Mexican Pork Chops Recipe

Serving: 4 | Prep: | Cook: 10mins | Ready in:

Ingredients

- 1 teaspoon ground cumin
- 1 teaspoon chili powder
- 4 boneless pork loin chops (4 ounces each and 1/2 inch thick)
- 1 tablespoon vegetable oil
- 1-1/4 cups salsa
- 1 teaspoon baking cocoa
- 1/8 teaspoon ground cinnamon
- 2 tablespoons minced fresh cilantro
- 1 green onion, chopped

Direction

- Combine cumin and chili powder; rub over both sides of pork. In a large skillet, brown pork chops in oil on both sides over medium heat.
- In a small bowl, combine the salsa, cocoa and cinnamon; pour over pork. Bring sauce to a boil. Reduce heat; simmer, uncovered, for 8-10 minutes or until meat is tender, turning chops once and stirring sauce occasionally. Sprinkle with cilantro and green onion.

193. Mexico Geista Casserole Recipe

Serving: 10 | Prep: | Cook: 30mins | Ready in:

Ingredients

- 2 pounds ground sirloin
- 1/2 teaspoon garlic
- 1/2 teaspoon onion salt
- 1/2 teaspoon chili powder
- 1/2 teaspoon oregano
- 1/2 teaspoon cinnamon
- 3 tomatoes
- 2/3 cup salad dressing
- 3/4 cup grated cheddar cheese
- 1 cup sour cream
- 1 medium white onion diced
- 2 cups baking mix
- 1/2 cup water
- 1 small can chopped green chilies

Direction

- Brown meat slightly.
- Add garlic, onion salt, chili powder, oregano and cinnamon.
- Cook until meat is browned.
- Drain well.
- Slice tomatoes.
- Mix salad dressing, cheese, sour cream and onion then set aside.
- Combine baking mix and water.

- Pat into bottom of well-greased rectangular baking dish.
- Add meat, tomato slices and green chilies then top with sour cream mixture.
- Bake at 350 for 30 minutes.

---

194. Mix N Match Skillet Meals Recipe

Serving: 4 | Prep: | Cook: 60mins | Ready in:

Ingredients

- Choose one (1) food from each of the following four (4) groups:
- 1) breads and cereals (1 cup raw)
- macaroni
- spaghetti
- rice (white or brown)
- noodles
- Bulgar
- Any pasta
- 2) Sauce (1 can soup plus 1.5 cans milk, broth or water)
- Cream of mushroom
- Cream of celery
- Cream of chicken
- Cream of potato
- tomato soup
- French onion soup
- 3) Protein (1 pound or 1 cup cooked)
- Chopped beef
- Chopped pork or ham
- ground beef or turkey
- chicken
- turkey
- tuna
- salmon
- Mackerel
- Cooked dry beans
- frankfurters
- Keilbasa
- 4) vegetables (1.5 to 2 cups canned, cooked or raw)
- carrots
- peas
- corn
- green beans
- lima beans
- broccoli
- spinach
- mixed vegetables green pepper
- Whatever you have around
- 1/2 to 1 cup cheese (any kind) can be stirred into sauce at the end of the cooking time.

Direction

- Choose one food from each of the four groups above.
- Stir together in skillet.
- Season to taste with salt, pepper, soy sauce, onion flakes, garlic, or whatever spices you enjoy.
- Bring to a boil.
- Reduce heat to lowest setting.
- Cover pan and simmer 30 minutes until pasta or rice is tender.
- Stir occasionally to prevent rice and pasta from sticking.
- Stir in cheese, if desired.
- Serve.
- Makes 4 to 6 servings.
- Or, to bake in oven: mix all ingredients in casserole dish and cover tightly; bake at 350 F for one hour.

---

195. Moms Carne Pizzaiola Recipe

Serving: 1 | Prep: | Cook: 15mins | Ready in:

Ingredients

- 1 cup of egg noodles cooked according to package instructions
- top round steak (any thin cut of meat will do)- about 1/3 lb cut in two pieces

- olive oil
- 2 cloves of garlic
- salt
- 1/2 cup chopped tomatoes (1 small tomato or 12 grape tomatoes or chopped canned tomatoes)
- white wine (optional)
- parsley
- grated parmesan cheese

Direction

- Heat enough olive oil to cover the bottom of a large shallow sauté pan on medium heat.
- While oil is heating, chop garlic-add to pan.
- While garlic is heating, chop tomatoes.
- Once garlics is starting to turn brown, remove the garlic with a slotted spoon and keep on a plate.
- Add the two pieces of meat to the pan with the garlic-flavoured oil and salt meat while in pan.
- Cook on both sides about 1-2 minutes per side.
- Remove meat and keep on plate with garlic.
- Add chopped tomato to olive oil and meat juices in pan and sauté, stirring occasionally until a sauce starts to form-about 5-7 minutes.
- Add meat and garlic back to the sauce to reheat, *add a splash of white wine at this time if desired* or you can just add water and allow to reduce slightly, about another 3-5 minutes. This increases the amount of sauce/juice.
- Chop parsley while meat reheats and sauce reduces.
- Turn off heat and add chopped parsley to pan.
- Place noodles on a dish, and lay meat on top of noodles using tongs.
- Spoon the rest of the sauce over the meat and the noodles.
- Sprinkle meat generously with parmesan cheese, avoiding the noodles.
- Be sure to sop up all the juices on the plate. That is the best part!
- Enjoy!

196.   Moms Swiss Steak Recipe

Serving: 4 | Prep: | Cook: 90mins | Ready in:

Ingredients

- Round or chuck steak, 2 " thick
- 1/2 c flour
- 2 t salt
- 1 t black pepper
- shortening
- 2 T Worchestershire
- 1 onion, sliced in rings
- 1 large can whole tomatoes (Hunts, or other that is NOT sweet)
- ** I usually add some seasoned salt, garlic pepper, and italian seasoning - just a few shakes of each **

Direction

- Mix together flour, salt and pepper
- Pound into both sides of steak
- Brown both sides of steak in deep electric skillet, in 1 - 2 T melted shortening
- Lay onion slices on top
- Sprinkle with Worcestershire
- Cover with tomatoes
- Shake other seasonings over all
- Heat to simmer
- Reduce heat to low
- Cover and cook 1 1/2 hours

197.   Mongolian Beef Recipe

Serving: 4 | Prep: | Cook: 4mins | Ready in:

Ingredients

- 2 Tbs soy sauce
- 1 tsp sugar
- 1 tsp cornstarch
- 2 tsp dry sherry
- 2 tsp hoisin sauce
- 1 tsp rice vinegar

- 1 tsp chile paste with garlic
- 1/4 tsp salt
- 2 tsp peanut oil
- 1 Tbs minced, peeled,fresh ginger
- 1 Tbs minced fresh garlic
- 1 lb. sirloin steak,thin sliced across the grain
- 16 medium green onions,cut in 2" pieces

Direction

- Combine first 8 ingredients, stirring till smooth.
- Heat peanut oil in large, nonstick skillet over med-high heat. Add minced ginger, minced garlic, and beef; sauté for 2 mins or till beef is browned. Add green onion pieces; sauté 30 seconds. Add soy sauce mixture; cook 1 min or till thickened, stirring constantly.

---

198. Moo Shi Beef Recipe

Serving: 4 | Prep: | Cook: 30mins |Ready in:

Ingredients

- Ingredients:
- 1 lb. sirloin tip steak 1/8" to 1/4" thick
- 3 cups fresh pkg. coleslaw mix
- 2/3 cup sliced green onions
- 1 Tbs. cornstarch, dissolved in ¼ cup water
- 8 medium floured tortillas, warmed
- 1/3 cup hoisin sauce
- marinade Ingredients:
- 2 Tbs. Reduced-sodium soy sauce
- 2 Tbs. water
- 1 Tbs. dark sesame oil
- 2 cloves garlic, crushed
- 2 tsp. sugar

Direction

- 1. Cut Steaks lengthwise in half and then crosswise into thin strips. In a medium bowl, combine marinade ingredients; add beef,

tossing to coat. Cover and marinate in refrigerator for 20 minutes.
- 2. Remove beef from marinade; discard marinade. Heat a large nonstick skillet over medium-high heat until hot. Add beef (½ at a time) and stir-fry 1 o 2 minutes or until outside surface is no longer pink. (Do not overcook). Add coleslaw mix, green onions and cornstarch mixture. Cook and stir until sauce is thickened and bubbly.
- 3. To assemble, spread one side of tortilla with2 tsp. Hoisin sauce. Spoon ½ cup beef mixture in center of each tortilla. Fold bottom edge up over filling. Fold sides to center, overlapping edges.
- Nutrition: Per serving: 501 calories; 34g protein; 62g carbohydrate; 13g fat (4g saturated fat); 6.3mg iron; 1,055mg sodium; 69mg cholesterol.

---

199. Morant Villas Jamaican Honey Ginger Pork Chops Recipe

Serving: 6 | Prep: | Cook: 120mins |Ready in:

Ingredients

- Marinade: -----------
- 8 medium pork chops (cut at least 3/4 inch thick, but 1 inch is better)
- 1 tsp garlic powder
- 1/4tsp ground allspice
- 2 Tbsp soy sauce
- 2 tsp Jamaican All Purpose seasoning (optional)
- 1 scotch bonnet pepper (optional if you want heat)
- salt and pepper -- to taste,
- Sauce: ----------
- 1 ounce ginger root -- finely grated
- 1/2 cup water
- 1/4 cup honey
- 1 Tbsp Pickapepper sauce

- 3/4 cup ketchup

Direction

- Season pork chops with garlic powder, allspice, soy sauce, all-purpose seasoning and pepper.
- Marinate in refrigerator for 3 to 6 hours.
- Note: Additional salt may not be necessary for seasoning the chops since the all-purpose seasoning and soy are both salty.
- Preheat oven to 375 degrees.
- Place pork chops in a shallow baking pan and bake for about 1-1/2 hours, turning once or twice to prevent chops from burning.
- While chops are cooking:
- MAKE THE SAUCE
- Grate the ginger then rinse any ginger from grater with the 1/2 cup water.
- Add honey, Pickapeppa and ketchup to ginger liquid mixing well.
- Spoon and spread the sauce over pork chops and bake for 1/2 hour more.
- Serve hot over rice.

---

200. Morroccan Pork Chops Recipe

Serving: 2 | Prep: | Cook: 20mins | Ready in:

Ingredients

- 1 tablespoon cumin seeds, toasted and coarsely ground
- 1 tablespoon coriander seeds, toasted and coarsely ground
- 3 garlic cloves, finely chopped
- 2 tablespoons olive oil
- 2 (3/4-inch-thick) pork chops
- 2 tablespoons coarsely chopped fresh cilantro
- Garnish: lime wedges

Direction

- Combine cumin, coriander, garlic, and 1 tablespoon oil. Pat pork chops dry and season with salt and pepper. Rub spice mixture on both sides of chops.
- Heat remaining tablespoon oil in a large heavy skillet over moderate heat until hot but not smoking, then cook chops until just cooked through, 5 to 7 minutes on each side.
- Serve pork chops sprinkled with cilantro and garnish with lime wedges.

---

201. Mushroom Roasted Garlic Pork Chops Recipe

Serving: 4 | Prep: | Cook: 25mins | Ready in:

Ingredients

- 1 tbsp. vegetable oil
- 4 bone-in pork chops, 1/2-inch thick (about 1 pound)
- 1 can (10 3/4 oz.) Campbell's® Condensed Cream of mushroom with roasted garlic Soup
- 1/2 cup milk
- Hot cooked egg noodles

Direction

- Heat the oil in a 10-inch skillet over medium-high heat. Add the pork chops and cook until the chops are well browned on both sides. Remove the pork chops and set them aside.
- Stir in the soup and milk. Heat to a boil. Return the pork chops to the skillet and reduce the heat to low. Cover and cook for 5 minutes or until the chops are cooked through but slightly pink in the center*.
- Serve with the noodles.
- TIP: *The internal temperature of the pork should reach 160°F.

202. Mushroom Tortellini Alfredo

Serving: 100 | Prep: | Cook: | Ready in:

Ingredients

- 2 (9 ounce) packages refrigerated cheese tortellini
- 6 tablespoons unsalted butter
- 1 (8 ounce) package sliced baby bella mushrooms
- 2 cups heavy cream, divided
- 1 ½ cups grated Parmesan cheese
- 1 teaspoon grated lemon zest
- 1 pinch freshly grated nutmeg
- sea salt and freshly ground black pepper to taste
- 1 tablespoon grated Parmesan cheese, or to taste
- 1 tablespoon chopped fresh parsley

Direction

- Fill a large pot with lightly salted water and bring to a rolling boil; stir in tortellini and return to a boil. Cook uncovered, stirring occasionally, until the tortellini float to the top and are tender yet firm to the bite, 2 to 3 minutes; do not overcook. Drain, reserving some pasta water.
- Meanwhile, melt butter over medium heat in a large skillet. Add mushrooms, and saute until tender and golden brown, about 5 minutes. Reduce heat to low, pour in 1 1/2 cups of cream, and simmer, stirring occasionally, 4 to 5 minutes.
- Remove the skillet from the heat and add drained tortellini; toss to combine. Stir in remaining 1/2 cup of heavy cream, 1 1/2 cups Parmesan cheese, lemon zest, nutmeg, sea salt, and pepper; toss until well incorporated.
- Place the skillet over low heat and cook until Parmesan has melted and sauce has thickened slightly, 1 to 2 remaining Parmesan and parsley.
- Nutrition Facts

- Per Serving:
- 1115.8 calories; protein 33.8g 68% DV; carbohydrates 67.1g 22% DV; fat 81.7g 126% DV; cholesterol 292.5mg 98% DV; sodium 1090.9mg 44% DV.

203. Mustard Crusted London Broil Recipe

Serving: 4 | Prep: | Cook: 18mins | Ready in:

Ingredients

- 3/4 cup panko (Japanese bread crumbs-found in bread crumb isle)
- 1 TBS. fresh thyme leaves
- 1 lb Top-round London Broil, trimmed
- 1 1/2 TBS Dijon mustard
- 2 cloves garlic

Direction

- Arrange oven rack on top position. Preheat oven to 450 degrees. Fit baking or roasting pan with a wire rack.
- Mix panko and thyme on a plate.
- Season both sides of London broil with salt and pepper to taste. Combine mustard and garlic in small bowl and cover meat with mixture.
- Coat London broil with panko mixture, pressing crumbs into meat so that they stick. Discard remaining crumbs. Place meat on rack and coat top and sides thoroughly with olive oil spray.
- Roast 16-18 minutes for medium doneness or until crumbs are golden and desires doneness is reached. If crumbs begin browning too much, cover beef loosely with foil. Remove from oven and let stand 10 minutes. Slice into thin strips and serve.
- Nutrition: 230 calories, 28 g protein, 9 gr carb, 8.5 gr fat, 3 gr. sat fat, 50 mg. cholesterol, 0 gr. fibre, 105 mg. sodium.

204. My Favorite Breakfast Lunch Dinner Or Late Night Snack Recipe

Serving: 4 | Prep: | Cook: 20mins | Ready in:

Ingredients

- 2 large potatoes, diced
- 1 med onion, diced
- Leftover meat, beef or pork roast, steaks, chops etc…, chopped
- 4-6 eggs
- garlic pepper
- Grated cheese, what ever kind you have in the fridge in whatever amount you like
- Optional: peppers-hot or sweet, left over veggies, mushrooms, olives, herbs or what ever strikes your fancy.

Direction

- Fry potatoes and onions in oil or butter till done to your liking. I cook mine till they are brown and crispy. Add meat and any optional ingredients and fry till heated. Add eggs, stir. Cook till done. Sprinkle with garlic pepper and cheese. Serve with whatever condiments you like. My husband likes ketchup and I prefer Emeril's green sauce or salsa and sour cream. My daughters want it without meat, maybe with some tofu. Add toast and hot chocolate and you have the perfect comfort meal.

205. My Philly Cheese Steak Sandwiches Recipe

Serving: 4 | Prep: | Cook: 10mins | Ready in:

Ingredients

- 2 fresh torpedo rolls, split in half crosswise
- 1 small sweet Maui onion, thinly sliced
- 1/2 large green bell pepper, thinly sliced
- 1 large clove crushed garlic
- kosher salt and fresh ground black pepper, to taste
- 1 pound rib-eye steak, very, very thinly shaved/sliced (put in freezer for about an hour to make it easier to slice)
- few splashes of soy sauce (yes, that's right!)
- 2 slices white American cheese
- 1 TBSP unsalted butter and 1 clove garlic (crushed), for toasting bread
- Mayo (optional, but in my book, mandatory!)

Direction

- Melt butter with garlic in skillet. Add bread, open face down and toast in skillet. Once light golden brown, remove and wrap rolls in foil; set aside.
- Preheat the oven to 200 degrees F.
- Heat the same skillet over medium-high heat. When hot add the oil and crushed garlic. Allow oil to become fragrant with the garlic then remove the garlic. Add the onion and bell peppers, and cook, stirring, until caramelized, about 6 minutes. Season lightly with salt and pepper and sauté for 30 seconds. Remove to a bowl and set aside.
- Add the meat to the hot pan and cook, stirring and breaking up with a spatula, until almost no longer pink, about 2 minutes. Season with salt, pepper and soy (go easy on the soy; you only need just a little). Add the sautéed vegetables back to the pan, sauté about 30 seconds; remove from heat.
- Spread a little mayo on the rolls. Add cheese slices and spoon the meat on top. Close the rolls and wrap in foil. Place in oven for about 8 minutes to slightly rewarm the rolls and melt the cheese.

206.   Nikkis Steak Saltimbocca Recipe

Serving: 6 | Prep: | Cook: 15mins | Ready in:

Ingredients

- 2 pounds beef skirt steak, trimmed of fat
- freshly ground black pepper to taste
- 6 ounces sliced aged provolone cheese
- 2 bunches fresh sage leaves
- 12 slices prosciutto
- 1/4 cup extra virgin olive oil

Direction

- Preheat the oven to 350 degrees F (175 degrees C).
- Cut the steak into approximately 4 ounce pieces, then pound each one to 1/4 inch thickness.
- Season with black pepper.
- On each piece of steak, lay one slice of provolone cheese, a few leaves of sage and 2 slices of prosciutto.
- Roll into pinwheels and secure with toothpicks.
- Heat the oil in a large skillet over medium-high heat. Quickly brown the pinwheels on the outside.
- Transfer to a baking dish if your skillet is not oven-safe.
- Bake for 7 minutes for medium rare, or 10 for medium.
- Let rest for 5 minutes before carving into thin pinwheels.
- Place the skillet back over medium-high heat, and add any remaining sage leaves.
- Fry until crispy and then use them to garnish steaks.

207.   Normandy Pork Chops Recipe

Serving: 4 | Prep: | Cook: 30mins | Ready in:

Ingredients

- 1 tbsp of olive oil
- 1 tbsp of unsalted butter
- 4 center cut boneless pork chops at least 3/4 to one inch thick
- 1/4 cup of white wine
- 2 medium shallots minced
- 1/8 cup of chicken broth
- 1 scant tbsp of Dijon mustard
- 2 granny smith apples, cored, peeled and sliced
- 1 tbsp of unsalted butter
- 1/4 cup of apple brandy or calvados
- 2 tbsp of red currant jelly

Direction

- Preheat the oven to 350 degrees.
- Heat the olive oil and the first tbsp. of butter in a large heavy bottomed skillet and sauté the pork chops on each side about 3 minutes each side.
- Transfer to a glass baking dish.
- Add wine to the skillet, scrape to deglaze the bottom of the pan and get all the goodies off the bottom, add the shallots, broth and mustard, stir well and cook until shallots are soft and liquid is reduced by 1/2.
- Pour over the chops, cover tightly with foil and bake for 20 minutes.
- In the same skillet, melt the remaining tbsp. of butter and add the sliced Granny Smith apples. Cook until these are soft about five minutes over medium high heat.
- Remove from heat, add the Calvados.
- Return to heat and stir in the currant jelly and cook until a glaze forms.
- Spoon the apples over the chops and bake another five minutes uncovered.

208.   Not My Mamas Swiss Steak Recipe

Serving: 6 | Prep: | Cook: 22mins | Ready in:

Ingredients

- 1 and half lbs round steak
- 2 Tbls flour
- 1/4 ts thyme
- 1/8 ts garlic powder
- salt and pepper to taste
- 1/2 medium onion chopped
- 1 green pepper diced
- 1 stalk celery
- 1 carrot chopped (optional)
- 1 clove garlic chopped or 1 ts minced garlic (more if you love garlic)
- 1 (14.5oz can) stewed tomatoes
- 1/4 cup red wine (or 1/4 can beef broth)
- 1 or more Tbls worchestershire sauce

Direction

- Cut ground steak into serving sized pieces.
- Mix flour, thyme, garlic powder, salt and pepper together.
- Dredge the meat pieces through the flour mixture and place in slow cooker.
- Chop the onion, green pepper, celery and carrot if using.
- Place the onion, green pepper, celery and carrot if using on top of the meat.
- Sprinkle minced garlic over the vegetables.
- Cover this all with the can of stewed tomatoes.
- Pour the Worcestershire sauce and wine or beef broth over all.
- Cook on low for 8 to 10 hours or high for 3 to 5 hours.
- Serve with mashed potatoes or pasta or whatever your heart desires.
- Enjoy!

209.   Old Fashioned Cabbage Rolls Recipe

Serving: 8 | Prep: | Cook: 90mins | Ready in:

Ingredients

- 1/2 pound ground beef
- 1/2 pound ground veal
- 1/2 pound ground pork
- 1 small onion, chopped
- 2 eggs, lightly beaten
- 1/2 cup dry bread crumbs
- 1 tea. salt
- 1 tea. molasses
- 1/4 tea. ground ginger
- 1/4 tea. ground nutmeg
- 1/4 tea. ground allspice
- 1 large head cabbage, separated into leaves
- 3 cups boiling water
- 1/4 cup butter
- 1/2 cup milk, plus additional if need be
- 1 Tab. cornstarch

Direction

- Combine meats and onion in large bowl. Combine eggs, bread crumbs, salt, molasses, ginger, nutmeg and allspice in medium bowl; mix well. Add to meat mixture, stir until well blended. Set aside
- Drop cabbage leaves into boiling water for 3 minutes. Remove with slotted spoon, reserving 1/2 cup of the boiling water
- Preheat oven to 375*. Place about 2 tablespoons meat mixture about 1 inch from stem end of each cabbage leaf. Fold sides in and roll up. Fasten with toothpicks if necessary.
- Heat butter in large skillet over medium-high heat. Add cabbage rolls. 3 or 4 at a time. Brown on all sides. Arrange rolls, seam side down, in single layer in casserole. Combine reserved boiling liquid with butter remaining in skillet, pour over cabbage rolls
- Bake 1 hour. Carefully drain accumulated pan juices into measuring cup. Return cabbage

rolls to over. Add enough milk to pan juices to make 1 cup.

- Pour milk mixture into small saucepan. Stir in cornstarch; bring to boil, stirring constantly until sauce is thickened. Pour over cabbage rolls. Bake 15 minutes more or until sauce is browned and cabbage is very tender

210. Once A Year Cholesterol Busting Burger Recipe

Serving: 3 | Prep: | Cook: 15mins | Ready in:

Ingredients

- 1 pound mixture of ground sirloin and ground chuck
- 4 tablespoons water
- seasonings (I use some garlic salt, pepper and a maybe a bit of steak seasoning)
- 1 large onion, sliced in rings
- 8 slices bacon, fried crisp
- real butter, and lots of it, for frying the onions (about 4 tablespoons)
- American or Velvetta cheese, any cheese that melts creamy (cheddar is a bit too "solid" for the topping – you want the cheese to "drip" off the burger a bit)
- 4 large eggs (why go small on this burger – you're splurging, remember??)
- 4 hamburger buns, cut sides spread with MORE real butter

Direction

- In a medium bowl, GENTLY combine meats with water and seasonings (yes, trust me, the water will give you an unbelievably moist burger), and shape into 3 patties.
- Melt butter in large skillet and fry onions until nicely browned and beginning to caramelize – you don't want a wimpy sauté for these…you want them FRIED.

- Remove onions from skillet and fry bacon in same skillet – no need to clean out first…the flavors blend well.
- Remove bacon from skillet and pour out MOST of the grease, but not all (leave about 1 tablespoon in the pan). Add a pat of butter (come on, you're splurging).
- Fry the burgers in the bacon drippings and butter. Place cheese slice on top of each burger just shortly before done (the cheese will finish melting as the cooked burgers "hold" while the eggs fry)
- While the burgers are frying in all that fat, butter the cut sides of the hamburger buns and toast them in a skillet or place under the broiler to get a nice crispy bun.
- While buns are toasting, finish frying the burgers and then set them aside. Add another pat of butter to that same skillet (we're getting a lot of use out of that one skillet).
- Now fry those eggs in that skillet (I break the yolks, because it's just too messy to eat the burger with the yolk running out).
- You are READY to assemble your masterpiece: bottom buttery toasted bun, cheese-topped burger, 1 fried egg, 2 slices of bacon, fried onions, a squirt of mustard (optional), and top it off with the remaining toasted top bun.
- You'll probably find this burger is easiest eaten with a knife and fork, but if you don't have company, pick it up and let it drip!

211. Oven Baked Bone In Pork Chops Recipe

Serving: 6 | Prep: | Cook: 40mins | Ready in:

Ingredients

- 4-8 Bone in pork chops ¼ - ¾ inch thick
- Donnie's cajun seasoning Mix (or equivalent) (Recipe on my recipe page)

Direction

- Let chops come to room temperature for 20-30 minutes.
- Rinse off chops with cold water.
- Pat dry with paper towels and place chops on a baking sheet or pan.
- Sprinkle seasoning mix on chops.
- Turn chops over and sprinkle seasoning mix on what was the bottom side of chops.
- If chops are ½ inch or thinner, preheat oven to 300 deg.
- If chops are ½ inch or thicker, preheat oven to 325 deg.
- Cook chops for 15 minutes then turn them.
- Cook chops for another 15 minutes.
- If the internal temperature is between 150-160 deg., remove chops from the oven.
- Cover pan with foil and let the chops stand for 5-10 minutes.
- Enjoy

212. Oven Fried Pork Chops Recipe

Serving: 4 | Prep: | Cook: 45mins | Ready in:

Ingredients

- 4 center cut boneless pork chops (about 1/2" thick)
- 1 tsp. salt
- 1 tsp. sugar
- 1/2 tsp. garlic powder
- 1 C. crushed saltine crackers
- 2 eggs, slightly beaten

Direction

- Preheat oven to 425°
- Combine salt, sugar and garlic powder and mix well.
- Sprinkle chops evenly with the salt mixture.
- Dip chops in egg then put in cracker crumbs and cover well.
- Place on greased rack sitting on a baking sheet.

- Lightly spray the chops with cooking spray.
- Bake for 12 to 15 minutes or until done.

213. Oven Smoked Tri Tip Recipe

Serving: 6 | Prep: | Cook: 90mins | Ready in:

Ingredients

- 1 tri-tip roast, slightly trimmed
- 1 Tb salt
- 1 Tb ground pepper
- 2 Tbs chili powder
- 1 Tb granulated garlic (or rub the roast with fresh chopped garlic)
- 3 Tbs Wrights Natural Hickory seasoning liquid

Direction

- Preheat the oven to 350 degrees.
- There is a layer of fat on the top of the tri-tip. I run a very sharp knife over that fat cutting lines across the fat then turn the roast and run the knife over the first lines, making "diamond" cuts across the top of the beef. Do not cut down into the beef if possible.
- Add all of the dry spices together in a bowl and mix.
- Sprinkle the entire roast with the dry seasonings, rubbing them well into the meat.
- Place the beef into a baking pan (I can fit 2 into a 13x9 pan)
- **Sprinkle the liquid smoke over the meat**
- Cover the pan completely with foil and place in oven for 60 minutes. (At 350 degrees!) .
- Remove foil and bake for 15 to 30 minutes, (depending on how rare you prefer your beef) and allow the top to brown.
- Baste your roast before placing back in oven.
- Remove beef, cover the pan with the foil and let the beef sit for 10 minutes before slicing.
- Slice against the grain and serve.

- *I must add that I always cook two of these at the same time. Two roasts fit a 13x9 pan perfectly.
- The leftover meat with some added BBQ sauce makes a wonderful sandwich! We chop up a few slices, add BBQ sauce to the meat, and heat it up, served on hamburger buns. Good stuff, Maynard!
- (It's great in tacos and burritos, too!)

214. PORK CHOPS AND APRICOTS Recipe

Serving: 4 | Prep: | Cook: 25mins | Ready in:

Ingredients

- INGREDIENTS;
- 1/2 cup, chopped dried apricots
- 1/2 cup orange juice
- 1/4 c. apricot preserves
- 2 tsp brown sugar
- 1/2 tsp curry powder
- 2 tsp olive oil
- 4 1/2-3/4 inch thick pork chops of your choice
- salt and ground black pepper to taste
- 2 scallions chopped

Direction

- DIRECTIONS:
- Pour apricots into a deep bowl
- Pour orange juice over apricots
- Add preserves, sugar and curry powder...
- Stir gently and set aside
- Heat a large skillet over medium high heat and add oil
- Cook chops 3 min on each side no more than golden brown
- Season lightly w/ salt and black pepper
- Reduce to low
- Add apricots and juice mixture
- Cover and simmer for 5 min

- Remove from heat and sprinkle w/ green onions

215. Paddy's Cheese Steak's Recipe

Serving: 4 | Prep: | Cook: 40mins | Ready in:

Ingredients

- 1- 1lb ribeye steak
- 1 red bell pepper
- 1 medium onion, chopped
- 1 cup baby bella mushrooms, chopped
- Salt to taste
- Pepper to taste
- Dash cayenne pepper
- 2 tbs olive oil, or butter
- 1 loaf Italian bread, unsliced
- 6 slices American cheese

Direction

- Season the steak with salt and pepper, and grill to rare/medium rare. Set aside (you will be cooking this again in a skillet, so rare is ok)
- Grill red bell pepper until skin has blackened slightly
- Peel burned skin from pepper, remove seeds and chop to small pieces
- Once steak has set for at least ten minutes, slice, or chop to bite sized bits.
- Heat a large skillet and add oil or butter
- Add chopped onion, mushrooms and chopped bell pepper and sauté for 3 minutes, or until onion is transparent
- Add steak
- Season all with salt and pepper (and a touch of cayenne, for a kick)
- Separate into four servings in the pan, and add American cheese, breaking it up and folding it into the servings until melted completely
- Remove pan from heat
- Meanwhile...
- BREAD:

- Heat oven to 400
- Cut the entire loaf into 4 quarters
- Using your hand, remove (scoop out) bread from inside the crust, leaving only about 1/2" of soft bread against the crust (save remainder for meatballs, or stuffing!)
- Sprinkle inside with olive oil, butter or mayonnaise and heat for 4 minutes in oven
- When ready, place steak servings in each quarter, and enjoy!

---

216. Panko Crusted Pork Chops Recipe

Serving: 4 | Prep: | Cook: 20mins | Ready in:

Ingredients

- 4 pork chops, bone in or boneless, 3/4-1 in. thick
- 2 eggs, beaten
- 1/2 cup flour
- 1 1/2 cups panko bread crumbs
- 1 tsp. thyme
- 1/2 tsp. ground sage
- salt and pepper to taste
- olive oil

Direction

- Preheat oven to 400
- In wide shallow bowl, add flour, salt, and pepper
- In another bowl, add eggs
- In another bowl, add bread crumbs, sage, thyme, and salt and pepper
- In sauté pan, heat olive oil to medium high heat
- In order, flour chop, egg it, then lastly, dredge in bread crumbs
- Cook in sauté pan until golden brown on both sides
- Put into oven, pan and all (if handle not heat resistant, wrap in foil)
- Cook until temp. Of 140-145

- Remove from oven
- Tent with foil
- Rest for 5 minutes

---

217. Parmesan Ranch Burgers Recipe

Serving: 8 | Prep: | Cook: 18mins | Ready in:

Ingredients

- 2. 5 lbs ground chuck or sirloin (15-20% fat - less will make for dry burgers)
- 1 package ranch dressing mix
- 1/4 c grated parmesan cheese
- 1 package beefy onion mushroom soup mix
- 1 egg, beaten
- 1 T minced garlic
- 3-4 T worcestershire
- 1 t liquid smoke, or 1 t charcoal grill taste dry rub
- 1 t seasoned salt
- 1 T garlic pepper
- 8 slices provolone cheese (or your fave)
- 1 white onion, sliced
- sliced fresh mushrooms

Direction

- Mix all ingredients - except provolone - well with hands, quickly (handling too much will make tougher burgers)
- Shape into 8 patties, large and about 1 inch thick
- Grill to desired doneness, turning once, AVOID mashing with the spatula!
- Add cheese slices
- Butter insides of rolls and place on grill.
- I sautéed onions and fresh mushrooms with olive oil, garlic, butter and Worcestershire for a topping.

218. Pat King Of Steaks Original Philly Cheesesteaks Recipe

Serving: 4 | Prep: | Cook: 10mins | Ready in:

Ingredients

- 2 lb. rib eye, thinly sliced (I put it in the freezer for an hour to make slicing easier)
- 6 tbls. oil
- Cheez Whiz
- 4 crusty Italian rolls
- 1 red onion
- Optional: sweet green and red peppers, sauteed

Direction

- Heat 3 tbsp. oil in skillet
- Sauté onions until tender
- Set aside
- Heat Cheez Whiz in microwave
- Add remaining oil and cook slices of meat quickly on both sides
- Put steak onto rolls
- Add onions
- Pour Cheez Whiz over top

219. Pepper Beef Recipe

Serving: 4 | Prep: | Cook: 20mins | Ready in:

Ingredients

- 2 tablespoons oil
- 3/4 pound top round or other
- inexpensive steak, uncooked and thinly sliced
- 2 cloves garlic, minced
- 1/4 cup coarsely chopped onions
- 1 green bell pepper, cut into
- 1-inch pieces
- 1 (14 1/2-ounce) can beef broth
- 1/4 cup soy sauce
- 2 tablespoons cornstarch

- 3/4 cup cold water
- Hot cooked rice

Direction

- Heat oil in wok or skillet over medium-high heat. Stir-fry steak until no longer pink. Remove with a slotted spoon. Stir-fry garlic, onions and green bell pepper for 2 minutes. Return steak to wok. Add broth and soy sauce. Bring to a simmer. Combine cornstarch and cold water. Add to wok to thicken sauce. Cook for 2 to 3 minutes, or until heated through. Serve over rice.
- Variations: Leftover beef roast works great in this recipe. Omit stir-frying meat.

220. Pepper Steak Recipe

Serving: 4 | Prep: | Cook: 30mins | Ready in:

Ingredients

- 2 round steaks cut in strips
- 1 stick butter
- 1 (15 oz) can tomato sauce
- 2 beef bouillion cubes
- 2 c hot water
- 1 green pepper cut in strips

Direction

- Melt butter in large skillet.
- Brown the meat and add the green pepper till cooked.
- Dissolve bouillon cubes in hot water.
- Add this and the tomato sauce to the meat.
- Simmer 20 minutes.
- Mix together: 1/2 cup cold water, 1 tsp. sugar, 1 tbsps. cornstarch, and 3 tbsps. soy sauce.
- Add this to meat mixture, stir till thickened.
- Serve over rice.

221. Pepper Steak Stir Fry Recipe

Serving: 4 | Prep: | Cook: 30mins | Ready in:

Ingredients

- 1 lb top round steak
- 3 tablespoons vegetable oil
- 1 cup water
- 2 cubes beef bouillon
- 1 medium onion, cut into 1/4 inch slices
- 1-2 garlic cloves, finely chopped
- 2 medium green bell peppers, cut into 1/2 inch-wide strips
- 8 oz fresh mushrooms, sliced
- 1 tablespoon cornstarch
- 2 tablespoons soy sauce
- 2 medium tomatoes, cut into thin wedges
- 6 cups hot cooked rice

Direction

- Cut beef into thin strips for stir fry. Heat oil in wok or skillet over medium-high heat. Cook beef until brown. Stir in water, onion, and garlic. Heat to boiling; reduce heat to low. Cover and simmer 12 to 15 minutes, adding bell peppers and mushrooms during last 5 minutes of simmering, until beef is tender and peppers are crisp-tender. Mix cornstarch and soy sauce; stir into beef mixture. Cook, stirring constantly, until mixture thickens and boils. Boil and stir 1 minute. Cut tomatoes into wedges and place on beef mixture. Cover and cook over low heat about 3 minutes or just until tomatoes are heated through. Serve over rice.
- Time Saver Tip – Get beef from the grocery store already pre sliced for stir fry. Get the onion, bell peppers and tomatoes from the salad bar at the grocery store.

222. Peppered Pork With Chive Sauce Recipe

Serving: 4 | Prep: | Cook: 20mins | Ready in:

Ingredients

- 4 boneless pork chops, 3/4 inch thick
- 1 tsp. coarsely ground pepper, black or tricolored
- 2 tsp. olive oil
- 1/4 cup water
- 3 tbls. dry sherry or chicken broth
- 1 3oz. pkg. cream cheese and chives (or 3oz. pkg plain cream cheese mixed with finely chopped chives)
- Fresh chives, chopped for garnish

Direction

- Lightly rub pepper into both sides of pork chops
- Heat oil in skillet and cook pork chops for 8-10 minutes until no longer pink, turning once
- Remove from skillet and keep warm
- Add water to hot skillet
- Add sherry or broth and heat until bubbling
- Add cream cheese
- Whisk until cheese is melted
- Pour sauce over pork
- Garnish with chopped chives

223. Peppered Ribeye Steak With Grilled Sweet Peppers Recipe

Serving: 8 | Prep: | Cook: 11mins | Ready in:

Ingredients

- 4 10- to 12-ounce beef ribeye steaks, cut 1 inch thick
- 1 tablespoon olive oil
- 1 tablespoon paprika
- 1 tablespoon garlic powder

- 2 teaspoons dried thyme, crushed
- 2 teaspoons dried oregano, crushed
- 1-1/2 teaspoons lemon-pepper seasoning
- 1 teaspoon salt
- 1/2 to 1 teaspoon ground black pepper
- 1/2 to 1 teaspoon cayenne pepper
- 1 recipe Grilled peppers (see recipe below)

Direction

- Trim fat from meat. Brush steaks with oil. In a small bowl, combine paprika, garlic powder, thyme, oregano, lemon-pepper seasoning, salt, black pepper, and cayenne pepper. Sprinkle paprika mixture evenly over meat; rub in with your fingers. Cover steaks and chill for 1 hour.
- Place steaks on the rack of an uncovered grill directly over medium coals. Grill until desired doneness, turning once. (Allow 11 to 15 minutes for medium-rare doneness [145 degree F] or 14 to 18 minutes for medium doneness [160 degree F].) Cut steaks into serving-size pieces. Serve with Grilled Peppers. Makes 8 servings.
- Grilled Peppers: Seed and quarter 4 yellow, red, and/or orange sweet peppers. Brush peppers with 4 teaspoons olive oil. Place pepper quarters on grill rack directly over medium coals. Grill for 12 to 15 minutes or until peppers are crisp-tender and lightly browned, turning once. Remove peppers from grill; cool slightly. Cut peppers into wide strips. Place peppers in bowl. Add 2 tablespoons snipped fresh basil and 2 tablespoons balsamic vinegar; toss well. Serve immediately or cool to room temperature.

224. Philly Cheese Steak Casserole Recipe

Serving: 6 | Prep: | Cook: 50mins | Ready in:

Ingredients

- (6 oz) wide egg noodles

- 1-1/2 lb. beef, boneless sirloin steak, about 3/4 inch thick
- 1/2 teaspoon pepper
- 2 medium onions, chopped
- 2 garlic cloves, minced or finely chopped
- 1 green bell pepper, chopped
- 1 (14 oz.) can fat-free and sodium reduced beef broth
- 1/4 cup Gold Medal all-purpose flour
- Note: The recipe calls for 1/4 cup but I find a couple of Tablespoons do the trick.
- 1/2 cup half-and-half, fat-free or regular
- 1 Tablespoon Dijon mustard
- 1 cup cheddar cheese, reduced-fat or regular, shredded

Direction

- Heat oven to 350 degrees F.
- Spray an 11 x 7 inch (2 quart) glass baking dish with cooking spray.
- Cook and drain noodles as directed on package.
- Meanwhile, remove any fat from beef.
- Cut beef into 3/4 inch pieces.
- Heat a 12 inch non-stick skillet over medium heat.
- Cook beef and pepper in skillet 3-4 minutes, stirring occasionally, until beef is lightly brown.
- Stir in onions and bell pepper.
- Cook 2 minutes, stirring occasionally.
- Spoon into baking dish.
- In medium bowl, beat broth and flour with wire whisk until smooth.
- Add to skillet and heat to boiling.
- Cook, stirring constantly, until mixture thickens.
- Remove from heat.
- Stir in half-and-half and mustard.
- Spoon over beef mixture.
- Stir in cooked noodles.
- Cover and bake for 40 minutes.
- Sprinkle with cheese.
- Bake uncovered about 10 minutes longer or until cheese is melted and casserole is bubbly.
- Makes 4-6 servings (1-1/3 cups each)

- From: Betty Crocker, Quick-to-Fix Casseroles

225. Philly Cheese Steak Pie Recipe

Serving: 10 | Prep: | Cook: 90mins | Ready in:

Ingredients

- For the filling:
- 3 tbsp. oil
- 3 poblano, or green bell peppers, seeded and julienned
- 3 colored sweet bell peppers (orange, red or yellow), seeded and julienned
- 8 oz. baby bella mushrooms, or portobello mushrooms, thinly sliced
- 1 large onion, thinly sliced
- 2 cloves garlic, minced
- 4 roma tomatoes, shredded through the cheese grater, skins discarded
- 1 tsp. salt
- 1/2 tsp. pepper
- 1 tsp. steak rub or seasoning
- 14 oz (396 gr.) shaved steak (like Philly steak or thinly sliced beef sirloin)
- 10 oz deli style roast beef
- 2 cups shredded cheese (like Mozzarella or Muenster)
- 2 beaten eggs + 1 more for glazing
- For the Crust:
- 4 cups all-purpose flour
- 1 tsp. salt
- 10 tbsp. shortening
- 2/3 cup milk

Direction

- First make the filling: In a skillet, sauté the peppers, mushrooms, onion and garlic in oil until soft, about 10 minutes.
- Stir in the shredded tomatoes, salt, pepper and steak seasoning. Cook for another 2 minutes.
- Stir in the shaved steak, roast beef and cheese. Stir until the cheese is melted. Remove from heat and cool slightly.
- Meanwhile, make the crust: Put the flour into a large bowl with the salt. Heat the shortening in a small pan with the milk until just beginning to boil. Set aside and leave to cool slightly.
- Using a spoon, stir the liquid into the flour until a stiff dough forms. Turn on to a work surface and knead until smooth. Cut 1/3 off the dough for the lid, wrap it in clear film (plastic wrap), and keep it in a warm place.
- Roll out the large piece of dough on a floured surface. Place the rolled dough into the well-greased 9-inch round springform pan. Press down the bottom and sides of the pan to distribute the dough evenly. Note*: work the dough while it is warm, it may crack if left to get cold.
- Stir the 2 beaten eggs into the cooled beef filling. Place the filling inside the crust.
- Roll out the rest of the dough and cover the filling, trimming any excess and sealing the edges with the last beaten egg.
- Make a steam hole, or slits in the lid and decorate with pastry trimmings (optional). Brush with beaten egg.
- Stand the springform pan on a baking tray to catch any juices that may seep from the pie during baking. Bake at 395F for 35 minutes, cover with foil and bake for 40 minutes more.

226. Philly Cheese Steak Sandwich Recipe

Serving: 2 | Prep: | Cook: 10mins | Ready in:

Ingredients

- 2 fresh Italian sandwich rolls or Kaiser buns, split in half crosswise
- 1 white onion, thinly sliced
- 1/2 large green bell pepper, thinly sliced

- 1 teaspoon minced garlic
- 1/2 teaspoon salt
- 1/4 teaspoon ground black pepper
- 1/2 pound rib-eye steak, very very thinly shaved or sliced
- 1/3 pound thinly sliced white American cheese, or provolone cheese OR 4 ounces melted Cheese Whiz
- ketchup, optional topping
- Italian pickled peppers, accompaniment

Direction

- Heat a cast-iron skillet or griddle over medium-high heat. When hot add the oil, onions and bell peppers, and cook, stirring, until caramelized, about 6 minutes. Add the garlic, salt, and pepper, and cook, stirring, for 30 seconds. Push off to 1 side of the griddle.
- Add the meat to the hot pan and cook, stirring and breaking up with the back of 2 metal spatulas, until almost no longer pink, about 2 minutes. Mix in the Sautéed vegetables. Top with cheese slices and melt. Spoon the cheesy meat mixture into the warm buns and serve immediately with condiments of choice or Put the meat in the bun and dip the spatula in the cheese whiz and then wipe the spatula down the inside of the bread.

---

227. Pineapple Beef Kabobs Recipe

Serving: 6 | Prep: | Cook: 10mins | Ready in:

Ingredients

- 1 can (6 ounces) unsweetened pineapple juice
- 1/3 cup honey
- 1/3- cup soy sauce
- 3 -tablespoons cider vinegar
- 1-1/2- teaspoons minced garlic
- 1-1/2- teaspoons ground ginger
- 1-1/2- pounds boneless beef top sirloin steak, cut into 1-inch pieces

- 1 -fresh pineapple, peeled and cut into 1-inch chunks
- 12 --large fresh mushrooms
- 1 -medium sweet red pepper, cut into 1-inch pieces
- 1 -medium sweet yellow pepper, cut into 1-inch pieces
- 1 -medium red onion, cut into 1-inch pieces
- 2-1/2 cups uncooked instant rice

Direction

- In a small bowl, combine the first six ingredients.
- Pour 3/4 cup into a large resealable plastic bag; add beef.
- Seal bag and turn to coat; refrigerate for 1-4 hours.
- Cover and refrigerate remaining marinade for basting.
- Coat grill rack with cooking spray before starting the grill.
- Drain and discard marinade.
- On 12 metal or soaked wooden skewers, alternately thread the beef, pineapple, mushrooms, peppers and onion.
- Grill, covered, over medium-hot heat for 8-10 minutes or until meat reaches desired doneness, turning occasionally and basting frequently with reserved marinade.
- Cook rice according to package directions; serve with kabobs. Yum
- Yield: 6 servings. ....
- *********************
- Note............
- I made this a couple of weeks ago I used boneless chicken tenders and cut into chunks..... It was delicious.....keep marinating them as they cook I really put a lot on and they were tender and moist.....

123

228.   Pineapple Teriyaki Beef Recipe

Serving: 8 | Prep: | Cook: 30mins | Ready in:

Ingredients

- 2 pound boneless beef top round steak cut 1-1/2" thick
- 8 ounce can crushed pineapple juice packed
- 2 tablespoons finely chopped green onion
- 2 tablespoons teriyaki sauce
- 1 teaspoon grated fresh ginger
- 1 teaspoon bottled minced garlic

Direction

- Trim fat from steak and place in a plastic bag set in a shallow dish.
- Drain pineapple reserving juice then cover and chill pineapple for sauce.
- In small bowl, stir together reserved juice, green onion, teriyaki sauce, ginger and garlic.
- Pour over steak and seal bag then marinate in refrigerator up to 24 hours turning occasionally.
- Drain steak reserving marinade then place steak on unheated rack of a broiler pan.
- Broil 5" from heat for 20 minutes turning once.
- In small saucepan, combine reserved marinade and pineapple.
- Bring to boiling and reduce heat then simmer uncovered for 5 minutes.
- Remove from heat then cut steak into serving size pieces.
- Spoon sauce over steak.

229.   Polish Meatballs Recipe

Serving: 5 | Prep: | Cook: 30mins | Ready in:

Ingredients

- 2 ½ cups French bread (about ½ loaf) cut into ½" cubes -firmly packed
- ¾ cup milk
- 1 T salt
- 1 tsp. pepper
- 2 lbs. ground beef (1/2 sirloin, ½ 80% fat)
- 1 large onion, divided
- 1 T. worcestershire sauce
- 1 egg
- 1 tsp. dried minced garlic
- 1/3 cup olive oil
- 1 scallion, peeled, finely diced
- ½ lb. mushrooms
- ½ cup dry sherry
- 5 cups beef stock or broth
- ½ cup water
- 3 T. cornstarch
- salt & pepper to taste

Direction

- Pour the milk into the measuring cup containing the bread and mash down with your fingers until it is fully saturated. The bread should now measure 1 cup. Finely dice ½ of the onion, and roughly chop the other half. Mix the meat, egg, diced onion, Worcestershire, garlic, salt and pepper, along with the bread mixture until everything is incorporated well. Form into large meatballs, 1 ½" – 2" in diameter. There should be 9-10. Heat a cast iron frying pan or other large, heavy pan on medium high and add the olive oil. Brown the meatballs on all sides, in two batches. Remove the hamburgers and place them in a Dutch oven. Lower the heat of the skillet to medium, and add the chopped onion, scallion, and mushrooms and sauté about 7-8 minutes. Add a pinch of salt and pepper. Remove the mixture to the Dutch oven and add the dry sherry, scraping up the bits from the bottom of the pan. Allow it to simmer for a few minutes, and add to the Dutch oven, along with the beef broth and bring to a boil. Heat the oven to 350°. Whisk together the water and cornstarch and add it to the Dutch oven, stirring carefully so as not to break apart the meatballs. Turn the heat off, cover and place it in the oven 30 minutes. Remove from

124

oven and re-season with salt and freshly ground black pepper, if needed.

- Serve with mashed potatoes, spaetzle, dumplings, or buttered noodles.

230. Polish Pork Cutlet Kotlet Schabowy Recipe

Serving: 4 | Prep: | Cook: 25mins | Ready in:

Ingredients

- 4 - 6 boneless pork chops
- Note: I also use boneless chicken breast or veal for this recipe.
- 2 eggs, beaten
- 3/4 - 1 cup all-purpose flour(separate plate)
- 3/4 - 1 cup seasoned breadcrumbs(separate plate)
- salt and pepper to taste
- bacon fat, lard or margarine

Direction

- To make more you can always cut the pork chops in half.
- With a mallet, pound each pork chop until thin but not too thin.
- I sometimes cover the meat with cling wrap.
- Rub salt and pepper into each chop on both sides.
- Dip the chops in flour, then beaten egg and finally seasoned breadcrumbs.
- Heat the fat / oil in the pan before placing the (cutlets) in the pan.
- Fry until they become a toasted golden colour.
- Serve the (cutlets) with potatoes and sauerkraut or mizeria (cucumber salad). These (cutlets) go well with a salad of your choice and a side vegetable such as beets.
- Polish tradition is to sprinkle fresh dill on the potatoes.

231. Pork Adobo Recipe

Serving: 2 | Prep: | Cook: 30mins | Ready in:

Ingredients

- 500g pork chops, cut into large pieces
- 5 garlic cloves, smashed
- 250ml water
- 125ml white vinegar
- 75ml dark soy sauce
- vegetable oil
- pinch of salt

Direction

- In a frying pan, add water, vinegar, garlic, salt and the pork chops.
- Simmer until the pork is cooked through; about 15 minutes.
- Remove pork and set aside liquid.
- Add the oil and fry the pork.
- Return liquid and soy.
- Simmer gently for 5 minutes.
- Serve with plan rice.

232. Pork And Cabbage Halushki Recipe

Serving: 8 | Prep: | Cook: 120mins | Ready in:

Ingredients

- 3 pounds pork chops
- Note: You can use smoked sausage or kielbasa in place of pork chops
- 1-1/2 - 2 cups flour, mixed with 2 tsp. garlic powder, 2 tsp. onion powder, 1/2 tsp. cumin, salt and pepper to taste
- 1 large onion, chopped
- 1 head of cabbage, either cut into chunks or thickly sliced
- 1 pound large egg noodles
- 2 Tablespoons of butter

- a pinch of caraway seeds tossed into the cabbage water (optional)

Direction

- Shake pork chops in a plastic bag with flour, garlic powder, onion powder, cumin, salt and pepper.
- Place them in a LARGE greased sauce pan or a LARGE deep skillet and fry until browned and cook completely.
- Add chopped onion during the last 10-15 minutes of cooking.
- It is fine if the pork chops stick a little, as the scrapings are necessary in this dish.
- When they are done, remove chops and onions and set aside.
- Add a little water to the saucepan or skillet and mix up the drippings/scrapings a bit.
- Place cabbage into the pot, and allow to cool down completely.
- In a separate large saucepan, boil the egg noodles until cooked to your liking.
- Drain noodles and mix in butter.
- Cut up the pork chops into chunks and set aside.
- When the cabbage has cooked down, add pork and cooked noodles and mix completely adding more butter if you wish.
- Note: You require a LARGE skillet or Dutch oven for this recipe.

233.   Pork And Sausage Jambalaya Recipe

Serving: 10 | Prep: | Cook: 120mins | Ready in:

Ingredients

- 1 lb. of sausage(I use smoked pork sausage), cut into 1/2 inch slices
- 1 lb. of lean cubed pork
- 3 onions, chopped
- salt, pepper, creole seasoning (LeBlanc's)
- 1 tsp. garlic powder

- 6 cups of water
- 3 cups of Mahatma long grain rice

Direction

- Spray pot with a non-stick spray
- Cook sausage until almost done, remove
- Add cubed pork, season with salt, pepper and creole seasoning
- Brown the pork and remove
- Add chopped onion and cook until onions are almost brown.
- Add a little water if necessary.
- Be sure to watch carefully so onions don't burn.
- Add the sausage and pork back into the pot.
- Mix well with onions
- Add about 1 cup of water, cover and lower heat and let it cook for about 30 minutes. Watch it to make sure it doesn't burn. Stir occasionally.
- Add 6 cups of water, and the rice. Add the seasonings to taste and the garlic powder.
- When it comes to a boil, cover, lower heat and let it simmer for 20 mins. Fluff rice and cover and let it simmer for about 15 more mins.
- Remove lid. Fluff the rice.
- We serve this with potato salad and bread. (Oh, and also a big pot of white beans goes well too!) ENJOY!!!

234.   Pork Burritos Recipe

Serving: 14 | Prep: | Cook: 480mins | Ready in:

Ingredients

- 1 boneless pork sirloin roast (3lbs)
- 1/4 c reduced-sodium chicken broth
- 1 envelope reduced-sodium taco seasoning
- 1 Ths dried parsley flakes
- 2 garlic cloves,minced
- 1/2 tsp pepper
- 1/4 tsp salt
- 1 can (16 oz) refried beans

- 1 can (4oz) chopped green chilies
- 14 flour tortillas (8") warmed
- optioal toppings:shredded lettuce,chopped tomatoes,guacamole,reduced-fat sour cream ,reduced-fat cheddar cheese,shredded.

Direction

- Cut roast in half, place in 4 to 5 qt. slow cooker. In a small bowl, combine broth, taco seasoning, parsley, garlic, pepper and salt. Pour over roast and cook on low for 8 to 10 hours or till meat is very tender.
- Remove pork from slow cooker, cool slightly. Shred with 2 forks; set aside. Skim fat from the liquid; stir in beans and chilies. Return pork to the slow cooker; heat through.
- Spoon 1/22 cup pork mixture down the center of each tortilla; add toppings of your choice. Fold sides and ends over filling and roll up.

235. Pork Chop And Potato Bake Recipe

Serving: 4 | Prep: | Cook: 45mins |Ready in:

Ingredients

- 1 tbs vegetable oil
- 4 pork chops
- 1 (10.75 ounce) can condensed cream of chicken or mushroom soup
- 1/2 cup milk
- 1/2 cup sour cream
- salt and pepper to taste
- 1 (20 ounce) package frozen hash brown potatoes, thawed
- 1 cup shredded cheddar cheese
- 1 1/2 cups French-fried onions, divided

Direction

- Preheat oven to 350 degrees F
- Heat oil in a large skillet over medium high heat. Add pork chops and sauté until

browned. Remove from skillet and drain on paper towel.
- In a medium bowl mix together soup, milk, sour cream and salt and pepper to taste. Stir in potatoes, 1/2 cup cheese and 1/2 cup onions. Mix together and spread mixture in the bottom of a 9x13 inch baking dish. Arrange pork chops over potato mixture.
- Cover dish and bake in the preheated oven for about 40 minutes, or until internal temperature of pork has reached 160 degrees F. Remove cover; top with remaining cheese and onions and bake uncovered for 5 more minutes.

236. Pork Chop With Apple Pie Filling And Stuffing Recipe

Serving: 6 | Prep: | Cook: 35mins |Ready in:

Ingredients

- 6 boneless pork chops
- 1 tbsp. vegetable oil
- 1 package (6 oz)stuffing mix
- 1 can (21 oz) apple pie filling
- dash of cinnamon

Direction

- In a large skillet, brown the chops in the oil over medium-high heat.
- Prepare the stuffing according to the package directions.
- Spread the apple pie filling on the bottom of a greased 9x13 baking dish. Place the chops on top of the filling and then spoon the stuffing over the chops.
- Cover and bake in a 350 degree oven for 35 minutes. Uncover and bake 10 minutes more.

237. Pork Chops A La Charcutiere Recipe

Serving: 4 | Prep: | Cook: 15mins | Ready in:

Ingredients

- 8 to 10 rib pork chops, not too thick
- 1 pint of Robert Sauce-posted
- 2 ounces of minced gherkins
- melted butter
- panko bread crumbs

Direction

- Season the chops with salt and pepper.
- Dip them in the melted butter and press the bread crumbs into the pork chops. Press in well.
- Sauté those gently in melted butter, basting them from time to time.
- Allow about 8 to 9 minutes per side.
- Don't dry them out or over cook.
- While the chops are cooking over medium low heat, gently heat the prepared sauce Robert in a sauce pan and add the gherkins to the sauce to make it a charcutiere sauce.
- Arrange chops on a warm serving platter and nap them with the charcutiere sauce.
- Garnish with minced parsley.
- Potatoes are a must with this dish, either roasted tiny new potatoes or a mashed potato prep drizzled with roasted garlic oil.
- Robert Sauce:
- 1 large onion, finely minced
- 1 tbsp. of butter
- 1/3 pint of white wine
- 1 pint of half glaze (demi-glace quick method)-posted
- 1 tsp. of dry mustard - fresh can - not something that has been sitting in the cupboard for years
- 1 generous pinch of powdered sugar
- 1 tsp. of beef base - purchased
- Melt butter.
- Add minced onion and sauté gently, do not let it brown.

- Add the white wine and reduce by 1/3, add the half glaze and allow to simmer for 20 minutes.
- Add the beef base, dry mustard and sugar.
- If this sauce has to wait to be used, it should be kept warm in a double boiler, it must not boil again. It is best suited for grilled or roasted pork.
- NOTE: Robert Sauce becomes a Charcutiere Sauce with the addition of 2 ounces of julienne or minced gherkins.

238. Pork Chops And Kraut Recipe

Serving: 8 | Prep: | Cook: 120mins | Ready in:

Ingredients

- 8 pork chops, seasoned with salt, pepper, etc
- 2 T cooking oil
- 2 med-lrg onions, sliced
- 2 large cooking apples, peeled/cored/sliced
- 1 large bag/can sauerkraut, drained, rinsed
- 1/2 c brown sugar
- 1 T dry mustard
- 1 t caraway seeds (optional)

Direction

- Brown the chops, set aside.
- Sauté the onions in the pan the chops were browned in. Pour off extra oil first if the chops gave off a lot of fat while cooking.
- Mix brown sugar, mustard, and caraway if using.
- In a 9x13 pan, put a layer of chops (4), onions, apples, kraut and the brown sugar mixture. Repeat.
- Add water to the pan to cover the bottom and cover with foil.
- Bake 2 hours or until pork is very tender.

239. Pork Chops And Potatoes In Creamy Gravy Recipe

Serving: 4 | Prep: | Cook: 25mins | Ready in:

Ingredients

- 4 Lean pork chops with bone in (about 5 ounces each), all visible fat discarded
- paprika to taste
- pepper to taste
- vegetable oil Spray
- 2 cups Fat-Free, low sodium chicken broth
- 8 red potatoes (about 2 ounces each), each cut into 8 wedges
- 2 medium onions, thinly sliced
- 2 medium carrots, thinly sliced
- 1/4 tsp. dried tarragon, crumbled
- 1/2 cup fat-free evaporated milk
- 2 Tbs. all-purpose flour
- 3/4 tsp. salt
- 4-ounce jar sliced pimientos

Direction

- Sprinkle one side of the pork chops with paprika and pepper.
- Heat a large skillet over high heat.
- Remove the skillet from the heat and lightly spray with vegetable oil spray (being careful not to spray near gas flame).
- Cook the pork chops with the seasoned side down for 1 minute. Remove from the skillet.
- In the same skillet, stir together the broth, potatoes, onions, carrots, and tarragon.
- Bring to a boil.
- Top with the pork chops with the seasoned side up.
- Reduce the heat and simmer, covered, for 12 minutes, or until the pork is no longer pink in the centre and the potatoes are tender.
- Using a large slotted spoon, transfer the vegetables to a serving platter with a rim or a large shallow bowl.
- Top with pork.
- Cover with aluminum foil to keep warm. Set aside.

- Increase the heat to high. Bring the broth to a boil.
- Boil for 2 minutes, or until reduced to 1 cup.
- Reduce the heat to medium.
- Whisk in the evaporated milk and flour until well blended.
- Stir in the salt. (If you use a flat spatula, you can scrape the skillet).
- Cook for 2 minutes.
- Remove from heat.
- Stir in the pimientos.
- Pour over the vegetables on the serving platter.

240. Pork Chops Fiesta Recipe

Serving: 4 | Prep: | Cook: 55mins | Ready in:

Ingredients

- 2 Tbsp sugar
- 2 Tbsp cornstarch
- 1/8 tsp ground allspice
- 1 cup water
- 1/4 cup orange juice
- 1/4 cup raisins or currants (I used the golden raisins)
- 1/4 cup ap flour
- 1/2 tsp salt
- 1/4 tsp fresh ground pepper
- 4 one inch thick pork chops
- 1 Tbsp shortening (I used light olive oil)
- 4 orange slices

Direction

- Combine sugar, cornstarch, and allspice in a small saucepan, add water and cook over low heat, stirring constantly, until mixture thickens.
- Stir in juice and raisins, remove from heat and set aside.
- Combine flour, salt, and pepper.

- Heat shortening or light oil over medium high heat. Dredge chops in flour mixture, then brown chops quickly on both sides.
- Pour mixture over chops, cover, reduce heat and simmer 45 minutes or until chops are tender.
- Top with orange slices.

241. Pork Chops In Chive Cream Recipe

Serving: 4 | Prep: | Cook: 40mins |Ready in:

Ingredients

- 4 pork chops, cut 1/2-inch thick
- salt and pepper
- 1 tablespoon butter
- 1 tablespoon vegetable oil
- 1 cup sliced fresh mushrooms
- 1/3 cup dry white wine
- 1/3 cup chicken or beef broth
- 2 tablespoons chopped chives
- 1/2 cup whipping cream
- 2 teaspoons dijon-style mustard
- salt and pepper to taste

Direction

- Sprinkle pork chops with salt and pepper.
- In frying pan just large enough to hold the chops, melt the butter and oil over medium heat.
- Add chops to the pan. Brown on both sides. Remove chops. Add mushrooms to the pan. Sauté for a few minutes.
- Add wine, broth and chives to the pan. Bring to a boil. Add chops.
- Cover. Reduce heat. Simmer until chops are tender, 35 to 40 minutes.
- Remove chops to a warm serving dish. Keep warm.
- Skim and discard fat from cooking liquid. Add cream and mustard.

- Bring to a boil, stirring. Cook until reduced and slightly thickened. Taste and add salt and pepper.
- Pour sauce over chops. Sprinkle with extra chives

242. Pork Chops In Mushroom Cream Sauce Recipe

Serving: 4 | Prep: | Cook: 70mins |Ready in:

Ingredients

- Oven 350 degrees
- 4 1" pork chops bone in
- 8-10 oz. package of mushrooms, sliced or whole
- 1/2 cup chicken broth
- 1 cup heavy or whipping cream
- 1 tsp fresh or dried parsley
- 2 tablespoons of butter
- 1/2 cup of dry white wine
- salt and pepper

Direction

- In a large skillet melt 1 tablespoon of butter on med high heat. Add all 4 pork chops. Fry for two minutes on each side. Remove the chops.
- Add the other tablespoon of butter and fry the mushrooms for 2 minutes. Remove the mushrooms.
- Add the wine and deglaze the skillet Add the chicken broth and cook for two minutes. Add the cream and cook for five minutes stirring. Add salt and pepper to taste.
- Add the pork chops to the skillet. Add the mushrooms and sauté for 1 minute.
- If the skillet is oven friendly you can wrap the pan tightly in aluminum foil, if not, pour the mixture into a baking dish; cover tightly and bake for one hour.
- Remove foil and bake for ten more minutes or until fork tender and the sauce thickens.

- Besides mushrooms in this dish, you can add sautéed onions, shallots, red peppers.
- Delicious served over buttered egg noodles.

243. Pork Chops In Mushroom Gravy Recipe

Serving: 4 | Prep: | Cook: 30mins |Ready in:

Ingredients

- 4-6 boneless pork chops
- Donnie's cajun seasoning Mix (or equivalent) (Recipe on my profile page)
- ½ of an onion sliced
- 1 10¼ oz. can of Campbell's beef gravy
- ½ can of water
- 1 clove minced garlic
- 1 small can of green giant sliced mushrooms
- Pam cooking spray

Direction

- Preheat oven to 350.
- Spray an 8x8 glass baking dish with PAM.
- Season pork chops with Donnie's Cajun Seasoning and let stand for 30 minutes.
- Mix the remaining ingredients (except the onions) in a bowl.
- Add enough of the gravy mixture to cover the bottom of the baking dish.
- Place pork chops in the baking dish and cover with the onions and the remaining gravy mixture.
- Bake uncovered for 20-30 minutes or until pork is completely cooked. (To an internal temperature of at least 155 deg.).
- Remove from oven cover with foil and let stand for 10 minutes.
- Enjoy.

244. Pork Chops Italiano

Serving: 0 | Prep: | Cook: |Ready in:

Ingredients

- 1 teaspoon olive oil
- 2 cups sliced mushrooms
- 2 tablespoons olive oil
- 6 eaches (3/4 inch thick) pork loin chops
- 2 cloves garlic, crushed
- 1 cup chopped onion
- 1 (14.5 ounce) can diced Italian tomatoes, undrained
- 1 teaspoon dried basil
- ½ teaspoon dried oregano
- ½ teaspoon salt
- ¼ teaspoon ground black pepper
- ½ cup water, if necessary
- 1 large green bell pepper, cut in 6 pieces

Direction

- Heat 1 teaspoon olive oil in a skillet over medium heat. Stir in mushrooms; cook and stir until mushrooms are tender, 5 to 7 minutes. Transfer the mushrooms to a bowl and set aside.
- Heat the remaining 2 tablespoons olive oil in the skillet over medium heat. Add the pork chops, browning on both sides, 7 to 10 minutes. Place the pork chops on a plate, then drain all but 1 tablespoon of drippings from the skillet. Stir in the garlic and onion; cook and stir until the onion has softened and turned translucent, about 5 minutes.
- Pour in the tomatoes, then season with basil, oregano, salt, and pepper. Transfer the pork chops back to the skillet; cover and simmer until the pork chops are tender and no longer pink in the center, about 45 minutes. Stir in some water if the mixture becomes too dry. Place the bell pepper on top of the pork, then add the reserved mushrooms. Continue to simmer until the bell pepper is tender, 5 to 10 minutes.
- Cook's Note

- Don't add the green pepper wedges until your chops are done, otherwise, they will turn to mush.
- Nutrition Facts
- Per Serving:
- 290 calories; protein 25.3g 51% DV; carbohydrates 7.8g 3% DV; fat 17.6g 27% DV; cholesterol 63mg 21% DV; sodium 339.1mg 14% DV.

---

245.   Pork Chops Marsala Recipe

Serving: 4 | Prep: | Cook: 25mins | Ready in:

Ingredients

- 4 boneless pork loin chops,1/2" thick(4 oz. ea.) trimmed of fat
- 3tsp. olive oil
- 1 pkg.(10 oz.) sliced cremini mushrooms
- 1 lg. shallot,chopped(1/4c)
- 1/2tsp dried thyme or 11/2tsp.fresh thyme leaves
- 1lb. asparagus,ends trimmed
- 1/2c reduced-sodium chicken broth
- 1/3c marsala wine

Direction

- Evenly season pork chops on both sides with 1/2tsp salt and 1/4 tsp. black pepper. In a 12" non-stick skillet, heat 2 tsp. oil on medium 1 min. Add chops and cook 6 mins or until browned on outside and still slightly pink in the centre, turning over once. Transfer chops to platter, keep warm.
- In same skillet, heat remaining oil 1 min. Add mushrooms, shallot and thyme; cook 5 mins. Or until mushrooms are browned and shallot is softened. Meanwhile, place asparagus in a glass pie with 2 Tbsp. water; cover and cook in microwave on high 3 mins. To 31/2 mins or till fork tender... Set aside. Add broth and wine to mushroom mixture; cook 2 mins.

Place chops on 4 dinner plates; top with wine sauce. Serve with asparagus, and if you like, rice.

---

246.   Pork Chops Recipe

Serving: 6 | Prep: | Cook: | Ready in:

Ingredients

- 6 pork chops, thin cut
- 3 (4 oz) bags of crushed saltine crackers
- 2 eggs
- 1/2 tsp onion powder
- 1/2 tsp garlic powder
- 3 tbsp vegetable oil

Direction

- Preheat the oven to 375 degrees F.
- Whisk eggs along with the onion and garlic powder in a shallow bowl or pie plate. Dump the cracker crumbs onto a separate plate. In a large sized skillet, heat the oil over medium-high heat. Dip pork chops into the egg first, then press in the cracker crumbs to coat evenly. Fry for 2-3 minutes per side, just until they become golden-brown. Remove and place on a baking sheet.
- Bake for 45 minutes, turning once. Remove, and serve immediately.

---

247.   Pork Chops Trattoria Recipe

Serving: 4 | Prep: | Cook: 10mins | Ready in:

Ingredients

- 4 12-ounce pork chops, bonless
- 2 tablespoons olive oil
- 1 tablespoon fresh rosemary, chopped
- 1 tablespoon fresh thyme, chopped

- 1 tablespoon onion powder
- 1 tablespoon garlic powder
- 1 teaspoon salt
- 1 teaspoon dry mustard
- 1 teaspoon black pepper
- 1 teaspoon fennel seed, crushed

Direction

- Preheat grill.
- Brush pork chops with olive oil.
- Combine all herbs and spices and spread evenly over the pork chops. Place chops on very hot grill and cook for 1 minute per side.
- Reduce heat or move to a cooler portion of the grill and continue grilling for about 3 minutes per side or until done.

248. Pork Chops With Apricot Dijon Glaze Recipe

Serving: 4 | Prep: | Cook: 30mins | Ready in:

Ingredients

- 4 center cut pork chops on the bone
- 1-1/2 cups dry white wine
- 1/2 teaspoon dried thyme leaves
- 1/2 teaspoon salt
- 1/4 teaspoon freshly ground black pepper
- apricot Dijon Glaze:
- 4 cups apricot preserves
- 1/2 cup rice wine vinegar
- 1 cup whole grain Dijon mustard
- 1/4 cup soy sauce

Direction

- Place pork chops in a shallow baking dish and pour white wine evenly over all four cuts.
- Cover and refrigerate 6 to 8 hours turning periodically.
- Remove chops and sprinkle both sides with seasonings.

- Place pork on a hot mesquite grill and char on each side.
- Be careful not to overcook.
- Smother the chops with the warm apricot glaze right before serving. To make the glaze combine all ingredients in a saucepan over low heat and stir until smooth.

249. Pork Chops Yum Yum Recipe

Serving: 4 | Prep: | Cook: 60mins | Ready in:

Ingredients

- 4 pork chops-1/2 to 3/4" thick
- 1/4c chicken broth
- 1/8c honey
- 1/8c soy sauce
- 1/4tsp ginger
- 1/8tsp garlic salt
- 1Tbs ketchup

Direction

- Brown chops on both sides.
- Place in greased casserole dish
- Mix all remaining ingredients and pour over chops. Bake, uncovered, at 350 for 1 hour!

250. Pork Chops And Apple Sauce Recipe

Serving: 8 | Prep: | Cook: 25mins | Ready in:

Ingredients

- 2 cups milk
- 3 teaspoons salt
- 8 (1/2-inch-thick) pork chops (with or without bone)

- 3 1/2 cups fresh bread crumbs (from firm white sandwich bread, ground in a food processor)
- 1 tablespoon minced garlic
- 2 teaspoons chopped fresh rosemary
- 2 teaspoons chopped fresh thyme
- 2 tablespoons vegetable oil, or as needed
- 2 tablespoons unsalted butter, or as needed
- 3 pounds mixed McIntosh and gala apples
- 1/4 cup water
- 3 tablespoons sugar
- 1 tablespoon cider vinegar
- 1 Turkish bay leaf
- 1/4 teaspoon ground allspice

Direction

- Marinate pork chops: Stir together milk and 2 teaspoons salt in a shallow 3-quart dish, then add pork chops. Marinate, covered and chilled, turning over once, at least 1 hour.
- Make applesauce while chops marinate: Peel, core, and coarsely chop apples, then stir together with remaining applesauce ingredients in a 3-quart heavy saucepan. Bring to a simmer, stirring occasionally, then reduce heat to moderately low and cook, covered, stirring occasionally, until apples are falling apart, 15 to 20 minutes. Discard bay leaf and mash apples with a fork. Keep applesauce warm, covered.
- Fry pork chops: Preheat oven to 200 degrees F.
- Stir together bread crumbs, garlic, rosemary, thyme, and remaining teaspoon salt in a shallow bowl.
- Lift pork chops from milk 1 at a time, letting excess drip off, and dredge in bread crumbs, lightly patting crumbs to help adhere, then transfer to a tray, arranging in 1 layer.
- Heat 2 tablespoons oil and 2 tablespoons butter in a 12-inch heavy skillet over moderately high heat until foam subsides, then sauté pork chops in 2 or 3 batches, without crowding, turning over once, until golden brown and just cooked through, 5 to 6 minutes per batch. Transfer as cooked to a

platter and keep warm in oven. (Add more oil and butter to skillet as needed.)
- Serve pork chops with applesauce.

251. Pork Chops And Potato Casserole Recipe

Serving: 6 | Prep: | Cook: 90mins | Ready in:

Ingredients

- 1 can cream of mushroom soup
- 1 carton sour cream
- 6 pork chops
- 1/2 cup flour
- 2 teaspoons parsley flakes
- 1 teaspoon salt
- 2 teaspoons freshly ground black pepper
- 5 cups sliced potatoes

Direction

- Combine soup and sour cream in bowl mixing well.
- Combine flour, parsley, salt and pepper then coat chops with flour mixture.
- Place potatoes in buttered casserole dish then arrange pork chops on top.
- Cover with sour cream mixture and bake at 350 for 1-1/2 hours.

252. Pork Chops With Apples And Parsnips Recipe

Serving: 4 | Prep: | Cook: 40mins | Ready in:

Ingredients

- 4 pork chops about 1/2" thick (about a pound)
- 3 medium parsnips, cut crosswise into 1/2" rounds
- 1 medium onion, sliced

- 1/2 C chicken broth
- 2 tsp dry mustard
- 1/4 tsp salt
- 1/4 tsp ground allspice
- 1/8 tsppepper
- 1 medium apple, cut into 1/4 " wedges
- 2 T chopped fresh parsley (use dried to taste)

Direction

- Cook chops in a large non-stick skillet over medium, turning once, until brown
- Place parsnips and onion on pork.
- Mix broth, mustard, salt, allspice and pepper; pour over vegetables and pork
- Heat to boiling, reduce heat
- Cover and simmer about 30 minutes or until chops are just tender
- Arrange apple on vegetables
- Cover and simmer about 3 minutes or until apples is tender
- Sprinkle with parsley and serve

---

253.   Pork Chops With Black Beans Recipe

Serving: 4 | Prep: | Cook: 20mins | Ready in:

Ingredients

- 4 pork chops, but 3/4 inch thick
- 1/8 tsp. ground red pepper
- 1/4 tsp. garlic powder
- 1 Tb. olive oil or cooking oil
- 1 (15 oz.) can black beans, drained and rinsed
- 1 C. salsa (I love Target's Archer Farms Original salsa)
- 1 Tb. snipped fresh cilantro or flat leaf parsley
- salt and black pepper to taste

Direction

- Trim fat from meat.
- Rub red pepper, black pepper, salt, and garlic powder onto chops.

- In a skillet, cook chops in hot oil over medium-high heat until brown, about 2 min. per side.
- Remove and drain off fat.
- In the same skillet, combine beans, salsa and cilantro or parsley.
- Add chops.
- Bring to a boil.
- Reduce heat and simmer, covered, for 5 to 6 minutes or till no pink remains and juices run clear.
- To serve, top bean mixture with chops.

---

254.   Pork Chops With Chili Apricot Glaze Recipe

Serving: 4 | Prep: | Cook: 20mins | Ready in:

Ingredients

- 1/4 cup apricot jam (or preserves)
- 1/4 cup chili sauce
- 1 tbls. sweet hot mustard (or brown mustard)
- 1 tbls. water
- 4 boneless pork chops, 1 inch thick

Direction

- Turn oven on to broil
- Combine apricot jam, chili sauce, mustard and water in a small saucepan
- Cook over medium heat until heated through
- Set aside
- Set chops onto broiler pan
- Broil 4-5 inches from heat for 8 minutes
- Turn chops over and baste with glaze
- Broil for 8-10 more minutes
- Spoon remaining glaze over top before serving

255. Pork Chops With Mushroom Bourbon Cream Sauce

Serving: 4 | Prep: | Cook: 60mins | Ready in:

Ingredients

- Mushroom Cream Sauce:
- 2 tablespoons extra virgin olive oil
- 1 pound sliced button or cremini mushrooms
- 1/4 cup chopped onions
- 2 large garlic cloves, chopped
- 1/2 cup dry white wine (e.g. Sauvignon Blanc)
- 1 cup chicken stock
- 1/2 cup heavy cream
- 1/4 cup bourbon whisky
- Salt and pepper
- Pork Chops:
- 1 large egg
- 2 tablespoons water
- 4 6-7 oz center-cut pork chops
- All purpose flour
- 2 cups fresh bread crumbs
- 3 tablespoons extra virgin olive oil
- 2 tablespoons minced fresh basil

Direction

- Make the mushroom bourbon cream sauce: Sauté onions, garlic, and mushrooms in 2 Tbsp of olive oil in a large wide skillet on medium high heat until the mushrooms are browned - about 10-15 minutes.
- Add the wine, increase the heat to high, and boil down until the liquid is reduced to almost a glaze, about 4 minutes.
- Add the chicken stock and bourbon, boil until reduced by two thirds.
- Add the cream and simmer several minutes until the sauce thickens.
- Dredge the chops: Whisk an egg and 2 Tbsp of water in a shallow baking dish. Sprinkle both sides of pork chops with salt and pepper. Dip chops into the flour, then egg mixture, then breadcrumbs, coating completely.
- Cook the chops on both sides: Heat olive or canola oil in a large skillet over medium-high heat. Add the pork chops and cook until brown, about 4 minutes per side. If your pork chops are thin cuts, this may be all the cooking they need. If thicker, lower the heat to low and cover the pot. Cook for a few minutes more until the chops are just cooked through, about 145°F.
- Finish the sauce: When about to serve the pork, bring the sauce to a simmer and add the chopped basil to it. Season to taste with salt and freshly ground black pepper.

256. Pork Chops With Mushrooms Recipe

Serving: 4 | Prep: | Cook: 25mins | Ready in:

Ingredients

- 1 tbsp. vegetable oil
- 4 boneless pork chops, 1" thick
- 2 cups sliced mushrooms
- 1 tsp. dried oregano leaves, crushed
- 2 cups Prego® Traditional Italian Sauce
- .

Direction

- Heat oil in skillet. Add chops and cook 10 min. or until browned. Remove chops.
- Add mushrooms and oregano and cook until tender. Add pasta sauce. Heat to a boil. Return chops to skillet. Cook over low heat 10 min. or until done.
- Tip: Serve with steamed broccoli flowerets.

257. Pork Chops With Walnut Sage Crust Recipe

Serving: 4 | Prep: | Cook: 10mins | Ready in:

Ingredients

- 1/2c chopped walnuts, toasted
- 1/3c panko crumbs
- 1/3c chopped fresh Italian parsley
- 6 med. fresh sage leaves
- 1 garlic clove 2Tbs olive oil, divided
- 1/2tsp salt
- 1/4tsp pepper
- 4 boneless pork chops(3/4" thick

Direction

- Heat oven to 450. Process walnuts, panko, parsley, sage, garlic, 2tsp.oil, salt and pepper in food processor until mixture resembles bread crumbs.
- Pat pork dry; rub both sides with 1tsp.oil. Press walnut mixture over top of chops.
- Heat large ovenproof skillet over medium high heat till hot. Add remaining 1 Tbs. oil; heat till hot. Cook pork, crust side up, 3 mins or till nicely browned on bottom. Place skillet in oven; bake 5-6 mins. Or till pork chops are pale pink in centre. Let stand 3 mins. Before serving.

---

258.   Pork Cube Steaks In Sour Cream Gravy Recipe

Serving: 4 | Prep: | Cook: 55mins | Ready in:

Ingredients

- 4 medium pork cubed steaks, boneless
- 1 1/2 cups saltine cracker crumbs
- 2 eggs, beaten
- 2 teaspoon Mrs. Dash original seasoning-- divided
- 1 teaspoon seasoning salt
- 1/2 teaspoon garlic powder
- 1/2 teaspoon black pepper
- 1 can cream chicken soup (may sub low sodium version)
- 8 oz sour cream (may sub light version)

- 1 tablespoon worcestershire
- 1 cup chicken broth
- 1/4 cup veg oil

Direction

- Place cracker crumbs and seasonings into a gallon-sized Ziploc bag. Dip boneless pork cube steaks into egg, then drop into cracker crumbs. Shake well and let sit in crumb mixture while heating oil.
- In small frying pan, heat oil over med-high heat.
- Fry coated steaks until well-browned on both sides.
- Place into 11x7 Pyrex baking dish, (glass dish is preferred) that you've sprayed with non-stick spray.
- In medium bowl, mix together cream soup, sour cream, chicken broth and Worcestershire. Add 1 teaspoon Mrs. Dash to the cream mixture. Mix well.
- Pour cream mixture over pork steaks. Cover dish with foil. Bake in 350 oven for about 50 minutes. Remove foil and let sit for 5-10 minutes before serving.
- Enjoy!

---

259.   Pork Garlic Adobo Recipe

Serving: 2 | Prep: | Cook: 45mins | Ready in:

Ingredients

- 1/4 kg pork with fat
- 7 cloves of garlic
- water
- salt
- any kind of edible oil (optional)

Direction

- Combine all ingredients in a pan (not plenty of water)
- Stir occasionally (every 10mins)

- Wait for the water to evaporate (35mins. rough estimate)
- Wait for the pork lard comes out
- Add oil if want (I do this if the fat isn't enough to roast the garlic)
- Stir-fry and stir-fry until the garlic has been roasted
- Scrape the garlic that sticked in the pan as you continue to stir-fry now, if you're happy with the garlic, remove from pan
- Serve with hot rice or fried garlic rice

260. Pork Loin Chops With Cascabel And Grapefruit Sauce Recipe

Serving: 4 | Prep: | Cook: 45mins | Ready in:

Ingredients

- 4 Double Thick pork loin chops
- 25 dried Cascabel Chiles
- 3 Cups water
- 6 cloves garlic
- 4 Cups grapefruit juice
- 1 Cup orange juice
- 3 Tbls toasted ground allspice
- 1 Tsp salt
- 4 Tbls olive oil

Direction

- Remove stems from Chiles. In a heavy skillet, dry toast Chiles 3-4 minutes while shaking pan. Do not allow to blacken. Meanwhile bring the 3 Cups of Water to a boil. Add Chiles to boiling Water. Reduce heat and simmer very low for 20 minutes to rehydrate.
- Allow to cool.
- Taste Chile Water. If not bitter (If it is use plain water.) add the chiles, garlic and 1/2 cup Chile water to a blender. Puree and strain.
- Add Fruit Juices, Allspice and Salt, then mix together.

- Place Pork Chops in the Marinade and refrigerate overnight.
- When ready to cook, remove Pork Chops and bring to room temp. Reserve Marinade.
- Preheat oven to 450 F
- In an oven proof skillet over high heat, bring olive oil to almost smoking. Sear Pork Chops until brown. (About 2 Minutes per side.) Remove Chops to a plate and pour off excess fat.
- Add Marinade to the skillet and reduce by 1/2. Add Pork chops and roast in oven for 40 Minutes. Add a little water to the pan if it gets too dry.
- Place chops on plate and drizzle with sauce from pan.
- Serve with Black Beans and Fried Sweet Potatoes.

261. Pork On Pork With Mushroom Bourbon Sauce Recipe

Serving: 4 | Prep: | Cook: 60mins | Ready in:

Ingredients

- 2 Tbsp olive oil
- 1 lb button mushrooms, sliced
- 4 large shallots
- 1/2 cup dry white wine
- 1 cup chicken stock
- 1/2 cup heavy cream
- 1/4 cup bourbon whisky
- salt and pepper
- 1 large egg
- 2 Tbsp water
- 4 6-7 oz center-cut pork chops
- 2 cups crushed pork rind, 1/2 cup cushed nearly powder-fine and 1 1/2 cups more coarsely crushed (similar to coarse bread crumbs)
- 3 Tbsp olive oil or grapeseed oil

138

Direction

- Prepare the sauce. Sauté shallots, and mushrooms in 2 Tbsp. of olive oil in a large skillet on medium high heat until the mushrooms are browned - about 10 minutes.
- Add the wine and boil down until the liquid is reduced to almost a glaze, about 4 minutes. Add the chicken stock, cream, and bourbon. Simmer until the sauce thickens, about 12 minutes.
- Prepare the pork. Whisk an egg and 2 Tbsp. of water in a shallow baking dish. Sprinkle both sides of pork chops with salt and pepper. Dip chops into the powdered rinds, then egg mixture, then back into the coarse crushed pork rinds, coating completely.
- Heat olive or Grapeseed oil in a large skillet over medium-high heat. Add the pork chops and cook until brown, about 4 minutes per side. Turn the chops one more time and lower the heat to med-low and cook an additional 5-8 minutes, until the internal temperature of the chop is at 140°F. Alternatively you can put the chops in a pre-heated oven at 400°F for 5-8 more minutes.
- When about to serve the pork, bring the sauce to a simmer and season to taste with salt and freshly ground black pepper.

262. Pork Saltimbocca Recipe

Serving: 4 | Prep: | Cook: 6mins | Ready in:

Ingredients

- 4 boneless pork chops,about 6 ozs. each,cut 1/2"thick
- 1/8 tsp salt
- 1/8 tsp pepper
- 8 fresh sage leaves
- 3 oz. prosciutto
- 2 Tbs olive oil
- 1/2 c beef broth
- 2 tsp cornstarch
- 1/2 c marsala wine
- 1 c shredded Fontina cheese(4oz)
- 1 roll prepared polenta,grilled (optional)

Direction

- Season pork with salt and pepper. Place 2 sage leaves on each chop and top with 1/4 of the prosciutto. With sharp side of chef's knife pointed up, gently pound pork so that prosciutto adheres to it.
- Heat oil in large non-stick skillet over med-high heat. Place pork, prosciutto-side down, in skillet; cook 2 mins. Remove to plate
- Stir together the beef broth and cornstarch. Off heat, add Marsala wine and beef broth mixture to skillet. Scrape browned bits from bottom. Add pork back to skillet, prosciutto- side up, and top each chop with 1/4 of the cheese. Cover, simmer 2 mins, until cheese melts and pork registers 155 on thermometer. Top each piece with 1 tbsp. of sauce.
- Serve with grilled polenta, if desired.

263. Pork Schnitzel Recipe

Serving: 6 | Prep: | Cook: 35mins | Ready in:

Ingredients

- 6 boneless pork chops
- 1/2 cup all purpose flour
- 1 teaspoon ground sea salt
- 1 teaspoon cajun seasoning (I prefer Chef Paul Prudhomme's pork and veal magic seasoning blend)
- 1/2 teaspoon ground pepper
- 2 eggs
- 1/4 cup milk
- 1 1/2 cups fresh breadcumbs
- 2 teaspoons paprika
- 6 full tablespoons olive oil
- 2 tablespoons all purpose flour
- 1/2 teaspoon dried dill
- 1 1/2 cups chicken broth

- 1 cup sour cream, room temperature

Direction

- Place pork chops between 2 pieces of wax paper and flatten to 1/4 - 1/2- inch thickness.
- Cut small slits around edges of the pork chops to prevent them from curling and then set aside.
- Combine 1/2 cup flour, salt, Cajun seasoning, and pepper in a shallow bowl or on another sheet of wax paper.
- Beat eggs with milk in another shallow bowl.
- Mix crumbs with paprika in another small bowl or another sheet of wax paper.
- Heat 3 tablespoons of the olive oil in a large skillet over a medium heat.
- Dip pork chops in the flour, then into the egg mixture.
- Coat pork chops with crumbs covering them completely.
- Add 3 pork chops to the skillet and sauté on both sides until the coating is golden brown and the meat is no longer pink, it should be around 3 -5 minutes per side.
- Transfer to a platter and keep warm.
- Repeat the procedure with the remaining pork chops and olive oil.
- Combine the remaining flour with the dill. Add to skillet, scraping up any brown bits clinging to the bottom of the pan.
- Add broth stirring constantly until very well blended.
- Stir in sour cream and cook until heated through.
- Spoon over pork chops and serve.
- **** Sometimes I sauté some mushrooms and serve them on top as well. ****

---

264.   Pork Schnitzel With Warm Fingerling Potato Salad Recipe

Serving: 2 | Prep: | Cook: 15mins | Ready in:

Ingredients

- For the schnitzel:
- 2 boneless, organic pork chops (1 pound total)
- kosher salt & fresh ground black pepper
- 1/2 cup all purpose flour
- 1 free range egg + 2 tablespoons heavy cream + pinch of freshly grated nutmeg
- 3/4 cup panko (or other plain, dry bread crumbs)
- 1/2 cup canola oil + 2 tbsp. unsalted butter, for frying
- ~~~~~~ ~~~~~~~~~~~~~~~~~~~~
- For the Warm Fingerling Potato Salad:
- 1 lbs. fingerling potatoes, cooked and peeled
- 1 small minced shallot
- 1 tbsp. minced parsley
- 3 tbsp. red wine vinegar
- 1 tbsp sugar (or more, to taste)
- 1/2 c olive oil
- 1 tsp. Dijon mustard
- pinch of kosher salt and fresh ground black pepper, to taste

Direction

- In between plastic sheets, use a rolling pin to pound the pork cutlets to 1/4-1/8 inch thickness. Season with salt and pepper.
- Set out 3 shallow bowls. One with a mixture of the flour, seasoned salt, and pepper. The second with the egg, cream and nutmeg beaten together. The third with the panko).
- Heat the oil & butter in a large skillet on medium high heat. Dredge the cutlets first in the seasoned flour, then dip the cutlets in the egg mixture, and then into the bread crumbs.
- Sauté the cutlets for 3-4 minutes on each side. Remove the cutlets from the skillet and cover with foil or place in a warm oven to keep warm.
- For the Warm Fingerling Potato Salad:
- Slice cooked and peeled potatoes in half (or more pieces if they are large or leave whole if they are small).

- Whisk all the vinaigrette ingredients together and pour on the warm potatoes. Let marinate at room temp for at least 20 minutes.
- Serve pork schnitzel with a slice of lemon and side of the fingerling salad, drizzling the extra vinaigrette around the plate. Garnish with minced fresh parsley.

265. Pork Steak Recipe

Serving: 4 | Prep: | Cook: 60mins | Ready in:

Ingredients

- 4-5 pork chops
- 1-2 tbsp calamansi or lemon juice
- 5 tbsp soy sauce
- 3 cloves garlic
- thumb of ginger
- 1/2 cup water, or more if necessary
- 1-2 large onions, rings
- 4 tbsp oil
- salt and pepper to taste

Direction

- 1. Combine calamansi or lemon juice, garlic, ginger, soy sauce and pepper. Add the pork chops and marinade for at least 30 minutes (overnight would be better).
- 2. Heat the pan then pour oil, add the marinated pork chops with marinade mixture then add 1/2 cup water or more if necessary, then cook slowly until done.
- 3. Add the onion rings and cook for 1-2 minutes.

266. Pork With Blueberry Sauce Recipe

Serving: 4 | Prep: | Cook: 20mins | Ready in:

Ingredients

- 4 boneless pork chops
- 1 Small red onion, finely diced
- 1/2 Pint Fresh Blueberry's
- 1 lime, zested and 1/2 juiced
- 1 Tbsp balsamic vinegar
- 1/4 Cup brown sugar
- 1 Tbsp canola oil
- salt & pepper, to taste
- To Garnish: parsley or cilantro, chopped finely

Direction

- Preheat oven to 400 degrees Fahrenheit.
- In a nonreactive bowl, mash the blueberry's with the brown sugar to desired consistency, then set aside.
- Heat sauté pan on medium. Season the pork chops with salt and pepper on both sides. Add canola oil to the sauté pan. Brown pork on both sides until golden and crispy, about 2-3 min on each side.
- Remove from pan and place on a baking dish to finish cooking in the oven. Depending on thickness of the pork. If it's thin keep warm aside until sauce is ready.
- In the same pan the pork was cooking in, add the chopped red onion, sauté until translucent. Then add in the mashed blueberry sugar mixture and balsamic vinegar. Cook until the sauce gets thick, about 2-3 minutes.
- Add in the lime zest and juice and season with salt and pepper. If you put the pork in the oven, remove and place on serving plates. Serve sauce on top and garnish with parsley or cilantro. Enjoy!

267. Pork With Spicy Orange Cranberry Sauce Recipe

Serving: 4 | Prep: | Cook: 15mins | Ready in:

Ingredients

- 1 tsp chili powder
- 1/2 tsp ground cumin
- 1/4 tsp ground allspice
- 1/4 tsp salt
- 1/4 tsp black pepper
- 4 boneless pork chops
- 1 tbsp canola oil
- 1 c whole cranberry sauce
- 1/2 tsp grated orange peel
- 1/4 tsp ground cinnamon
- 1/8 tsp red pepper flakes

Direction

- Combine chili powder, cumin, allspice, salt & black pepper in small bowl. Mix well. Sprinkle evenly over both sides of the chops. Set aside.
- Place oil in large skillet over medium heat till hot. Add chops. Cook 5 to 6 mins on each side or till barely pink in centres.
- Combine cranberry sauce, orange peel, cinnamon & pepper flakes in small bowl. Mix well. Serve sauce with pork chops.

268. Puebla Chicken And Potato Stew Recipe

Serving: 4 | Prep: | Cook: 60mins | Ready in:

Ingredients

- 2 lb chicken thighs (with skin and bone)
- 6 cups water
- 1 large white onion, quartered
- 2 teaspoons salt
- 2 garlic cloves (not peeled)
- 1 (14-oz) can whole tomatoes in juice
- 4 teaspoons chopped canned chipotle chiles in adobo*
- 1 teaspoon dried oregano (preferably Mexican)
- 1 (1 1/2-oz) link dried Spanish chorizo* (spicy cured pork sausage), finely chopped
- 1 tablespoon vegetable oil
- 1 lb boiling potatoes

- 2 oz crumbled queso fresco*, ricotta salata, or farmer cheese (1/2 cup)
- Accompaniments: avocado slices; warm corn tortillas

Direction

- Bring chicken, water, 2 onion quarters, and 1 teaspoon salt to a boil, covered, in a 4- to 5-quart pot over moderately high heat. Boil 10 minutes, then remove from heat and let stand, covered, until chicken is just cooked through, about 10 minutes. Transfer chicken to a plate, reserving broth with onion. When cool enough to handle, coarsely shred chicken, discarding skin and bones.
- While chicken is cooking, heat a dry well-seasoned small cast-iron skillet over moderate heat until hot, then brown garlic and remaining 2 onion quarters on all sides, turning with tongs, about 5 minutes. Peel garlic and transfer with onion to a blender. Add tomatoes with juice, chilies, and oregano, then purée until smooth.
- Cook chorizo in oil in a 12-inch heavy skillet over moderately high heat, stirring, until fat is rendered, about 2 minutes. Carefully add purée (it will splatter and steam) and cook, stirring frequently, until thick, about 10 minutes.
- Peel potatoes and cut into 3/4-inch pieces, then add to reserved broth with remaining teaspoon salt. Simmer, covered, stirring occasionally, until potatoes are almost tender, about 10 minutes.
- Add potatoes and onions to chorizo mixture along with 2 cups broth (save remainder for another use). Stir in chicken and simmer 10 minutes. Serve sprinkled with cheese.
- *Available at Latino markets and some specialty foods shops.

269. Put Some South In Your Mouth Pinto Beans Recipe

Serving: 10 | Prep: | Cook: 4mins | Ready in:

Ingredients

- DRY beans, YOUR CHOICE OF PINTO OR LIMA (BABY OR LARGE) I USE THE CAMELLIA BRAND DRY beans
- 3 LARGE yellow onions (CHOPPED OR DICED)
- CAN ALSO ADD 1 -2 CUPS OF green onions (CHOPPED), I USE THE green onions ALONG WITH THE yellow onions
- 5 SLICES OF JALEPENO pepperS
- seasoning MEAT (YOUR CHOICE OF bacon, SMOKED pork, ham, ham hock , salt MEAT OR A pork chop)
- seasoning (I USE NATURES seasoning)
- 3 TABLESPOONS OF sugar OR SPLENDA (CAN USE MORE, DEPENDS ON YOUR TASTE)
- PARLSEY
- black pepper (TO YOUR TASTE)
- salt (TO YOUR TASTE).. ADD salt TOWARDS THE END OF THE COOKING PROCESS)
- garlic powder (TO YOUR TASTE)
- 2 JALEPENOS SLICES (OPTIONAL)
- A PINCH OF cayenne pepper (OPTIONAL)
- YOU DONT WANT YOUR beans TO HOT TO THE TASTE OR TOO SWEET, SO KEEP TASTE TASTING YOUR beans

Direction

- SOAK YOUR BEANS OVER NIGHT, FOR A FEW HOURS OR YOU CAN PAR BOIL THEM (BRING TO A BOIL, DRAIN WATER AND ADD WATER AGAIN)
- ONCE YOUR BEANS ARE SOAKED, CLEANED OR PAR BOILED, ADD WATER TO THE HALFWAY POINT IN YOUR POT
- ADD YOUR ONIONS, SEASONINGS, MEAT AND THE OPTIONALS
- BRING YOUR WATER LEVEL TO ALMOST THE TOP. BRING TO A BOIL
- BOIL FOR A FEW MINUTES
- BRING YOUR HEAT DOWN TO MEDIUM. HALFWAY COVER THE POT WITH THE LID
- KEEP CHECKING THE WATER LEVEL SO BEANS WONT STICK. ADD WATER TO YOUR DESIRED CONSISTENCY. SOME LIKE THEIR BEAN JUICE THICK AND SOME LIKE IT THIN.
- COOK THESE BEANS FOR 3-5 HOURS OR UNTIL BEANS ARE VERY TENDER
- SERVE OVER RICE WITH CORNBREAD OR JUST SERVE WITH CORNBREAD.
- IN MY PINTO BEANS ABOUT 30 MINUTES BEFORE THEY ARE DONE, I ALSO ADD SLICED SMOKEY HOLLOW CAJUN SAUSAGE. THIS IS GREAT OVER RICE
- I COOK MY BEANS IN A CAST IRON POT BUT YOU CAN USE YOUR FAVORITE POT.
- I ALSO COOK MY PURPLE HULL PEAS THE SAME WAY
- DRY BEANS CAN BE SERVED ALSO WITH SLICED TOMATOES, FRIED OKRA, CHICKEN (FRIED OR BAKED), A ROAST, SMOTHERED POTATOES AND SQUASH.
- I HAVE ALSO PUT A HALF CAN OF ROTEL OR DICED TOMATOES IN MY PINTO BEANS FOR A DIFFERENT TAKE ON OCCASION.

270. Quick Cassoulet Meats And Beans Recipe

Serving: 6 | Prep: | Cook: 45mins | Ready in:

Ingredients

- 3 cans white beans - navy beans (or cook dry beans)
- 4 TBSP. olive oil
- 2 large onions, chopped
- 3 cloves of garlic, minced

- 4 slices of bacon, cut into pieces
- 3 thick pork chops, cooked and cut into cubes or leftover pork roast
- 2 boneless chicken breasts- cooked , cut into cubes
- 3 lamb steaks (optional) cooked, and cut into cubes (I skip this)
- 1 lb hot italian sausage, cooked and cut into slices (I use more!)
- 1/2 - 1 teasp. thyme
- parsley - approx a handful
- bay leaf
- salt and pepper to taste
- 1 8 oz. can of tomato sauce
- 1/4 cup dry red wine (optional)
- beef broth
- bread crumbs- regular or gluten Free

Direction

- Drain beans and place in a large casserole dish
- Heat oil in a frying pan and sauté onion and garlic until soft but not brown
- Add to the beans along with the spices. Stir
- Fry bacon until almost done... add to the beans
- Brown the pork chops, chicken, and lamb in the bacon fat. Cut into cubes
- Add to the beans
- Prick sausage and put in the frying pan with some water. Cook until done. Cut into slices and add to the beans
- Mix the bean and meat mixture gently
- Pour over mixture the tomato sauce, wine, and enough beef broth to just cover the mixture.
- Bake at 350'F for approx. 45 mins or until bubbly
- Sprinkle the top with bread crumbs and bake for 5 - 10 mins more

271.   RRs Smoky Beer Burgers Recipe

Serving: 4 | Prep: | Cook: 15mins | Ready in:

Ingredients

- 2 pounds lean ground sirloin
- 1/3 pound smoked gouda cheese, diced into 1/4 to 1/2-inch cubes
- 1 medium onion or 1/2 large onion
- 2 teaspoons smoked sweet paprika, 2/3 palm full
- 1 teaspoon ground cumin, 1/3 palm full
- Grill seasoning (recommended: Montreal steak seasoning)
- coarse salt and freshly ground black pepper
- 2 cloves garlic, grated or finely chopped
- Generous handful finely chopped fresh flat-leaf parsley
- 1 tablespoon worcestershire sauce
- 1/2 (12-ounce) bottle beer
- extra-virgin olive oil, for drizzling
- 1/2 cup spicy brown mustard
- 1/4 to 1/3 cup sour cream
- 2 to 3 tablespoons chopped fresh dill or 1 teaspoon dried dill
- 4 crusty kaiser rolls, split and lightly toasted
- Green or red leaf lettuce, for topping
- Sliced sweet bread and butter pickles, for topping

Direction

- Preheat grill over medium-high heat.
- Place the meat in a bowl and add the cheese.
- Peel the onion and halve it, if using the medium onion.
- Grate about 3 to 4 tablespoons of onion directly over the meat into the bowl.
- Finely chop the remaining onion and reserve for topping.
- Add spices to meat: paprika, cumin and about 1 tablespoon of grill seasoning and/or some salt and pepper.
- Add garlic, parsley and Worcestershire and beer then form 4 large patties making them a little thinner at the center than at edges. Burgers plump when you cook them so this will prevent burger bulge.
- Drizzle a little olive oil over the burgers then grill about 4 minutes on each side for medium

rare, 5 minutes on each side for medium and 6 to 7 minutes on each side for well done.

- Mix mustard and sour cream with dill.
- Serve patties on bun bottoms and top with lettuce, pickles, chopped raw onion.
- Slather bun tops with sauce and serve.

272. Ramen Stir Fry Recipe

Serving: 4 | Prep: | Cook: 15mins | Ready in:

Ingredients

- 1 pound beef boneless sirloin
- 1 tablespoon vegetable oil
- 2 cups water
- 1 package (3 ounces) Oriental-flavor ramen noodle soup mix
- 1 package (16 oz) fresh stir-fry vegetables (broccoli, cauliflower, celery, carrots, snow pea pods and bell peppers) (4 cups)
- 1/4 cup stir-fry sauce

Direction

- Remove fat from beef. Cut beef into thin strips.
- In 12-inch skillet, heat oil over medium-high heat. Cook beef in oil 3 to 5 minutes, stirring occasionally, until brown.
- Remove beef from skillet; keep warm.
- In same skillet, heat water to boiling. Break up noodles from soup mix into water; stir until slightly softened.
- Stir in vegetables.
- Heat to boiling. Boil 5 to 7 minutes, stirring occasionally, until vegetables are crisp-tender.
- Stir in contents of seasoning packet from soup mix, stir-fry sauce and beef. Cook 3 to 5 minutes, stirring frequently, until hot.

273. Rib Eye Steaks With A Soy And Ginger Marinade Recipe

Serving: 2 | Prep: | Cook: 80mins | Ready in:

Ingredients

- 1/2 cup soy sauce
- 1/4 cup real maple syrup
- 6 cloves garlic, minced
- 1 tablespoon grated fresh ginger
- 1 teaspoon mustard powder
- 1/2 teaspoon sesame oil
- 1/4 teaspoon hot pepper sauce
- 1/2 cup beer
- 4 (10 ounce) beef rib eye steaks

Direction

- In a medium size mixing bowl, combine soy sauce, maple syrup, garlic, ginger root, mustard powder, sesame oil, and Tabasco sauce; mix well to blend. Now add beer, and stir lightly to mix.
- Prepare steaks by scoring any fatty outside areas on steak with a knife, (this prevents the steaks from curling when barbecuing). Place steaks in a casserole dish, and pour marinade over. Using a fork, punch holes in steaks so that the marinade penetrates into the steaks. Turn steaks over, and repeat punching holes.
- Cover with clear wrap or foil, and let marinate in the refrigerator for at least 1 hour or longer. You can also refrigerate and marinate overnight.
- Prepare and preheat barbecue to high heat. Place steaks directly on grill and sear one side for about 15 seconds. Turn steaks over and cook for about 5 minutes, then turn over and cook for another 5 minutes for medium-rare, depending on thickness.
- Test for doneness by cutting into the middle of the steak

274. Rib Eyes With Honey Bourbon Caramelized Onions Recipe

Serving: 4 | Prep: | Cook: 60mins | Ready in:

Ingredients

- 2 2 lb. bone in rib eyes
- salt and pepper to taste
- 2 large onions, sliced
- 1/4 cup butter
- Olive oil
- 1/4 cup plus 2 tbls. Honey bourbon

Direction

- Melt butter and 2 tsp. olive oil in skillet over medium low heat
- Add onions and cook, stirring often until onions become light brown in color....About 20 minutes
- Stir in honey bourbon and cook another 3-4 minutes
- Season steaks with salt and pepper
- Heat grill pan to high and cook 3-4 minutes per side...More if medium rare isn't wanted.
- Rest for 5 minutes

275. Rib Eye Steaks With Gorgonzola Butter And Crispy Sweet Onion Rings Recipe

Serving: 6 | Prep: | Cook: 16mins | Ready in:

Ingredients

- gorgonzola butter:
- 2 heads of garlic, top 3/4 inch cut off to expose cloves
- 2 tablespoons olive oil
- 1/2 cup (1 stick) unsalted butter, room temperature
- 1/3 cup crumbled gorgonzola cheese (about 2 ounces)
- 2 tablespoons chopped fresh parsley, plus extra for garnish
- ~~~~~~~~~~~~~~~~~~~~~~~~~~~~~~~~~~~~
- Onion rings:
- 3 cups buttermilk
- 2 jumbo sized sweet onions (such as Vidalia or Walla Walla), thinly sliced into rounds, then separated into rings
- 3 cups unbleached all purpose flour
- 3 tablespoons onion powder
- 3 tablespoons garlic powder
- 2 teaspoons baking powder
- 1 1/2 teaspoons kosher salt
- 1 1/2 teaspoons ground black pepper
- ~~~~~~~~~~~~~~~~~~~~~~~~~~~~~~~~~~~~
- 4 cups canola oil (for frying)
- ~~~~~~~~~~~~~~~~~~~~~~~~~~~~~~~~~~~~
- Steaks:
- 6 10- to 12-ounce rib-eye steaks
- kosher salt
- ~~~~~~~~~~~~~~~~~~~~~~~~~~~~~~~~~~~~
- Balsamic Green Beans:
- 8 oz french green beans, steamed
- good quality aged balsamic vinegar
- extra virgin olive oil
- kosher salt and fresh ground black pepper, to taste

Direction

- For gorgonzola butter:
- Preheat oven to 350°F. Place garlic on piece of foil; drizzle with olive oil. Enclose garlic in foil. Bake until garlic is very soft, about 1 hour. Cool. Squeeze garlic cloves out from papery skins into medium bowl; mash garlic with fork. Mix in butter, cheese, and parsley. Season with salt and pepper. Transfer Gorgonzola butter to sheet of plastic wrap. Using plastic wrap as aid, form butter into 1 1/4-inch-diameter log, wrapping plastic tightly around

butter. Chill until firm. (Can be made 2 days ahead; keep chilled.)

- For French Green Beans:
- Season steamed beans with a few splashes of balsamic, extra virgin olive oil, salt & pepper. Can be served cold, warm or at room temp.
- For onion rings:
- Pour buttermilk into large bowl. Add onion rings; toss to coat. Let stand 1 hour, tossing occasionally. Mix flour, onion powder, garlic powder, baking powder, salt, and pepper in another large bowl.
- Preheat oven to 350°F. Pour enough oil into heavy large skillet to reach depth of 3 inches. Heat over medium-high heat to 350°F. Working with a few onion rings at a time, shake off excess buttermilk, and then turn onion rings in flour mixture to coat. Fry onion rings until deep golden brown, adjusting heat as necessary for each batch to maintain temperature at 350°F, about 2 minutes. Transfer onion rings to paper towels to drain, then place on baking sheet and keep warm in oven while frying remaining onion rings.
- For steaks:
- Sprinkle steaks with salt and leave at room temp for 10 minutes. Grill steaks to desired doneness, about 8 minutes per side for medium-rare, depends on how hot your charcoal is. Remove steaks from grill to a plate, tent lightly with foil and let rest 10-15 minutes. Top each steak with about 1 tablespoon of room temp gorgonzola butter the last 2 minutes of resting.
- Transfer steaks to dinner plates and serve with green beans and onion rings. Sprinkle with minced parsley.

276.　　Roasted Pork Chops And Potatoes Recipe

Serving: 4 | Prep: | Cook: 60mins | Ready in:

Ingredients

- 4 large pork chops (with or without bone)
- potatoes
- olive oil
- 5 cloves of garlic
- Dried oregano
- salt
- pepper
- fresh lemon juice

Direction

- Chop the potatoes into pieces and place in an oven proof baking dish.
- Place the pork chops, pealed whole garlic gloves, olive oil, oregano, salt and pepper into the dish and mix well with hands until everything is covered with a generous amount of olive oil and other ingredients.
- Place in the oven at 200 degrees for about an hour (but do check after 45 mins or so.)
- Serve with a generous squeeze of fresh lemon juice and a crisp salad.

277.　　Roasted Whole Turkey With Gravy And My Mothers Stuffing Recipe

Serving: 12 | Prep: | Cook: 240mins | Ready in:

Ingredients

- For roasted Whole Turkey:
- 1 twenty- to twenty-one-pound fresh whole turkey, giblets discarded and neck removed from cavity and reserved. Note: Brine turkey over night with water, kosher salt (be generous) black peppercorns, bay leaf
- 1 1/2 cups unsalted butter (3 sticks), melted, plus 4 tablespoons at room temperature
- 1 bottle dry white wine
- ~~~~~~~~~~~~~~~~~~~~~~~~~~~~~~
  ~~~~~~~~~~~~~~~~~~~~~
- Mom's Stuffing:
- 2 bunches sliced green onions

- 6 stalks of celery, finely chopped
- 2 sticks unsalted butter
- 3 small packages of white mushrooms, finely chopped in food processor (you can use any type/mix of mushrooms)
- 4 bags Colombo brand French bread croutons (homemade French bread croutons are great too of course!)
- Fresh thyme, rosemary, parsley and sage, chopped fine
- spice Island poultry seasoning (or use the little packets of seasoning that comes with bagged croutons)
- ground pork and chicken and homemade stock (below)
- kosher salt, freshly cracked black and white pepper to taste
- ~~~~~~
- ground pork and chicken and homemade stock:
- 4 whole chicken breasts, with bone & skin
- 4 pork loin chops, bone in center cut
- Reserved turkey neck
- 1 onion, quartered
- 2 stalks of celery
- Bouquet garni: whole allspice, parsley with stems, thyme, bay leaves and black, pink and white peppercorns (put all these things together in cheesecloth, making a big baggie, twist and secure with butcher's twine)
- kosher salt
- ~~~~~~
- Gravy: please see directions below

Direction

- Homemade Stock:
- Cover meat with water. Add remaining ingredients. Bring to a boil then simmer, covered for 1 hour, skimming off the scum that rises occasionally. Take off heat and let sit for another hour, uncovered.
- Take meat off bones, discarding chicken skin. In batches, add pieces of meat to food processor and process until finely ground.

Season with salt & pepper if needed. Reserve for stuffing.
- ~~~~~~
- For Stuffing:
- Sauté the celery, mushrooms and half the green onions in large skillet with butter until mushrooms have released most of their moisture, season with kosher salt & white pepper to taste. Transfer to large aluminum tray. Add ground meat and remaining green onions, stir to combine. Add French bread croutons, stir and add seasoning & herbs. Moisten with hot stock.
- Note: If placing stuffing inside turkey, be careful not to over moisten with the stock, as the turkey will release juices as it bakes that will further moisten the stuffing.
- ~~~~~~
- For Whole Roasted Turkey:
- Remove thawed turkey from brine and dry with paper towels. Let stand for 1 hour at room temperature.
- Heat oven to 450° with a rack on the bottom. Combine melted butter and white wine in a bowl. Fold a large piece of cheesecloth into quarters and cut into a 17-inch, four-layer square. Immerse cheesecloth in the butter and wine; let soak.
- Place turkey, breast side up, on a roasting rack in a heavy metal roasting pan. If the turkey comes with a pop-up timer, remove it; using an instant-read thermometer later will give a more accurate indication of doneness. Fold wing tips under turkey. Sprinkle 1/2 teaspoon salt and pepper inside turkey. Fill large cavity with as much stuffing as it will hold comfortably; do not pack tightly. (Cook any remaining stuffing in a buttered baking dish at 375°). Tie legs together loosely with kitchen string (a bow will be easy to untie later). Fold neck flap under and secure with toothpicks. Rub turkey with the softened butter and sprinkle with remaining 1 1/2 teaspoons salt and pepper.

- Lift cheesecloth out of liquid and squeeze it slightly, leaving it very damp; reserve remaining liquid. Spread it evenly over the breast and about halfway down the sides of the turkey; it can cover some of the leg area. Place turkey, legs first, in oven. Cook for 30 minutes. Using a pastry brush, baste cheesecloth and exposed parts of turkey with butter-and-wine mixture. Reduce oven temperature to 350° and continue to cook for 2 1/2 more hours, basting every 30 minutes and watching pan juices; if the pan gets too full, spoon out juices, reserving them for gravy.
- After the third hour of cooking, carefully remove and discard cheesecloth. Turn roasting pan so that the breast is facing the back of the oven. Baste turkey with pan juices. If there are not enough juices, continue to use the butter-and-wine mixture. The skin will get fragile as it browns, so baste carefully. Cook 1 more hour, basting after 30 minutes.
- After the fourth hour of cooking, insert an instant-read thermometer into the thickest part of the thigh, avoiding any bones. The temperature should reach 180° (stuffing should be between
- 140° and 160°) and the turkey should be golden brown. The breast does not need to be checked for temperature. If legs are not yet fully cooked, baste turkey, return to oven, and cook another 20 to 30 minutes.
- When fully cooked, transfer turkey to a serving platter and let rest for about 30 minutes.
- ~~~~~~
- For Gravy:
- Pour all of the pan juices from turkey into a glass measuring cup. Let stand until fat rises to the surface, about 10 minutes, then skim it off and reserve 1/4 cup. Add turkey fat to saucepan with 2 tablespoons of butter and 4 tablespoons of flour, making a roux. Add 1/2 cup dry white to the pan. Bring to a boil. Using a whisk, add reserved pan juices and some stock from the stuffing to pan until it is the consistency you like. Stir well and bring back

to the boil. Lower heat to medium and add 1/4 cup cream. Season to taste with kosher salt and white pepper and cook for 10 minute more. You should have about 2 1/2 cups of gravy. Pour into a warm gravy boat, and serve with turkey

278.	Round Steak Sauerbraten Recipe

Serving: 4 | Prep: | Cook: 90mins | Ready in:

Ingredients

- 1 1/2 pounds boneless round steak
- 1 tablespoon vegetable oil
- 2 cups water
- 1/4 cup onion, minced
- 1/2 teaspoon salt
- 2 tablespoons red wine vinegar
- 2 tablespoons brown sugar
- 1 envelope brown gravy mix
- 1 teaspoon worcestershire sauce
- 1/2 teaspoon ground ginger
- Hot cooked buttered noodles

Direction

- Cut round steak into 1 inch cubes or into thin strips.
- In large skillet, brown beef in oil over medium-high heat.
- Remove meat from skillet and set aside.
- In same skillet, add remaining ingredients except noodles.
- Heat, stirring, until smooth.
- Return meat to skillet.
- Simmer 1 1/2 hours.
- Serve over buttered noodles.

279. SAN FRANCISCO STYLE PORK CHOPS Recipe

Serving: 4 | Prep: | Cook: 45mins |Ready in:

Ingredients

- 4 pork chops ½ to ¾ inch thick, about 1 ½ lbs.
- 1 Tbs. oil
- 1 garlic clove, minced
- Sauce:
- 2 tsp. oil
- 4 Tbs. dry sherry or broth
- 4 Tbs. soy sauce
- 2 Tbs. brown sugar
- ¼ tsp. Crushed red pepper
- 2 tsp. cornstarch
- 2 Tbs. water

Direction

- 1 Trim pork chops of fat.
- 2 heat oil in skillet. Brown chops on both sides.
- 3 Remove and add a little more oil if needed.
- 4 Sauté garlic for a minute, being careful not to burn it.
- 5 Combine oil, sherry or broth, soy sauce, brown sugar and red pepper.
- 6 Place chops in skillet. Pour sauce over them. Cover tightly.
- 7 Simmer over low heat until chops are tender and cooked through, 30 to 35 minutes. Add a little water, 1 to 2 Tbsp. if needed to keep sauce from cooking down too much. Turn once.
- 8 Remove chops to platter. Stir in cornstarch dissolved in water. Cook until thickened.
- 9 Pour over chops and serve.
- Tips:
- Boneless pork loin chops can be used. Trim fat and pound to ¼ inch thickness. Cooking takes only 20 minutes.
- Good served with:
- Thin spaghetti or noodles with butter and sauce.

280. SO EASY CHEESY CHOPS Recipe

Serving: 4 | Prep: | Cook: 25mins |Ready in:

Ingredients

- 4 boneless pork chops 3/4 in thick.
- 4 medium potatoes sliced about 1/4 thick. Leave skin on.
- 1 small onion sliced thin and seperated.
- 1 can chedder cheese soup
- 1 can milk
- 1/2 teaspoon garlic minced
- parsley
- salt and pepper to taste.

Direction

- Spray pan with non-stick spray, add 1-2 teaspoons oil.
- Quick brown the chops and remove
- Add onions and stir for a minute or two, add garlic and give quick stir.
- Add soup and milk stir add salt and pepper.
- Add sliced potatoes, stir.
- Add chops on top.
- Simmer for about 20-25 min add parsley, stir.
- Serve and enjoy.
- Good with broccoli as a side.

281. SWEET BEEF LO MEIN Recipe

Serving: 6 | Prep: | Cook: 20mins |Ready in:

Ingredients

- 1 lb package thin spaghetti, prepared according to directions
- 1½ lbs round steak, sliced into thin strips about 1 inch x 3 inches
- 1 large onion, sliced

- 1 clove garlic, finely minced
- ginger root to taste, freshly peeled and grated
- ½ cup Kikoman™ soy sauce
- ½ cup sugar
- salt and black pepper to taste

Direction

- Prepare pasta according to package directions. Drain and retain for later.
- Add beef, onion, garlic, ginger, soy sauce and sugar into a heavy wok. Season the mixture with salt and black pepper.
- Stir fry over medium heat. The onions and meat will add liquid to the wok as they cook.
- Continue cooking until the liquid, sugar and soy sauce form a thick (almost a glaze) sauce.
- Add pasta to the wok and mix with meat and onions. Cook until pasta is hot.
- Serve hot

---

282. San Francisco Chops Recipe

Serving: 4 | Prep: | Cook: 36mins | Ready in:

Ingredients

- 4 pork chops
- 1 clove garlic, minced
- 1 tablespoon oil
- 2 teaspoons oil
- 4 tablespoons dry sherry
- 4 tablespoons soy sauce
- 1/4 teaspoon crushed red pepper
- 2 teaspoons cornstarch
- 2 tablespoons water
- 2 tablespoons brown sugar

Direction

- Trim fat off pork chops; heat 1 tablespoon of oil in skillet and brown pork chops on both sides.

- Sauté garlic for 1 minute being careful not to burn it, add to chops.
- Combine oil, sherry, soy sauce, brown sugar, and red pepper.
- Place chops back in skillet and pour sauce over them.
- Cover tightly.
- Simmer 30 to 35 minutes.
- Add 1 to 2 tablespoons water if needed.
- Remove chops to platter.
- Stir in cornstarch dissolved in water.
- Cook until thickened.
- Pour over chops and serve over noodles or rice...

---

283. Saucy Sizzle Pepper Steak Recipe

Serving: 6 | Prep: | Cook: 35mins | Ready in:

Ingredients

- 1 green bell pepper, cut into thin strips
- 1 red bell pepper, cut into thin strips
- 1 yellow bell pepper, cut into thin strips
- 1 medium onion, cut into strips
- 1 cup green onions
- 1 lb. well-trimmed boneless beef sirloin steak, cut into strips
- 2 cloves garlic, minced
- black pepper to taste
- 3 Tbsp. soy sauce (can use lite soy sauce)
- 1/2 cup KRAFT Original barbecue sauce or your favorite barbeque sauce
- 2 cups hot cooked rice

Direction

- HEAT large nonstick skillet sprayed with cooking spray on medium-high heat. Add bell peppers and onions; cook and stir 6 to 8 min. or until vegetables are crisp-tender. Transfer to large bowl; keep warm.
- ADD meat, garlic and black pepper to same skillet; cook and stir 3 min. Add soy sauce;

cook 1 min. or until meat is cooked through. Add barbecue sauce; cook until heated through.

- SPOON meat mixture into bowl with vegetables; toss gently. Serve over rice

---

284. Saucy Steak Skillet Recipe

Serving: 4 | Prep: | Cook: 30mins |Ready in:

Ingredients

- 1 pound boneless round steak
- 1/4 cup all purpose flour
- 1 tablespoon vegetable oil
- 1 large white onion chopped
- 1/4 cup catsup
- 1 tablespoon worcestershire sauce
- 1 bell pepper diced
- 1 teaspoon salt
- 1/2 teaspoon dried mushrooms
- 1 package frozen green beans
- 1 jar sliced pimientos drained
- 2 potatoes boiled reserving liquid

Direction

- Coat beef with flour and pound into meat then brown in oil in heavy skillet.
- Push beef aside and cook and stir onions in oil until tender then drain well.
- Add enough water to potato liquid to measure one cup.
- Mix with peppers, salt, Worcestershire sauce, marjoram and pepper.
- Pour over meat and add onions then heat to boiling and reduce heat.
- Cover and simmer until beef is tender then rinse beans under running cold water and separate.
- Add potatoes, beans and pimentos to skillet then heat to boiling and reduce heat.
- Cover and simmer until beans are tender.

285. Sauerbraten Recipe

Serving: 8 | Prep: | Cook: 240mins |Ready in:

Ingredients

- 4 lb beef Rump Or sirloin Tip
- 1 1/2 c vinegar
- 1 c dry red wine
- 3/4 c water
- 3 medium onions, sliced
- 2 stalks celery, sliced
- 2 carrots, sliced
- 10 whole peppercorns
- 10 whole cloves
- 3 bay leaves
- 2 tablespoons sugar
- 1 1/2 teaspoons salt
- flour
- 3 tablespoons oil
- Gravy:
- 3 c drippings plus strained marinade
- 5 tablespoons flour
- 5 tablespoons ginger snap crumbs

Direction

- Place meat in a large plastic bag.
- In a large bowl, thoroughly combine vinegar, wine, water, onions, celery, carrots, pepper, cloves, bay leaves, sugar and salt; pour over meat.
- Fasten bag tightly and lay flat in a 9" X 13" pan.
- Refrigerate 2-3 days, turning bag each day. (If you like sour sauerbraten, let marinate for 4 days.)
- When ready to cook, remove meat (saving marinade) and dry well. Rub the surface lightly with flour.
- In a Dutch oven, heat oil and slowly brown the meat well on all sides.
- Add 1 cup of the marinade liquid plus some of the vegetables and bay leaves.

- Cover tightly and simmer on surface heat or in a preheated 350° F oven for 3 to 4 hours until the meat is fork tender.
- If needed, add more marinade during the cooking time to keep at least 1/2 inch liquid in the Dutch oven.
- Remove the meat and keep warm until ready to slice.
- Into a large measuring cup, strain the drippings.
- Add several ice cubes and let stand for a few minutes until the fat separates out.
- Remove the fat, then make the gravy.
- TO MAKE THE GRAVY:
- In the Dutch oven, combine the gravy ingredients, stir and cook for about 5 minutes over medium heat until gravy has thickened.
- Taste for seasonings and adjust if necessary.
- This makes about 3 cups of gravy.

286. Savory Pork Chops Recipe

Serving: 4 | Prep: | Cook: 15mins | Ready in:

Ingredients

- 1/4c each honey and lemon juice
- 2T. sou sauce
- 1T dry sherry
- 2 cloves garlic,minced
- 4 boneless center cut lean pork chops(about 4 oz each)

Direction

- In small bowl, combine all ingredients except pork chops. Place chops in a shallow baking dish; pour marinade over pork. Cover and refrigerate 4hours or overnight. Remove pork from marinade. Heat remaining marinade in a small saucepan over med. heat to simmer. Broil pork chops 4 to 6 inches from the heat for 12 to 15 mins, turning once during cooking and basting frequently with marinade.

287. Schwibraches Recipe

Serving: 6 | Prep: | Cook: 50mins | Ready in:

Ingredients

- 2 lbs.. boneless sirloin steak, cut into thin strips (you can use a tough cut of meat here)
- 3 slices of bacon diced
- 1/4 cup of unsalted butter
- 1 medium onion, minced
- 2 cloves of garlic, minced
- 1 teaspoon of caraway seeds
- 1/4 teaspoon of marjoram (don't fret if you don't have it)
- 1 tablespoon of parsley flakes
- 2 tablespoons of flour
- 2 cups of red wine
- 2 medium dill pickles diced
- 1 small can of anchovies in oil rolled with capers, drained and minced
- 1 tablespoon of Dijon mustard
- fresh ground pepper
- dash of paprika
- 1 cup of sour cream

Direction

- In skillet, sauté bacon in butter to render out fat and cook bacon done but not overly crisp.
- Remove bacon and reserve.
- In the pan drippings, sauté onion and garlic.
- Add caraway seeds, parsley and marjoram.
- Fry meat lightly on all sides, don't crown the pan.
- Dust with flour and cook a minute or two more.
- Add red wine, reduce heat to low.
- Cover pan and simmer for 20 minutes.
- Add pickles, anchovies, mustard, and reserved bacon, stir occasionally and cook slowly for another 20 minutes.
- Just before you want to eat bring the sauce and meat up to the boil and cook until the sauce

reduces to your desired consistency, stirring so it doesn't stick and the meat is tender.
- Take off the heat and stir in the sour cream and sprinkle with the paprika.
- Serve over wide buttered noodles, rice or dumplings.

288.   Simple Filipino Beef Steak Recipe

Serving: 3 | Prep: | Cook: 1hours | Ready in:

Ingredients

- 1/4 kg beef
- 4 cloves of garlic
- red onion
- ground pepper
- salt
- soy sauce
- 3 calamansi

Direction

- Pound the beef using the back of the knife to make it tender
- Sauté garlic and onion
- Add beef then add a pinch of salt and pepper
- Add some soy sauce, add water
- Mix well
- Let it simmer and leave it for about 30 - 40 minutes
- Wait until it is cooked
- Remove from heat
- Add calamansi

289.   Sirloin Beef And Lamb Burgers With Feta And Cilantro Mint Sauce Recipe

Serving: 6 | Prep: | Cook: 10mins | Ready in:

Ingredients

- For the cilantro - mint Sauce
- 1/3 cup plain non-fat yogurt or Greek style yogurt
- 3 tablespoons chopped green onion
- 1/3 cup fresh mint leaves, lightly packed, coarsely chopped
- 3/4 cup cilantro leaves, lightly packed
- 1 1/2 tablespoon minced jalapeno
- 2 cloves garlic, minced
- salt, to taste
- For the Burgers:
- 3/4 pound lean ground sirloin
- 3/4 pound lean ground lamb
- 1 large clove garlic, minced
- 1/3 cup feta cheese, crumbled
- 1/4 cup kalamata olives, finely chopped
- 2 tablespoon extra virgin olive oil
- 1 teaspoon ground cumin
- 1 teaspoon dried mint leaves
- 1/2 teaspoon ground coriander
- 1/2 teaspoon salt
- 1/4 teaspoon pepper
- Additional ingredients:
- 6 hamburger buns, preferably whole grain
- 6 slices ripe tomatoes
- 6 slices red onion
- Red lettuce or spinach leaves

Direction

- Make the Cilantro-Mint Sauce: combine all the ingredients in the work bowl of a blender or food processor. Pulse until the vegetables are finely minced and all is well combined. Cover and refrigerate until ready to serve.
- Make the Burgers: combine all the ingredients in a large bowl. Using your hands mix to combine. Divide and form 6 patties.
- Preheat the grill to medium high. When the grill is ready, place the patties on; cover and cook, turning once, about 4 minutes per side, or to your desired degree of doneness. Remove and cover to keep warm.
- Place the bun halves on the grill and grill until lightly toasted.

- To Serve: Place a patty on each bun, top with Cilantro-Mint sauce, add tomato slice, onion, lettuce or spinach and serve.
- Per Serving: 536 Calories; 37g Fat (13g Sat, 15g Mono, 3g Poly); 26g Protein; 25g Carbohydrate; 3g Dietary Fiber; 92mg Cholesterol; 870mg Sodium.

290. Sirloin Steak With Pepper Faux Filet Au Poìvre Recipe

Serving: 4 | Prep: | Cook: 15mins | Ready in:

Ingredients

- 4 sirloin steak 6 to 8 oz each
- 2 fl oz cognac
- 4 Tspoons sour cream
- 20 crushed peppercorns
- 2 Tspoons olive oil
- 2 Tspoons of butter
- salt to taste

Direction

- - Drag the steaks into the peppercorns and fry them at your convenience into the oil and butter (in a non-stick pan). French way is to cook it rare to medium rare (about 5 minutes).
- - Get them out from the pan and keep in a covered hot plate during the time you prepare the sauce (don't turn flame off). - Deglaze the pan with the cognac and flambé it (you need to pour the cognac in the pan, let it get hot, then tip the pan up and put a flame near the alcohol, with care !...wait for the flame to stop by itself, it just takes a few seconds).
- - Add the cream to the pan and mix everything together; top the steaks with the sauce, add salt, and serve right away with boiled (and peeled) potatoes.

291. Sirloin Steak With Garlic Butter Recipe

Serving: 4 | Prep: | Cook: 12mins | Ready in:

Ingredients

- 1/2 C. butter
- 2 t. garlic powder
- 4 cloves garlic, minced
- 4 1/2 inch thick sirloin steaks
- coarsely ground salt and pepper to taste

Direction

- In a small saucepan, melt butter and add in garlic powder and minced garlic. Set aside.
- Heat a bit of oil in a frying pan over medium heat.
- Sprinkle steaks with salt and pepper.
- Place steaks in frying pan and pour in the garlic butter mixture.
- Cook for 4-5 minutes on each side, until done.
- Serve on a warmed plate with a nice side of vegetables.

292. Sizzling Steak Tacos Recipe

Serving: 4 | Prep: | Cook: 10mins | Ready in:

Ingredients

- 4 tablespoons olive oil
- 2 green bell peppers thinly sliced
- 1 red onion thinly sliced
- 1 pound skirt or flank steak cut 1/4" thick long strips
- 1 jalapeño pepper minced with seeds
- 1 teaspoon cumin
- 1 teaspoon chili powder
- 1/2 teaspoon salt
- 1 teaspoon freshly ground black pepper
- 1-1/2 cups canned corn drained
- 2 plum tomatoes seeded and chopped

- 1 avocado peeled and diced
- 2 tablespoons minced fresh cilantro
- 1 teaspoon cider vinegar
- 1 teaspoon vegetable oil
- 8 corn tortillas

Direction

- Heat oil in heavy large skillet over medium heat.
- Add bell pepper and onion then sauté until tender about 5 minutes then transfer to bowl.
- Add steak to skillet and cook until no longer pink about 2 minutes.
- Add jalapeño, cumin, chili powder, salt and pepper then transfer to heated bowl.
- In medium bowl, combine corn, tomatoes, avocado, cilantro, vinegar and oil.
- Warm tortillas over gas flame or electric burner until they begin to color.
- Stuff tortillas with steak, peppers, onions and corn mixture then serve immediately.

293. Skillet Pork And Peppers Recipe

Serving: 4 | Prep: | Cook: 25mins | Ready in:

Ingredients

- 1 large pork tenderloin (about 11/2 pounds), trimmed
- Kosher salt
- 3 tablespoons extra-virgin olive oil
- 1 small onion, thickly sliced
- 2 red and/or yellow bell peppers, sliced into wide strips
- 6 cloves garlic, smashed
- 16 fresh sage leaves
- 2 tablespoons tomato paste
- 1/4 cup sliced pickled pepperoncini, plus 2 teaspoons liquid from the jar
- 1/3 cup dry white wine
- 2/3 cup low-sodium chicken broth

- 1/4 cup grated parmesan cheese

Direction

- Preheat the broiler. Slice the pork on an angle into 1-inch-thick pieces; season with salt. Heat a large ovenproof skillet over medium-high heat; add 1 tablespoon olive oil. Add the onion and bell peppers; season with 1/2 teaspoon salt and cook until the vegetables are crisp-tender and slightly browned, 4 to 6 minutes. Transfer to a plate.
- Add the remaining 2 tablespoons oil to the skillet. Add the pork and sear over high heat until browned, 2 to 4 minutes per side. Transfer the pork to the plate with the onion and peppers.
- Reduce the heat to medium and add the garlic, sage and tomato paste to the skillet. Cook, stirring, until the tomato paste turns brick-red, about 1 minute. Add the pepperoncini slices and their liquid, then pour in the wine and bring to a boil. Add the broth and return to a simmer. Arrange the pork in a single layer in the skillet; add the onion and peppers and sprinkle with cheese. Transfer to the oven and broil until the pork is cooked through, 4 to 7 minutes.
- Serve with rice or eat alone with some crusty bread to soak up the sauce
- Per serving: Calories 380; Fat 18 g (Sat. 4.4 g; Mono. 10.5 g; Poly. 2 g); Cholesterol 115 mg; Sodium 586 mg; Carbohydrate 10 g; Fiber 2 g; Protein 40 g

294. Skillet Pork Chops With Potatoes And Onions Recipe

Serving: 2 | Prep: | Cook: 50mins | Ready in:

Ingredients

- 2 Tbsp vegetable oil
- 4 pork chops, 1/2 - 3/4 inch thick, trimmed
- 2 Tbsp AP flour

- 1/3 grated parmesan cheese
- 1/2 tsp salt
- 1/4 tsp pepper
- 4 yukon gold potatoes, peeled, thinly sliced
- 2 medium onions, sliced thin
- 3 cubes beef bouillon
- 3/4 cup hot water
- 1 Tbsp lemon juice

Direction

- Heat oil in a large skillet over medium heat. Coat the pork chops flour, and place in the skillet. Brown ~ 4 minutes on each side.
- In a small bowl, mix the Parmesan cheese, salt, and pepper. Sprinkle 1/2 the Parmesan cheese mixture over the pork shops.
- Layer pork chops with potatoes.
- Sprinkle with remaining Parmesan cheese mixture.
- Top with onion slices.
- In a small bowl, dissolve beef bouillon cubes in hot water. Stir in lemon juice then pour over the layered pork chops.
- Cover skillet, and reduce heat to a simmer, simmer for 40 minutes, until vegetables are tender and pork chops internal temperature is between 140-160 F.
- Serve immediately.

295. Slow Cooked Apple Pear And Apricot Pork Chops Recipe

Serving: 6 | Prep: | Cook: 22mins | Ready in:

Ingredients

- 6 Smithfield pork chops
- 1 cup fresh Anjou pear -- roughly chopped
- 1 cup red apple -- roughly chopped
- 1 cup dried apricots -- chopped
- 1 medium onion -- chopped
- 3 ribs celery -- roughly sliced
- 1 tablespoon fresh thyme leaves

- 3/4 cups apple juice
- 1/2 cup dark brown sugar
- 1/4 cup white wine
- salt and pepper to taste
- 2 tablespoons cornstarch mixed with 2 tablespoons water
- Apple and pear slices for garnish

Direction

- In a slow cooker, or Dutch oven combine all ingredients, except cornstarch and water. Cover and cook on LOW for 7 to 9 hours, or 3 1/2 to 4 1/2 hours on HIGH. 30 minutes before serving, skim off any excess fat.
- Stir in cornstarch mixture and return broth to slow cooker. Continue cooking on low until sauce is smooth and thickened.
- Garnish with apple and pear slices.
- Serving Suggestions:
- Serve alongside a fresh green salad.

296. Slow Cooker Barbacoa Shredded Beef Recipe

Serving: 6 | Prep: | Cook: 7mins | Ready in:

Ingredients

- 3 pound tri tip or chuck roast, some fat trimmed off(leave some for flavor) Cut into about 4 or 5 large pieces
- 1/2 a yellow onion quartered
- 2 large garlic cloves cut in quarters
- 1 jalapeno, chopped- stem and seeds removed if you dont want to spicy
- 2 tbs of chili powder
- 1/2 tsp of garlic powder
- 1/4 tsp onion powder
- 1/2 tsp pepper
- salt to taste, I add about 1 1/2 tsp salt
- 1 -2 cups of water

Direction

- Place all ingredients in slow cooker, and add enough water. Set on low and let cook for about 7-8 hours until very moist and shreds easily. There should be enough liquid to keep it moist; or cook on high for about 4-5 hours. Enjoy!

297. Slow Cooker Hawaiian Beef Recipe

Serving: 5 | Prep: | Cook: 22mins | Ready in:

Ingredients

- 1/3 cup firmly packed brown sugar
- 1/3 cup cider vinegar
- 1 (8-ounce) can pineapple chucks, drained, erserve juice
- 3 tbs soy sauce
- 1 tps finely chopped freah garlic
- 2 tbs butter
- 1 1/2 pounds round steak, cut into 1 1/2-inch pieces
- 1 cup baby-cut carrots, halved crosswise
- 1 large onion, cutinto 1- inch pieces
- 3 tbs cornstarch
- 3 tbs cold water
- 1 large green bell pepper, cut into bite-size pieces
- Hot cooked rice
- green onion slices, if desired

Direction

- Combine brown sugar, vinegar, reserved pineapple juice, soy sauce and garlic in small bowl, stir until sugar is dissolved. Set aside.
- Melt 1 tbsp. butter in 12-inch skillet until sizzling, add half of steak pieces. Cook over med-high heat. Repeat with remaining butter and steak pieces.
- Add carrots and onion to slow cooker. Pour pineapple juice mixture over vegetables. Cover, cook on Low heat setting for 7 to 9 hrs,

or on High setting for 3 to 4 hrs or until meat is tender.
- Dissolve cornstarch in cold water in small bowl. Stir cornstarch mixture, pineapple chunks and green pepper into beef mixture. Cover, continue cooking 30 mins or until green pepper is crisply tender and juices are thickened. Serve over hot rice.

298. Slow Cooker Philly Style Cheese Steak Sandwiches Recipe

Serving: 6 | Prep: | Cook: 480mins | Ready in:

Ingredients

- 1 1/2 lbs beef round steak
- 1 medium green pepper, sliced thin
- 1 medium onion, sliced thin
- 1 (14 oz) can vegetable broth (can use beef - I've even used chicken in a pinc h)
- 1 envelope Italian dressing mix
- 1 large loaf French bread, siced into sandwich lengths
- 6 slices provolone cheese

Direction

- Spray crock pot with cooking spray
- Cut meat into strips, place in slow cooker
- Add green pepper, onion, broth, and dressing mix
- Cover and cook on low 7-8 hours, or high 3-4 hours
- Spoon meat mixture onto bread, top with a slice of cheese
- Another option is to toast bread in a 375 oven for 5-10 minutes, add meat, cover with cheese, then bake an additional 5 minutes to melt the cheese.

299. Slow Cooked Pepper Steak Recipe

Serving: 68 | Prep: | Cook: 360mins | Ready in:

Ingredients

- 1 1/2 - 2 lbs. beef round steak
- 2 Tbsp. cooking oil
- 1/4 cup soy sauce
- 1/2 cup chopped onion
- 1 clove garlic, minced
- 1 tsp. sugar
- 1/2 tsp. salt
- 1/4 tsp. pepper
- 1/4 tsp. ground ginger
- 4 tomatoes, cut into eighths
- 2 large green peppers, sliced into strips
- 1/2 cup cold water
- 1 Tbsp. cornstarch
- rice or noodles

Direction

- Cut beef into 3 x 1-in. strips; brown in oil
- Transfer to slow cooker.
- Combine next 7 ingredients; pour over beef.
- Cover and cook on low 5-6 hours.
- Add tomatoes and green pepper.
- Cook on low 1 hour longer.
- Make paste out of water and cornstarch.
- Stir into liquid in slow cooker and cook on high until thickened.
- Serve over rice or noodles.

300. Smokey Pan Carne Asada Recipe

Serving: 12 | Prep: | Cook: 20mins | Ready in:

Ingredients

- 6 pounds skirt steak sliced thin
- 2 large red onions sliced thin
- 1 teaspoon cumin
- 3 heads crushed fresh garlic
- 6 tablespoons chopped fresh cilantro
- 6 tablespoons fresh squeezed lime juice
- 1/2 teaspoon salt
- 1 teaspoon freshly ground black pepper
- 2 fresh jalapeno peppers sliced
- 1/2 freshly squeezed orange juice
- 2 tablespoons liquid smoke

Direction

- Place all ingredients in a large plastic bag and marinate overnight.
- When marinated put meat into a fry pan and cook to desired doneness.
- Serve with hot tortillas and desired garnishes.

301. Smothered Pork Chops Recipe

Serving: 4 | Prep: | Cook: 30mins | Ready in:

Ingredients

- 4 pork loin chops
- 1 teaspoon plus 1 tablespoon salt, divided
- 1 teaspoon plus 1 tablespoon ground black pepper, divided
- 2 cups plus 2 tablespoons all-purpose flour, divided
- 1/2 cup vegetable oil
- 1 large onions, coarsely chopped
- 1 green bell peppers, cored, seeded and
- coarsely chopped
- 1 stalks celery, coarsely chopped
- 2 cups water

Direction

- Trim excess fat from the edges of the pork chops. Sprinkle each with some of the 1 teaspoon salt and pepper. Season 2 cups flour with the remaining 1 tablespoon salt and pepper. Dredge chops in the flour until coated on all sides, shaking off excess flour.

- Pour the vegetable oil in a deep, heavy skillet, such as cast iron, over medium-high heat. When the oil begins to shake slightly, add as many pork chops as will fit without crowding. Fry, turning once, until well-browned on both sides, about 5 minutes. Remove chops to a plate and repeat with remaining chops.
- Pour off all but 1/4 cup drippings from the skillet. Reduce the heat to medium and add onions, green peppers and celery. Cook until brown and soft, about 10 minutes. Sprinkle 2 tablespoons flour over the vegetables and bottom of the skillet. Cook, stirring, until flour is golden brown. Slowly pour in 2 cups water. Stir, then cook until thickened.
- Place pork chops in a Dutch oven or divide between two skillets. Top with the gravy and vegetables. Cover tightly and cook over low heat until pork chops are cooked through, about 15 minutes.

302.   Snitzel Recipe

Serving: 4 | Prep: | Cook: 10mins |Ready in:

Ingredients

- 2 cups Italian bread crumbs
- 4 pieces of sliced pork tenderloin or pork chop will due
- 2 eggs
- 4 slices of American cheese
- 1 to 2 cans asparagus or 12 fresh asparagus(just a tip: If you can get
- fresh asparagus, do!!)
- frying oil
- 1 can cranberry sauce

Direction

- So, you want to heat your frying oil before starting. So, go ahead and pour a pan half full of oil. I use a deep fryer, but you can use a cast iron pan or whatever you use to fry.

- Whip your eggs in something you can dip your pork
- Put crumbs on a plate
- Dip the pork into the egg and then lay it on the crumbs so it coats well! I double coat =) Makes it taste better, I think.
- After they're coated fry them up!
- They should be a golden brown or darker when they're done. Be careful because of all the juices from the pork it might splatter oil.
- Put them on a plate and lay your asparagus, a piece of American cheese, and cranberry sauce over the top! Yay, it's done. I like it with red sauerkraut and mashed potatoes=) Yummy.

303.   Southern Fried Pork Chops Recipe

Serving: 8 | Prep: | Cook: 4mins |Ready in:

Ingredients

- 8 CENTER CUT pork chops (ON THE BONE)
- salt
- pepper
- garlic powder
- 1 TEASPOON cayenne pepper
- flour
- 1 CUP vegetABLE OR canola oil

Direction

- MIX THE SPICES
- SPRINKLE ON BOTH SIDES OF THE PORK CHOPS
- REFRIGERATE FOR A FEW HOURS OR LONGER (I LEAVE MINE IN THE REFRIGERATOR ALL DAY)
- WHEN READY TO FRY, HEAT THE OIL IN A CAST IRON OR HEAVY SKILLET OVER MEDIUM HIGH HEAT FOR ABOUT 3-5 MINUTES
- DIP THE PORK CHOPS IN FLOUR THEN SHAKE OFF EXCESS FLOUR
- PLACE PORK CHOPS IN HOT OIL

- DO NOT OVERCROWD THE PORK CHOPS, WILL TAKE TWO BATCHES OF FRYING
- COOK FOR ABOUT 3 MINUTES ON EACH SIDE
- DO NOT OVERCOOK OR THE MEAT WILL BE DRY
- DRAIN ON PAPER TOWELS AND SERVE
- CAN SERVE WITH RICE AND GRAVY, CORNBREAD, ETC...
- SAVE YOUR PORK CHOP DRIPPINGS, ADD FLOUR & WATER TO MAKE A PORK CHOP GRAVY TO GO OVER THE RICE.

304. Southern Fried Steak With Gravy Recipe

Serving: 4 | Prep: | Cook: 30mins | Ready in:

Ingredients

- 1-1/2 pounds round steak cut into square servings
- 2 medium white onions sliced
- 1 tablespoon shortening
- 2 tablespoons flour
- 2 cups hot water
- 1/2 teaspoon Kitchen Bouquet
- 1 teaspoon ketchup
- 1 teaspoon salt
- 1/2 teaspoon freshly ground black pepper
- 1/2 teaspoon cayenne pepper

Direction

- Beat steaks with meat mallet or the edge of a plate to break down tissues.
- Sprinkle with salt and pepper then brown the steaks in hot shortening and set aside.
- In the same hot fat brown the onions adding more shortening if necessary.
- Blend in the flour and add 2 cups hot water and season with salt, pepper and cayenne.
- Add steaks to the gravy then add the Kitchen Bouquet and ketchup.
- Cover pan and let simmer until tender.

305. Southern Style Pork Chops Recipe

Serving: 6 | Prep: | Cook: 35mins | Ready in:

Ingredients

- 6 pork chops
- 2/3 c rice
- 1 c. water
- 2 t salt
- 1 chopped onion
- 1 16oz. can tomatoes
- 1 can whole kernel corn
- 1/4 t pepper

Direction

- Brown chops in large skillet. Remove and pour off fat. Spread rice in pan and add water. Sprinkle 1 t. salt over rice. Arrange chops over rice. Sprinkle remaining 1 t. salt over chops. Spread onions, then tomatoes over chops. Spoon on corn. Sprinkle with pepper. Bring to boil and reduce heat. Cover and cook for 35 minutes.
- * I sometimes cook this in the oven in a covered casserole dish for about an hour at 375.

306. Spicy Pork In Fermented Shrimps Recipe

Serving: 3 | Prep: | Cook: | Ready in:

Ingredients

- 1/4 kg pork (40% fat)
- 4 cloves of garlic
- onion
- tomato

- 3 tablespoons of fermented shrimps (small)
- salt and pepper
- chili (depends upon your taste)

Direction

- Sauté garlic, onion and tomato
- Add pork
- Stir fry
- Wait till the fat of the pork comes out
- Add a pinch of salt and pepper
- Add water (not too much)
- Mix well
- Simmer for 30 - 40 mins till the meat is tender
- Add chilies and the fermented shrimps
- Mix well

307. Spicy Pork In Sizzling Ketchup Recipe

Serving: 3 | Prep: | Cook: | Ready in:

Ingredients

- 1/4 kg pork
- 3 cloves of garlic
- 1 onion
- red chili (As many as you desired)
- tomato ketchup
- banana ketchup
- little amount of vinegar
- Pinch of salt

Direction

- Sauté garlic and onion
- Add pork and banana ketchup
- Add water and let it simmer about 30 mins
- Add tomato ketchup and vinegar
- Add red chili
- Mix well
- Wait until it's cooked

308. Spicy Pork Tausi In Tomato Sauce Recipe

Serving: 3 | Prep: | Cook: | Ready in:

Ingredients

- 1/4 kg pork
- tomato sauce
- 4 cloves of garlic
- onion
- pepper
- tomato
- salt
- chili
- Tausi (salted black beans)
- 6 Vienna sausages
- pinch of sugar

Direction

- Sauté garlic, onion and tomato
- Add pork then add tausi, pepper and salt
- Add water, mix well
- Let it simmer for 30 minutes
- Add tomato sauce
- Add chili (as much as you desired) then add the sausages
- Mix well
- Wait until it's cooked

309. Steak Chicken And Vegetable Tacos Recipe

Serving: 6 | Prep: | Cook: 10mins | Ready in:

Ingredients

- steak
- 2 ounces pressed tamarind from a pound block, cut into 3/4-inch pieces
- . 3/4 cup hot water
- 4 unpeeled garlic cloves
- 3 scallions, chopped
- 1 1/2 teaspoons thyme leaves

- 1 tablespoon pure ancho chile powder
- 2 tablespoons extra-virgin olive oil
- 3/4 cup Coca-Cola
- salt and freshly ground pepper
- 1 1/2 pounds skirt steak, cut into 4-inch lengths
- vegetables AND chicken
- 1/2 cup extra-virgin olive oil
- 2 garlic cloves, minced
- 1 serrano chile, thinly sliced
- 2 medium zucchini, thinly sliced lengthwise
- 2 chayote—peeled, halved lengthwise, pitted and thinly sliced crosswise
- 2 large carrots, thinly sliced on a sharp angle
- 1 fennel bulb—trimmed, cored and thinly sliced
- salt and freshly ground pepper
- 4 skinless, boneless chicken breast halves, butterflied
- 36 corn tortillas, warmed
- salsa verde and pico de gallo, cilantro sprigs and sour cream, for serving

Direction

- Prepare the steak: In a microwave-safe bowl, combine the tamarind and water and microwave on high power for 2 minutes. Cover and let stand until the tamarind is softened, about 30 minutes
- .
- Meanwhile, preheat a small skillet. Add the garlic and cook over moderate heat, turning occasionally, until the cloves are blackened in spots, about 8 minutes. Peel the garlic.
- Mash the tamarind to a pulp. Strain the puree through a fine sieve into a blender. Discard the seeds and fibres. Add the roasted garlic and the scallions, thyme, chile powder and olive oil to the blender and puree until smooth. With the machine on, add the Coca-Cola in a thin stream until blended. Season generously with salt and pepper. Transfer the mixture to a shallow baking dish. Add the steak and turn to coat. Cover and refrigerate overnight.
- Prepare the vegetables and chicken: Preheat a grill pan. In a large bowl, combine the oil,

garlic and Serrano chile. Add the sliced vegetables and a generous pinch each of salt and pepper and toss to coat. Grill the vegetables over high heat, turning occasionally, until tender and lightly charred, about 8 minutes. Transfer the vegetables to a cutting board and coarsely chop them.
- Brush the chicken with some of the remaining oil from the vegetable bowl and season with salt and pepper. Grill the chicken over high heat, turning once until cooked through and lightly charred, about 8 minutes. Let rest for 10 minutes, then cut into thin strips.
- Scrape most of the marinade off the steaks. Grill the steaks over high heat, turning occasionally, until charred in spots, about 10 minutes for medium-rare. Transfer the steaks to a cutting board and let rest for 10 minutes, then thinly slice across the grain.
- Mound the steak, chicken and vegetables in 3 bowls and serve with the tortillas, Salsa Verde, Pico de Gallo, cilantro and sour cream.

310.　　　Steak Frites Recipe

Serving: 4 | Prep: | Cook: 8mins | Ready in:

Ingredients

- 4 beef steaks, such as porterhouse, sirloin, rib eye, or fillet mignon (1/2 pound each and 3/4 to 1 in thick), or one 2-pound steak
- 5 tablespoons unsalted butter
- 1 tablespoon water
- salt and freshly ground black pepper, to taste

Direction

- With a sharp knife, make small incisions, about 1 1/2 inches apart in the fat around the outside of each steak.
- Melt 3 tablespoons of the butter in a large heavy skillet or sauté pan over high heat until hot but not smoking. Add the steaks and sear for 1 minute on each side. Reduce the heat to

medium. Season the steaks generously with salt and pepper and continue cooking, turning the steaks every other minute, until you see little pearls of blood come to the surface, about 6 to 8 minutes. The steaks should be cooked rare to medium for juicy, tender meat.

- Remove the steaks and place them on warmed plates. Over medium heat, deglaze the pan with the water and swirl in the remaining 2 tablespoons butter. Drizzle these pan juices over the meat and serve at once with fries. Serves 4.
- Matt says: Don't forget a big glass of beer. Or wine. Lots.

311.   Steak Po Boy Recipe

Serving: 4 | Prep: | Cook: 20mins | Ready in:

Ingredients

- Four 1/2 inch thick strip steaks (about 6 to 8 oz each), trimmed of excess fat
- 1/4 cup worcestershire sauce
- 2 to 3 tablespoons olive oil
- 1 garlic clove, crushed
- 2 large green or red bell peppers (or one of each), seeded and cut into 6 wedges
- Four 1/4 inch thick slices, cut from a large yellow onion
- 1 teaspoon creole seasoning (available at most supermarkets)
- 1/4 teaspoon ground black pepper
- 4 slices Swiss, Muenster or provolone cheese
- 4 sandwich rolls, French bread or hoagie rolls

Direction

- Place the steaks in a plastic zipper closure bag; add the Worcestershire sauce, 1 tablespoon olive oil and the crushed garlic.
- Seal and shake the bag to distribute the ingredients evenly. Marinate for at least 20 minutes or overnight in a refrigerator.
- Preheat the grill to medium-high.

- Brush the bell peppers and onion slices with the remaining oil. Grill until soft and lightly browned, about 6 to 10 minutes.
- Transfer to a plate and cover with aluminum foil.
- Remove the steaks from the bag and wife off the excess marinade. Season the meat with Creole seasoning and ground pepper.
- Grill for 3 to 4 minutes, turn over and continue cooking 2 to 3 minutes.
- Place a slice of cheese on each steak and allow it to melt.
- Place the bun cut side down on the grill until lightly toasted and warm.
- Place 1 steak on each roll, break up the slices of onions into rings and divide among each sandwich; top with bell pepper slices.
- Serve immediately.

312.   Steak Quesadillas With Roasted Peppers And Bousin Recipe

Serving: 4 | Prep: | Cook: 18mins | Ready in:

Ingredients

- 2 strip steaks(about 1")thick
- salt and pepper
- 1Tbs veg. oil
- 1(5.2oz)pkg bousin cheese(crumbled)
- 11/2c shreaded cheddar cheese
- 4(12") flour tortillas
- 1/2c drained jarred roasted red peppers,patted dry with paper towels and sliced thin
- 4 scallions,sliced thin

Direction

- Pat steaks dry and season with salt and pepper. Heat oil in lg. non-stick skillet over med-high heat until just smoking. Cook steaks till well browned 3-5 mins each side. Transfer to a plate and let rest 5 mins, then slice against the grain. Wipe out skillet.

- While steaks rest, combine boursin, cheddar, ½ tsp salt and 1 tsp. pepper in a bowl. Divide cheese mixture evenly over o1/2 of each tortilla, leaving 1.2" border around edge. Top with peppers, scallions and sliced steak. Fold tortilla over filling and press down firmly.
- Add 2 quesadillas to empty skillet and cook over med-high heat until golden and crisp 1-2 mins. Using spatula, flip quesadillas and cook until golden brown and cheese is melted, 1-2 mins. Transfer to cutting board and repeat with remaining quesadillas. Cut into wedges and serve.

313.   Steak Rolls Recipe

Serving: 8 | Prep: | Cook: 90mins | Ready in:

Ingredients

- 2 lbs top round or strip steak
- 1 cp fine bread crumbs
- 2 tsp basil
- 1 cp fresh parsley chopped
- 1 tbs finely chopped garlic
- 1/2 cp finely chopped yellow onion
- 1 cp parmesean cheese
- 1 tsp oregano
- 1/2 cp shredded carrot
- 1/2 cp finely chopped celery
- 8 slices thick bacon
- 1 can diced tomatoes with juice (can use theones that contain chilis for a great taste)
- salt and pepper
- olive oil for frying

Direction

- Cut each steak into four equal pieces.
- Pound with mallet until very thin.
- Sprinkle with salt and pepper.
- Combine all dry ingredients.
- Add tomatoes and mix well.

- Let sit a few minutes so juices are absorbed.
- Place 1/2 cup of bread mixture in center of each steak piece.
- Roll up tucking in ends.
- Wrap each roll in one strip of bacon and secure with toothpicks.
- Gently brown in olive oil.
- Place in casserole dish cover and bake in a 325 oven for about 1 1/2 hrs. or until everything is tender and juicy. Serve with steamed rice and fresh broccoli. Yummy!

314.   Steak Saltimbocca Recipe

Serving: 6 | Prep: | Cook: 15mins | Ready in:

Ingredients

- 2lbs, beef skirt steak,trimmed of fat
- fresh ground black pepper to taste
- 6 oz. sliced aged provolone cheese
- 2 bunches fresh sage leaves
- 12 slices prosciutto
- 1/4c extra virgin olive oil

Direction

- Preheat oven to 350. Cut the steak into 4oz. pieces, then pound each one to 1/4" thickness. Season with black pepper. On each piece of steak, lay 1 slice of provolone cheese, a few leaves of sage and 2 slices of prosciutto. Roll into pinwheels and secure with toothpicks.
- Heat the oil in a large skillet over med-high heat. Quickly brown the pinwheels on the outside. Transfer to a baking dish if your skillet is not oven-safe.
- Bake for 7 minutes for med-rare, or 10 minutes for medium. Let rest for 5 minutes before carving into thin pinwheels. Place the skillet back over med-high heat, and add any remaining sage leaves. Fry till crispy and then use them to garnish the steaks.

315.   Steak Skillet Dinner With Green Beans Dated 1926 Recipe

Serving: 30 | Prep: | Cook: 30mins | Ready in:

Ingredients

- 1 pound boneless beef round steak, cut into serving pieces
- 1/4 cup all purpose flour
- 1 tablespoon vegetable oil
- 1 chopped white onion
- 1 can whole white potatoes, reserve liquid
- 1/4 cup ketchup
- 1 tablespoon worcestershire sauce
- 1 teaspoon beef bouillon granules
- 1 teaspoon salt
- 1 teaspoon freshly ground black pepper
- 1 can green beans, drained

Direction

- Coat beef pieces with flour then brown beef and onion in oil in skillet and set aside.
- Add enough water to reserved potato liquid to measure 1 cup.
- In small bowl, mix liquid, ketchup, Worcestershire, bouillon granules, salt and pepper.
- Pour over beef and onion then heat to a boil.
- Reduce heat then cover and simmer until beef is tender about 30 minutes.
- Add potatoes and green beans to skillet then heat to boil and reduce heat.
- Cover and simmer 15 minutes longer.

316.   Steak Tacos With Chipotle Sour Cream Recipe

Serving: 4 | Prep: | Cook: 15mins | Ready in:

Ingredients

- 1 flank or top round steak, cut approximately 1-inch thick
- 2 bell peppers, cut into quarters
- 1 medium onion, cut crosswise into 1/2-inch slices
- 1 Tbsp. olive oil
- 8-10 small flour tortillas, warmed
- +++++++++++++++++++++++++++++++++++
- Zesty Southwestern marinade
- 1/4 cup olive oil
- 3 Tbsp. fresh lime juice
- 1 Tbsp. packed brown sugar
- 2 tsp. ground cumin
- 2 large cloves garlic, minced
- 3/4 tsp. dried oregano leaves, crushed
- +++++++++++++++++++++++++++++++++++ +++
- Chipotle Cream
- 1/2 cup sour cream
- 1 Tbsp. chopped fresh cilantro
- 1 tsp. adobo sauce from canned chipotle peppers
- Combine marinade ingredients in small bowl.

Direction

- Place steak and marinade in sealable plastic bag; turn steak to coat. Refrigerate 6 hours to overnight, turning occasionally.
- Remove steak from marinade; discard marinade.
- Brush bell peppers and onion lightly with oil; season with salt and pepper, as desired.
- Place steak and vegetables on rack in broiler pan so surface is 2-3 inches from heat. Broil flank steak 13-18 minutes for medium rare to medium doneness, turning once. Broil peppers and onion 13-15 minutes, or until crisp-tender, turning once.
- Cut vegetables into thin strips; combine. Carve steak across the grain into thin slices. Serve with Chipotle Cream.
- For Chipotle Cream: Combine sour cream, cilantro and adobo sauce. Cover and refrigerate until ready to serve.

317. Steak Tips With Peppered Mushroom Gravy Recipe

Serving: 4 | Prep: | Cook: 15mins | Ready in:

Ingredients

- 2 c uncooked egg noodles
- cooking spray
- 1 lb. top sirloin steak, cut in 3/4" pieces
- 1 Tbs butter
- 2 Tbs fine chopped shallots
- 1 (8oz) pkg pre-sliced baby bella mushrooms
- 1 tsp minced garlic
- 1 Tbs low-sodium soy sauce
- 3 Tbs flour
- 1-1/2 c less-sodium beef broth
- 1/2 tsp black pepper
- 1/4 tsp salt
- 3 fresh thyme sprigs
- 1 tsp fresh thyme leaves (optional)

Direction

- Cook noodles, according to pkg. directions, omitting salt and fat; drain
- While noodles cook, heat large non-stick skillet over med-high heat. Coat pan with cooking spray. Add steak, sauté 5 mins, browning on all sides. Remove from pan; cover
- Melt butter in pan over med-high heat. Add shallots and mushrooms, sauté 4 mins. Add garlic; sauté 30 seconds. Stir in soy sauce.
- Sprinkle flour over mushroom mixture; cook 1 ministering constantly. Gradually add broth, stirring constantly. Add pepper, salt and thyme sprigs. Bring to a boil; cook 2 mins or till thickened.
- Return beef to pan; cook 1 min. or till thoroughly heated. Discard thyme sprigs. Garnish with thyme leaves, if desired.

318. Steak And Dip Recipe

Serving: 6 | Prep: | Cook: 45mins | Ready in:

Ingredients

- 1 cup mayonnaise
- 2 tablespoons chopped parsley
- 2 tablespoons capers
- 2 tablespoons chili sauce
- 2 teaspoons prepared mustard
- 1 clove garlic
- 1 envelope meat marinade mix
- 2 pounds beef round steak 1" thick

Direction

- Place first 6 ingredients in blender and blend at high speed for 30 seconds. Cover and chill 1 hour. Marinate and cook meat according to package directions. Cut into cubes. Serve sauce as dip for steak cubes.

319. Steak Bits Recipe

Serving: 8 | Prep: | Cook: 20mins | Ready in:

Ingredients

- 1 boneless sirloin steak
- [about 2 pounds
- 1/4 cup soy sauce
- 2 tbs. dry sherry
- 2 Tbs. chili sauce
- 2 tsp. cornstarch
- 1/2 cup salad oil
- 2 medium sized onions cut into wedges

Direction

- Cut steak into 1 1/2 inch cubes.
- In medium-sized bowl, combine meat, soy sauce, sherry, chili sauce and corn starch. In 12 inch skillet over medium heat in hot oil, cook onions stirring until crisp tender.

- Increase heat to high; add meat mixture; cook, stirring about 4 minutes for rare-or desired doneness. Serve immediately or refrigerate and serve next day.

320. Steakhouse Fajitas From Peerless Restaurant Recipe

Serving: 2 | Prep: | Cook: 8mins | Ready in:

Ingredients

- NY Strip steak, Black Angus
- 1 Texas sweet onion, large, cut into pedals
- 1 roasted red pepper, cut into strips
- 1 fresh tomato, large, sliced (reserve small slice and chop into guacamole)
- 1/2 cup white corn or fresh corn
- chopped garlic
- fresh avocado
- lime
- creme fresh or mayo
- 2 T. olive oil or corn oil
- Mexican Spices: (a few light shakes of each)
- oregano
- chili powder
- cumin
- Peerless' GK steak seasoning
- salt & fresh ground black pepper
- Fresh cilantro
- Fresh squeezed lime juice
- Sour cream, shredded cheese
- white corn or flour tortillas

Direction

- GUACAMOLE:
- Prep avocado then mash with a fork, add a squeeze of lime, salt, pepper, crème fresh or mayo, and a pinch of fresh chopped cilantro.
- STEAK FAJITAS:
- Your sauté pan should be HOT with a couple oz. of corn oil or olive oil.
- Grill steak to Medium Rare.

- Meanwhile, while steak is cooking, pan sauté onions, peppers, tomatoes, and corn all at once- add salt and pepper to taste. Caramelize your veggies but do not overcook.
- Finish steak, seasoning it generously with the Mexican spices.
- Cut steak on bias.
- Place steak on top of Veggies and serve in skillet, with 1/2 a fresh lime on top of final dish.
- May add sour cream and cheddar cheese if desired.
- Serve with warm or lightly grilled white corn tortillas

321. Steakhouse Mushroom Burgers On Texas Toast With Creamed Spinach Sauce Recipe

Serving: 4 | Prep: | Cook: 14mins | Ready in:

Ingredients

- BURGERS
- 8 oz button mushrooms, sliced
- 2 T EVOO, divided
- 1 t minced garlic
- 1.5 lb ground sirloin, 85% lean
- 1/2 t each - kosher salt and fresh ground black pepper
- 4 slices Texas toast
- Parmesan for garnish
- CREAMED spinach SAUCE
- *Can be made a day ahead. After cooking the sauce, let it cool completely; cover and refrigerate, then reheat over medium low heat.
- 2 T unsalted butter
- 1/4 c minced onion
- 2 T all-purpose flour
- 1/2 c half and half
- 1/2 c chicken broth
- kosher salt, cayenne pepper and nutmeg to taste
- 4 c chopped fresh spinach

- 1 T grated parmesan
- 1/2 t fresh lemon juice

Direction

- BURGERS
- Preheat grill to medium high
- Sauté mushrooms in 1 T EVOO over medium high heat
- Cook until begin to brown, 3-4 minutes
- Stir in garlic and cook 1 minute
- Season with salt and pepper
- Remove pan from heat slightly cool mushrooms
- Combine ground sirloin with soy sauce, 1/2 t salt, 1/2 t pepper and mushroom mixture by hand in large mixing bowl
- Divide into 4 equal portions and shape into patties
- Grill uncovered on direct heat, turning only once, and not mashing with the spatula
- Cook to desired doneness, remove from grill and tent with foil
- Allow to rest
- Reduce grill heat to medium low
- Brush toast with remaining 1 T EVOO
- Place toast slices on grill and heat until lightly browned, 1-2 minutes per side
- Serve place each burger on open piece of toast and to with Creamed Spinach Sauce
- Garnish with parmesan and serve as open-faced sandwiches
- CREAMED SPINACH SAUCE
- Melt butter in a saucepan over medium low heat
- Add onion and cook until translucent, 3-4 minutes
- Stir flour into onion, cook 1 minute
- Whisk in half and half, broth, salt, cayenne, and nutmeg
- Bring sauce to a boil; reduce heat
- Simmer for 2 minutes
- Add spinach, stirring until wilted
- Mix in 1 T parmesan and lemon juice

322. Steam Vegetable With Beef Curry Recipe

Serving: 4 | Prep: | Cook: 1hours | Ready in:

Ingredients

- broccoli
- cabbage
- red bell pepper
- salt
- pepper
- tenderloin
- ouster sauce
- cinnamon powder

Direction

- Preheat the oven
- Steam all the vegetables
- After the veggies steam the pork
- Toast the pork after steaming
- Serve

323. Stuff Yourself Stroganoff Recipe

Serving: 4 | Prep: | Cook: 35mins | Ready in:

Ingredients

- 1-1/2 lb. sirloin
- 2-3 slices bacon, diced
- 1/2 cup chopped onion
- 1/2 tsp salt (or to taste)
- 1/4 tsp paprika
- Dash black pepper
- 1 can cream of mushroom soup
- 1/8 lb. chopped fresh mushrooms (opt.)
- Hot buttered noodles with dashes of oregano and thyme

Direction

- Lightly freeze sirloin - just until easily sliced.

- Slice steak paper thin, or it will be tough.
- Spray skillet with cooking spray.
- Brown steak with bacon.
- Add onion; cook until onion is softened, but not caramelized.
- Drain part of grease.
- Add seasonings; stir in soup (and mushrooms, if using).
- Cook slowly, uncovered, 20 minutes, stirring frequently.
- Serve over noodles.

324. Stuffed Chops Kraut And Kielbasa Recipe

Serving: 4 | Prep: | Cook: 90mins | Ready in:

Ingredients

- Stuffing
- 1 cup finely chopped onion
- 1 garlic clove, minced
- 2 Tbsp minced fresh sage or 2 teaspoons crumbled dried
- 2 Tbsp unsalted butter
- 3 Tbsp dry bread crumbs
- pork chops, kielbasa, and sauerkraut
- 4 1-inch thick rib pork chops (about 1/2 pound each)
- 1 Tbsp grapeseed oil or canola oil
- 1/2 pound kielbasa, cut diagonally into 3/4-inch-thick slices
- 1 large onion, sliced
- 1 1/2 to 2 pounds sauerkraut, drained, rinsed well, and drained again
- salt and pepper
- 3/4 cup dry white wine
- 1/2 cup chicken broth
- 1 bay leaf
- 2 Tbsp thinly shredded fresh sage leaves or 2 teaspoons crumbled dried
- 1 Tbsp cornstarch dissolved in 2 Tbsp cold water
- 1 Tbsp minced fresh parsley

Direction

- Make the stuffing.
- In a heavy skillet cook the onion, the garlic, and the sage in the butter over low heat, stirring, until the onion is softened.
- Remove the skillet from the heat, and stir in the bread crumbs and salt and pepper to taste.
- Set aside.
- With a paring knife, make a 3/4-inch long horizontal incision along the fat side of each chop and cut a deep wide pocket in the chop by moving the knife back and forth carefully through the incision. (Your butcher will be glad to do this for you)
- Fill the chops with the stuffing.
- Pat the chops dry.
- In a large Dutch oven, heat the oil over medium high heat.
- Brown the chops on both sides, removing the chops from the pan to a plate when done.
- Add the kielbasa slices to the pan, browning them lightly on both sides, removing to another plate when done.
- Drain off all but 1 Tbsp. of fat.
- Cook the onion over medium heat, until softened.
- Add half of the sauerkraut, spreading it to form a layer on the bottom on the pan.
- Cover the sauerkraut with the pork chops.
- Add salt and pepper.
- Add the kielbasa.
- Spread the remaining sauerkraut over the chops and kielbasa.
- Add the wine, broth and bay leaf.
- Bring the liquid to a simmer and simmer the mixture, covered for 1 1/2 hours, or until the chops are tender. Discard the bay leaf. Transfer the chops and the kielbasa to a plate; cover with and keep warm.
- Add the sage to the sauerkraut mixture, bring mixture to a simmer. Add the cornstarch mixture to the sauerkraut then stir, and simmer for 2 minutes.
- Spoon sauerkraut on to a large platter.
- Place the chops and kielbasa on top of the sauerkraut, sprinkle with fresh parsley.

- Serve hot.

325.   Stuffed Flank Steak Recipe

Serving: 3 | Prep: | Cook: 17mins | Ready in:

Ingredients

- Thin Cut beef (or flank steak)
- red pepper
- basil
- goat cheese
- olive oil
- garlic salt
- pepper
- toothpicks or Twine

Direction

- I don't think I actually used flank steak last night, but I found a very thin cut of meat. Came with 3 large pieces. I seasoned both sides generously in garlic salt and pepper.
- Then, add a bunch of basil, a handful of chopped red peppers, and a good amount of goat cheese. Roll up, and seal with a toothpick or kitchen twine.
- I then oiled up a pan, places the 3 rolls of meat on top and drizzled with olive oil. I tossed it into an oven at 350° for about 15-20 minutes.
- It's a quick dish to prep and make, and it looked good! You could plate it with a salad or soup or more veggies or potatoes for a complete meal.

326.   Sun Dried Tomato And Basil Pesto Stuffed Pork Chops Recipe

Serving: 4 | Prep: | Cook: 15mins | Ready in:

Ingredients

- 1 bunch fresh basil
- 4 garlic cloves, halved
- 1 cup sun dried tomatoes, drained and chopped
- 1/2 cup parmegiano reggiano, grated
- 1/2 cup ricotta cheese
- salt and pepper
- 4 thick cut boneless pork chops
- 1 tablespoon olive oil

Direction

- In a food processor add the basil, garlic, sundried tomatoes, Parmigiano reggiano, and ricotta cheese.
- Chop until it forms a dry paste.
- Cut a pocket into the side of each pork chop and stuff with the pesto.
- Add 1 tablespoon olive oil to a skillet over medium high heat.
- Season both sides of the pork chops with salt and pepper.
- Place chops in the skillet and cook 4 to 5 minutes per side.

327.   Sunday Meat Loaf Recipe

Serving: 8 | Prep: | Cook: 75mins | Ready in:

Ingredients

- * 6 ounces garlic-flavored croutons
- * 1/2 teaspoon ground black pepper
- * 1/2 teaspoon cayenne pepper
- * 1 teaspoon chili powder
- * 1 teaspoon dried thyme
- * 1/2 onion, roughly chopped
- * 1 carrot, peeled and broken
- * 3 whole cloves garlic
- * 1/2 red bell pepper
- * 18 ounces ground chuck
- * 18 ounces ground sirloin
- * 1 1/2 teaspoon kosher salt

- * 1 egg
- For the glaze:
- * 1/2 cup ketchup
- * 1 teaspoon ground cumin
- * Dash worcestershire sauce
- * Dash hot pepper sauce
- * 1 tablespoon honey

Direction

- Heat oven to 325 degrees F.
- In a food processor bowl, combine croutons, black pepper, cayenne pepper, chili powder, and thyme.
- Pulse until the mixture is of a fine texture. Place this mixture into a large bowl.
- Combine the onion, carrot, garlic, and red pepper in the food processor bowl. Pulse until the mixture is finely chopped, but not pureed.
- Combine the vegetable mixture, ground sirloin, and ground chuck with the bread crumb mixture.
- Season the meat mixture with the kosher salt. Add the egg and combine thoroughly, but avoid squeezing the meat.
- Pack this mixture into a 10-inch loaf pan to mold the shape of the meatloaf.
- Onto a parchment paper-lined baking sheet, turn the meatloaf out of the pan onto the center of the tray. Insert a temperature probe at a 45 degree angle into the top of the meatloaf.
- Avoid touching the bottom of the tray with the probe. Set the probe for 155 degrees.
- Combine the ketchup, cumin, Worcestershire sauce, hot pepper sauce and honey. Brush the glaze onto the meatloaf after it has been cooking for about 10 minutes.
- As loaf is cooking, drain grease.
- Should cook within 1 hour or possibly 1 1/2.
- Serve with your favorite vegetables and salad.

328. Sweet And Sour Hawaiian Meatballs Recipe

Serving: 6 | Prep: | Cook: 30mins | Ready in:

Ingredients

- Meatballs:
- 2 pound ground chuck (I've used 1 pound ground sirloin and 1 pound unseasoned ground pork with good results, too)
- 1 teaspoon garlic powder
- 1 teaspoon salt
- few shakes of black pepper
- Batter:
- 2 eggs
- 4 tablespoons flour
- salt and pepper, to taste
- For frying meatballs:
- about ½ cup peanut oil for frying
- Sauce:
- 2 cups chicken stock, divided
- 2 large green peppers (or any color or combination - I especially like yellow and red), cut into bite-size pieces
- 1 large sweet onion, cubed
- 1 can sliced water chestnuts
- 3 or more tablespoons cornstarch (use enough to thicken sauce to your liking)
- 3 or more tablespoons soy sauce (to your taste)
- ¼ cup cider vinegar
- ½ cup pineapple juice
- ½ cup white or brown sugar (I like to use ¼ cup of each)
- 2 slices fresh or canned pineapple, cubed
- NOTE: The sauce amounts are really up to your taste buds - I keep tasting this as I go along until I get the balance of sweet and sour and salty that I prefer)

Direction

- Combine meatball ingredients and shape meat into large meatballs (if serving as main course) or cocktail size meatballs (if serving as an appetizer).

- Combine batter ingredients, and whisk together to make a smooth batter.
- Heat peanut oil in large, deep skillet to about 350 degrees.
- Dip meatballs in batter and fry in hot oil until browned on all sides.
- Remove meatballs from skillet; set aside.
- Remove all but about 1 tablespoon oil from pan, and add 1 cup broth, green pepper, onion and water chestnuts; cover and cook over medium heat for 10 minutes.
- NOTE: I've also stir-fried the veggies in the 1 tablespoon oil for a minute or two so they can grab the full flavor from the bottom of the pan, but it's not necessary if you prefer not to fry the veggies - the original recipe just cooks them in the stock.
- Blend in cornstarch to remaining 1 cup broth; stir into skillet mixture, then add soy sauce, vinegar, juice and sugar.
- Cook, stirring constantly, until sauce boils and thickens.
- Return meatballs to skillet; add pineapple chunks, and heat mixture thoroughly.
- For a main course, serve meatballs and sauce over hot rice, or place them in a crockpot to keep warm and serve as an appetizer.

329. Sweet Potato Apple And Pork Packets Recipe

Serving: 4 | Prep: | Cook: 22mins | Ready in:

Ingredients

- 1 large sweet potato, peeled and thinly sliced
- Dash of salt
- 2 Tbsp. butter or margarine
- 4 pork boneless smoked chops
- 2 medium apples, peeled and sliced
- Dash of ground cinnamon
- 4 med. green onions, sliced (1/4 cup)

Direction

- Heat coals or gas grill for direct heat.
- Cut four 18x12-in. pieces of heavy-duty aluminum foil.
- Spray with cooking spray.
- Place one-fourth of the sweet potato slices on one side of each foil piece.
- Sprinkle with salt.
- Cut butter into small pieces; sprinkle over sweet potato.
- Top with smoked pork chop and apples.
- Sprinkle with cinnamon.
- Fold foil over pork mixture so edges meet.
- Seal edges, making tight 1/2-in. fold; fold again.
- Allow space on sides for circulation and expansion.
- Cover and grill packets 4-5-in. from medium heat 20-22 minutes or until sweet potatoes and apples are tender.
- Place packets on plates.
- Cut large X across top of each packet; fold back foil.
- Sprinkle with onions.

330. Swiss Steak Stew Recipe

Serving: 6 | Prep: | Cook: 78mins | Ready in:

Ingredients

- 1/4 cup all-purpose flour
- 1/2 teaspoon salt
- 1 1/2 pounds boneless round steak, cut into bite size pieces
- 1 (14.5 ounce) can Italian-style diced tomatoes
- 3/4 cup water or beef broth
- 3 cups peeled and quartered new red potatoes
- 1 onion, diced
- 1 cup frozen or can corn
- 1 cup frozen or can green beans
- 1 garlic bulb minced
- 1 cup carrots sliced
- 2 to 3 bay leaves
- pepper to taste

Direction

- In medium bowl, combine flour and salt; mix well. Add beef and coat well.
- Coat a nonstick skillet with cooking spray and heat over medium heat. Add beef and cook until browned.
- In a slow cooker, layer potatoes, beef and onion and carrots. Stir tomatoes with juice, water and any remaining flour mixture together. Pour over top. Cover and cook on low setting for 7 to 8 hours or until beef is tender. Add green beans and corn and cook for about 10 to 15 minutes; cook till warm.

---

331. Szechwan Crispy Beef Recipe

Serving: 6 | Prep: | Cook: 15mins | Ready in:

Ingredients

- 1 pound, beef (flank or sirloin steak is good)
- 2 medium, carrots
- 1 tablespoon, minced ginger
- 2 scallions (spring onions, green onions), white parts only
- 1 tablespoon black sauce (or substitute hoisin sauce)
- 3 teaspoons chili paste or chili sauce
- 8 tablespoons peanut (Groundnut) oil
- ¼ teaspoon salt
- 1 tablespoon Shao hsing wine *
- ½ teaspoon sugar
- ½ teaspoon roasted Szechwan peppercorns**

Direction

- Cut the beef across the grain into thin slices less than ¼ inch thick and 2½ to 3 inches long. Wash, peel and julienne the carrots and celery into thin strips about 1/8 of an inch thick and 2½ to 3 inches long. Mince the ginger and cut the scallion into lengths about 2 ½ inches long, and then into thin shreds.

- In a small bowl, combine the black bean sauce and chile paste set to one side, Preheat the wok on a medium high heat for at about 30 seconds. (The wok is ready when you can feel the heat when holding the palm of your hand 2 to 3 inches above the wok's surface).
- Add 1 ½ tablespoons of oil to the pre-heated wok, drizzling down the sides. When the oil is hot, add the carrots and celery, stir fry for a couple of minutes, stirring in the salt, do not brown the veg, remove from the wok.
- Heat 6 tablespoons of oil in the wok over a medium to high heat, when the oil is hot, add the beef and stir fry for about 10 minutes, until the beef is crispy and dark brown and chewy (you will hear the beef sizzle as it dries out). Splash the beef with the rice wine or dry sherry during the later stages of cooking.
- Push the beef up to the sides and drain all but 2 tablespoons from the wok, add the bean sauce and chili paste or sauce mixture. Stir-fry for a few seconds, and then add the ginger and scallions. Stir-fry for a few seconds, until aromatic, then return the carrots and celery to the wok, stir in the sugar and the roasted Szechwan peppercorn, taste and adjust the seasonings if desired.
- * Usually, you shouldn't cook with any wine you wouldn't drink, and you should never ever buy cooking wine in the supermarket. And yet, here I am, telling you to do just that, to buy Chinese shao hsing (or shao xing) wine, for the reason that without it you will certainly not be able to recreate genuine Chinese dishes.
- What I buy from my Chinese supermarket is not the sort of shao hsing wine that is matured and mellow but at less than 2 quid a bottle what would you expect, nevertheless it is perfect for cooking and adding a touch of authentic flavor. You can substitute dry sherry in equal amounts for shao hsing wine, but it's not quite the same. Shao hsing keeps forever in the pantry, stored at room temperature.
- ** How to Roast Szechwan Peppercorns

- This simple technique for roasting Sichuan peppercorns will add an interesting flavor to your meals.
- Time: 10 to 15 minutes
- Method:
- Place Szechwan peppercorns in a frying pan on medium-low heat.
- Heat peppercorns, shaking pan occasionally, until they begin to darken and become fragrant.
- Remove from pan and cool.
- When cooled, grind peppercorns with a mortar and pestle, or crush with a rolling pin.
- Use as called for in a recipe, or store in a covered jar until needed.

---

332.   Tacos Al Pastor Recipe

Serving: 4 | Prep: | Cook: 30mins | Ready in:

Ingredients

- 2lbs of pork steaks, or pork chops bones removed
- 1 1/4 tbs chile powder
- 1/4 tsp of cayenne pepper, I usually add more, but i like it w/a kick
- 1 tsp garlic powder
- 1 bay leaf
- about 1 1/2 tsp salt, or to taste
- 1 tbs adobo sauce
- 1/2 tsp oregano
- 1/2 white onion coarsely chopped
- 1/4 cup of orange juice
- 1/4 cup of natural pineapple juice(or use juice from canned pineapple, not the syrup, but natural juices)
- small pinch of ground cloves, becareful, a little goes a long way, when i say pinch i mean pinch!
- corn tortillas
- cabbage, diced small
- onion diced small
- cilantro diced small
- your favorite chile
- lemon

Direction

- Chop up pork steaks or chops into a smaller chop, not too small, but not to big (kind of how meat is cut at the taco trucks, sorry if poor direction) mix all marinade ingredients together, add all ingredients for marinating to pork. Toss well, and let marinade for at least two hours. Once ready, you can either cook on the stovetop, by adding to a sauce pan(with juices) and letting it cook until cooked, and juices are almost "dried out" add some cooking oil and let it slightly fry. OR you can also bake it, which is what I always do. I line a baking sheet with foil, or use a baking dish, lightly oiled. IF using the foil lined sheet, I brush or drizzle about 2 tbsp. oil so that it gets a "fry". I add the meat with the juices. Bake at 400 for about 20 mins, or until browned, and I like it kind of crisped, the foil might get crisped or kind of burned on the edges but that's because of the sugars in the juices. Just get a spatula and remove meat.
- Mix the cilantro, onion.
- On a griddle, heat hot. Lightly spray tortillas with an oil based cooking spray. And heat on the griddle, top with meat, and add cilantro and onion mix, cabbage, chile, and lemon.

---

333.   Tacos Recipe

Serving: 8 | Prep: | Cook: 10mins | Ready in:

Ingredients

- I like these tacos and they go well with the beans below.
- Carne Asada Tacos
- 1 lb. good quality tender beef - I use a good sirloin. Cut into thin strips about 1 and 1/2 long about 1/4 inch wide.
- small amount of cooking oil.

175

- salt and pepper
- garlic powder
- cilantro and onion chopped for garnish
- 8 flour or corn tortillas - This is allowing 2 ozs. of meat for each taco, but my kids stuff their tacos,so this is just a guideline .
- slices of lime if desired. Can hold tortillas in a cloth towel and warm up in microwave.
- This is the same way I cook steak. I don't like to add a whole lot of different spices to a good cut of steak. I want to taste the steak.
- Open Kitchen windows
- Using a paper towel, coat skillet (very light)with Pam.
- Heat cast iron skillet (10 inch skillet is good) til the pan starts to smoke a little.
- salt, pepper and add garlic to meat.
- add about half the meat and cook til done enough for your taste, if you like it well done put a lid on skillet and lower heat til done enough.
- You can warm tortillas in a dry warm skillet. Let everyone make their own tacos and garnish with cilantro, onion, and a squeeze of lime. Fresh pico de gallo is also an option , I sent that recipe a few weeks ago. Cooking some sliced onions and bell pepper in the skillet after the meat is done is also an option.
- I had lunch with my Sister and Brother-in-law and the restaurant served this rice and it was called white Spanish rice and it is different. I would cut back on the lime a little.
- cilantro and lime rice
- Ingredients
- 3 cups cooked brown rice (or white)
- 1 teaspoon lime zest, minced
- 1-2 tablespoons fresh lime juice
- 2-3 tablespoons cilantro, finely minced
- Directions
- Toss lime zest, lime juice, and cilantro with the cooked rice. Serve warm or cold.
- Bunuelos:
- Fry tortillas (corn is best, but flour could work)til crisp. Drain on paper towels. Then dip in orange juice and dip into a mixture of cinnamon and sugar. This is quick and not

bad. I suppose you could cut the tortillas into chips and fry them.
- bacon avocado Guacamole:
- 4 ripe avocados - peeled, pitted, and mashed
- 4 slices bacon, cooked until crisp, drained and crumbled
- 1 large tomato, seeded and finely chopped
- 1 onion, finely chopped
- 1 clove garlic, minced
- salt and pepper to taste
- 1 dash hot pepper sauce to taste (optional)
- 1 jalapeno De-seeded and De-veined optional,just leave off the hot sauce and add a little mayo.
- Found this recipe online and sounds good, You can Shortcut by using a can of rotel green chilies and tomatoes. Also can use about a tsp.(or to taste) of garlic powder instead of fresh garlic:
- Borracho beans
- Serves 16 (cut in 1/2 or a 1/4, but I like leftover beans and they will hold for a couple of days).
- 4 cups uncooked beans (preferably pinto beans)
- 4 quarts water
- 1 pound bacon or salt pork, chopped (peppered bacon an option, so is a peppered jerky ground in a food processor, if you cant eat pork)
- 2 serrano chilies, chopped (can use jalapeno be sure to De-seed and De-vein)
- 1 cup cilantro, chopped
- 1 tomato, chopped
- 3 cloves garlic, peeled
- 1 teaspoon freshly ground pepper
- salt to taste
- 1 can beer (optional)
- In a large stockpot, combine all ingredients and boil for 2 to 3 hours, until the beans are tender.

Direction

- This is the same way I cook steak. I don't like to add a whole lot of different spices to a good cut of steak. I want to taste the steak.

- Open Kitchen windows
- Using a paper towel, coat skillet (very light) Pam.
- Heat cast iron skillet (10 inch skillet is good) till the pan starts to smoke a little.
- Salt, pepper and add garlic to meat.
- Add about half the meat and cook till done enough for your taste, if you like it well done put a lid on skillet and lower heat till done enough.
- You can warm tortillas in a dry warm skillet. Let everyone make their own tacos and garnish with cilantro, onion, and a squeeze of lime. Fresh pico de gallo is also an option, I sent that recipe a few weeks ago. Cooking some sliced onions and bell peppers in the skillet after the meat is done is also an option.

334. Tennessee Whiskey Pork Chops Recipe

Serving: 4 | Prep: | Cook: 20mins | Ready in:

Ingredients

- 1/2 cup Jack Daniel's Tennessee whiskey
- 1/2 cup apple cider
- 2 tablespoons light brown sugar
- 1 tablespoon Dijon mustard
- 1/8 teaspoon cayenne pepper
- 1/2 teaspoon vanilla extract
- 4 teaspoons cider vinegar
- 4 bone-in, center-cut pork chops, about 1-inch thick
- 2 teaspoons vegetable oil
- 1 tablespoon butter
- salt and pepper to taste
- mashed potatoes to serve under the chops.

Direction

- In a bowl, whisk together whiskey, cider, brown sugar, mustard, cayenne pepper, vanilla and 2 teaspoons vinegar.

- Transfer 1/4 of the whiskey mixture to a gallon-sized Ziploc plastic bag. Reserve remaining marinade.
- Add pork chops, press the air out of the bag, and seal.
- Turn bag to coat the chops with the marinade. Refrigerate for 2 hours.
- Remove chops from the bag and pat with paper towels. Discard that marinade.
- Heat oil in a large skillet over medium-high heat until just beginning to smoke.
- Season chops with salt and pepper and cook until well browned on both side. Using a paring knife, peek into the thickest part of a chop. It should still be a little pink. 3-4 minutes per side usually works.
- Transfer the chops to a plate and cover tightly with aluminum foil.
- Add reserved whiskey mixture to the skillet.
- Bring to a boil and scrape up any browned bits with a wooden spoon.
- Cook until reduced to a thick glaze, 3-5 minutes.
- Reduce heat to medium-low and tip the plate with the chops on over the skillet to drain any juices that accumulated back into the skillet.
- Add remaining 2 tablespoons vinegar, whisk in butter and simmer until glaze is thick and sticky. Watch closely during the last few minutes of cooking. It should have small bubbles when it is the right temperature. (2-3 minutes)
- Remove pan from heat.
- Return chops to skillet and let them rest in the pan until the glaze clings to the pork chops.
- Turn chops occasionally to evenly coat both sides.
- It is best to check with a meat thermometer at the thickest part of the chop. It should read at least 145°. It takes 5-7 minutes.
- Serve over mashed potatoes and pour over remaining glaze.

335. Tequila Chili Marinated Pork Chops Recipe

Serving: 4 | Prep: | Cook: 10mins | Ready in:

Ingredients

- 1 c chopped cilantro
- 4 bone-in rib pork chops(1" thick)
- 2 jalapeno chilies,minced
- 1/4 c lime juice
- 1/4 c vegetable or olive oil
- 3 Tbs tequila or water
- 1 T grated lime peel
- 1 Tbs minced garlic
- 1 Tbs ground chipolte chili or chili powder
- 1 Tbs chopped fresh oregano or 1 tsp dried
- 2 and 1/2 tsp salt
- 1 and 1/2 tsp ground cumin
- 1 tsp pepper
- 1/2 tsp ground allspice

Direction

- Place pork in large resealable bag. Combine all marinade ingredients in a small bowl; pour over pork. Refrigerate overnight, turning bag occasionally.
- Heat grill. Remove pork from marinade, leaving as much marinade on as possible; discard remaining marinade.
- Grill, covered over med. heat 7 to 10 mins, or till no longer pink in centre, turning once. Place on serving platter, cover loosely with foil. Let stand 5 mins.

336. Tex Mex Fajitas Recipe

Serving: 5 | Prep: | Cook: 20mins | Ready in:

Ingredients

- 2 tablespoons olive oil
- 4 cups lean steak strips
- 1 tablespoon chipotle pepper
- 1 cup thinly sliced green bell peppers
- 1-1/2 cups thinly sliced white onions
- 1 tablespoon minced garlic
- 2 tablespoons lemon juice
- 10 large flour tortillas
- 2 cups salsa
- 1 pint sour cream
- 2 cups shredded extra sharp cheddar cheese
- 1 teaspoon salt

Direction

- Put olive oil and garlic in preheated wok.
- Stir-fry steak then add salt and cook until it is almost done.
- Add onions, peppers, juice and chipotle then cook until onions and peppers are limp.
- When finished, pour into bowl and prepare fajitas on tortillas with salsa, sour cream and cheese.

337. Thai Style Ground Beef Recipe

Serving: 6 | Prep: | Cook: 25mins | Ready in:

Ingredients

- cooking spray
- 1 cup thinly sliced leek
- 1 teaspoon bottled minced garlic
- 1 pound lean ground sirloin
- 1 teaspoon red curry paste
- 1 cup tomato sauce
- 1/2 cup light coconut milk
- 1 tablespoon brown sugar
- 1/4 teaspoon grated lime rind
- 1 1/2 tablespoons fresh lime juice
- 1 tablespoon Asian fish sauce
- 3 cups hot cooked short-grain rice
- iceberg lettuce wedges (optional)
- Chopped cilantro
- Chopped green onions (optional)

Direction

- Heat a large skillet over medium-high heat. Coat pan with cooking spray. Add leek; sauté 5 minutes. Add garlic; sauté 1 minute. Add beef; cook 7 minutes or until lightly browned, stirring to crumble. Stir in curry paste and tomato sauce; cook until half of liquid evaporates (about 2 minutes). Add coconut milk, brown sugar, lime rind, lime juice, and Asian fish sauce. Cook 2 minutes or until slightly thickened. Serve with the rice and lettuce wedges, if desired. Garnish with cilantro and green onions, if desired.

---

338.   The Best Greek Lamb Chops Recipe

Serving: 0 | Prep: | Cook: 35mins | Ready in:

Ingredients

- 4 loin lamb chops(I used rib),about 6 oz ea
- 3 large garlic cloves,minced
- 2 TB chopped fresh rosemary
- 1 TB dried thyme
- 1 TB oregano
- 1 c dry red wine
- 1/2 c extra virgin olive oil
- salt and fresh ground black pepper
- 2 lemons,cut in half for garnish

Direction

- Trim, rinse and dry lamb chops.
- Using spice grinder or mortar and pestle, pulverize garlic, rosemary, thyme and oregano. Should be a paste (add a little oil if necessary). Rub lamb chops all over with mixture. Place in single layer in shallow bowl and pour in the wine and olive oil. Cover and marinate for 2 to 24 hours in refrigerator. Let stand at room temperature for 30 minutes before grilling.
- Heat grill to hot. Season chops with salt and pepper. Grill the chops. They will need about 6 to 8 mins for rare,8 to 10 mins for med,12 to 15 mins for well-done Serve with lemon halves and crusty bread

---

339.   Threadgills Chicken Fried Steak Recipe

Serving: 8 | Prep: | Cook: 35mins | Ready in:

Ingredients

- FIRST STAGE: Mix the following and store in a jar where it is cool.
- 1/2 cup kosher salt
- 1/4 cup black pepper , fresh grind
- 2 tablespoons white pepper, fresh grind
- 1 1/2 teasopoons cayenne
- 2 table spoon dry onion flakes
- 1 1/2 tablespoons ground cumin
- 1/4 cup granulated garlic
- 2 tablespoons paprika
- SECOUND STAGE:
- 2 large eggs
- 1 quart whole milk at room temperature
- 1 1/4 cup all purpose flour
- canola oil to fry, at least 2 cups in a flat pan.
- 8 6 ounce beef chuck cutlets, flattened and tenderized with a mallet
- 1/2 teaspoon worcestershire sauce
- 1/4 - 1/2 teaspoon Tabasco sauce
- salt
- black pepper.

Direction

- Whisk eggs and 2 cups mild in a bowl, reserve.
- Mix 2 teaspoons of the seasoning and 2 cups flour in a bowl, reserve.
- Heat oil in a large cast iron skillet to 350
- Dredge each beef cutlet in flour
- Dip in egg wash, let extra drip off
- Dredge in flour again, shake off extra flour

- Use LONG tongs to lower into oil
- Cook until golden brown about 3-4 minutes, flip cook another 3 minutes remove with a spider, place on paper towel to drain
- Cook all, keep warm
- GRAVY
- Drain all but 3 tablespoons oil from skillet.
- Heat the oil over medium stir in the 1/4 cup flour, keep stirring... make a WHITE roux.
- Gradually add the remaining 2 cups milk, slowly. Stir until it is as thick as you like.
- Remove from heat season with Worcestershire, Tabasco, salt and pepper.
- Place a cutlet on each plate, drench with gravy. Serve with potatoes and veggie.
- Now when they make it there.... they deep fry it... I do the same at home. They also make the gravy 16, gallons at time and add roasted bone marrow to that... I have used the packaged white gravy that I get from a restaurant supply company or Sam's as it speeds things up, Just season it up like listed above. But, this is how they listed it and I wanted to share...
- YOU CAN MAKE THESE, FREEZE ON A WAXED PAPER LINED COOKIE SHEET. WHEN FROZEN PUT IN ZIP BAG. DO NOT THAW TO FRY. ADD 2-4 MINUTES IN A DEEP FRYER.
- So take off your boots, grab a Lone Star beer and ENJOY LIFE! And if you're down Texas way.... stop in and try the REAL thing!

---

340. Three Cheese Black Bean Chili With Cheddar Crust Recipe

Serving: 8 | Prep: | Cook: 120mins | Ready in:

Ingredients

- *I like to add lean ground sirloin
- 2 large onions, diced
- 2 tbsp olive oil
- 1/4 cup tomato paste
- 1 tbsp chili powder
- 1 tbsp cocoa powder
- 1 tsp cumin seed
- 3 medium carrots, chopped
- 2 ribs celery, sliced
- 3 small jalapeño peppers, seeded and minced
- 1 28-ounce can crushed tomatoes
- 2 cups cooked or canned black beans, rinsed
- 6-12oz. tomato juice
- 1 cup (4 oz.) shredded mozzarella cheese
- 1 cup (4 oz.) reduced fat shredded monterey jack cheese
- 1 cup (4 oz.) shredded sharp cheddar cheese

Direction

- Sauté onions, carrots and celery in oil over medium high heat in large saucepan until translucent, about three minutes.
- Add jalapeño, tomato paste, chili powder, cocoa powder, and cumin, and cook until mixture caramelizes to a dark brown, about ten minutes.
- Add crushed tomatoes and beans.
- Stir in tomato juice to your preferred consistency.
- Simmer for at least an hour, but only up to two hours.
- Transfer to large (or individual) oven-proof dish (es).
- Preheat broiler.
- Stir Mozzarella and Monterey Jack cheese into chili and top with shredded Cheddar.
- Broil until cheese is bubbly, about four minutes.

---

341. Three Pepper Roasted Pork Chops Recipe

Serving: 4 | Prep: | Cook: 18mins | Ready in:

Ingredients

- 8 thin sliced center pork chops or breakfast chops

- 1 green bell pepper
- 1 yellow bell pepper
- 1 red bell pepper
- 1/2 cup chicken broth
- 1/4 cup white wine
- garlic salt to taste
- cracked black pepper to taste
- 1 large onion, sliced
- 1 cup thinly sliced celery
- 2 cloves garlic, thinly sliced
- 2 teaspoons olive oil, divided
- dash of creole seasoning

Direction

- Preheat oven to 400 degrees.
- Drizzle 1 teaspoon of the oil in a large cookie sheet or pan
- In a large bowl, mix together the peppers, onion, garlic, and celery.
- Add remaining 1 teaspoon oil and toss.
- Spoon onto prepared cookie sheet.
- Season pork with seasoning to taste and place over vegetables.'
- Roast in 400 degree oven for 10 minutes
- Turn pork chops and continue to roast for an additional 5 minutes.
- Remove pan and spoor broth and wine over pork
- Cover with foil and cook an additional 3 to 5 minutes.
- Serve

342. Top Sirloin Meatloaf Mashed Potatoes And Baby Carrots Recipe

Serving: 10 | Prep: | Cook: 60mins |Ready in:

Ingredients

- 5 pounds ground top sirloin
- 5 whole eggs beaten
- 3 cups mushrooms chopped
- 1/2 cup onions chopped
- 1/4 cup minced garlic
- 1/4 cup fresh thyme
- 1/2 cup ketchup
- 1/4 cup soy sauce
- 1/4 cup worcestershire sauce
- 1/4 cup chili sauce
- 1/4 cup butter
- 1 teaspoon salt
- 1 teaspoon pepper
- Potatoes:
- 1/4 pound yukon gold potatoes
- 1/2 cup grated horseradish
- 1 cup soft butter
- 1 teaspoon salt
- 1 teaspoon white pepper
- Baby Carrots:
- 32 baby carrots
- 1 teaspoon honey
- 2 ounces butter
- 1/2 cup water
- 1 teaspoon salt
- 1 teaspoon white pepper

Direction

- Cook onion and garlic with butter until done then add fresh thyme leaves and mushrooms.
- Cook another 5 minutes then let cool off and mix with remaining meatloaf ingredients.
- Place mixture in oiled loaf pans and cook at 350 for 1 hour.
- For potatoes cook unpeeled potatoes in salted water until done.
- Drain and mash in large pot with all other ingredients or press through a food mill.
- Cook carrots with all other ingredients until water is evaporated or until done.

343. Tortellini Alfredo With Fresh Spinach

Serving: 4 | Prep: | Cook: 60mins |Ready in:

Ingredients

- 2 quarts water
- 1 teaspoon salt
- 1 (16 ounce) package dry tortellini
- 1 (8 ounce) package cream cheese, cubed
- 1 cup whole milk
- ½ stick butter
- ¼ cup grated Parmesan cheese
- 2 teaspoons garlic powder
- 1 teaspoon Italian seasoning
- salt and ground black pepper to taste
- 2 cups fresh spinach
- 1 tomato, diced
- 2 tablespoons grated Parmesan cheese, or to taste

Direction

- Fill a large pot with 2 quarts water and 1 teaspoon salt and bring to a rolling boil; stir in tortellini and return to a boil. Cook uncovered, stirring occasionally, until the tortellini float to the top and the filling is hot, 10 to 12 minutes.
- Meanwhile, heat cream cheese, milk, butter, 1/4 cup Parmesan cheese, garlic powder, Italian seasoning, salt, and pepper in a large saucepan over medium heat; stir until cheeses have melted and sauce is smooth, 5 to 7 minutes. Reduce heat to low, add spinach, and stir occasionally until spinach has wilted, about 3 minutes.
- Drain tortellini, add to the sauce, and stir to combine. Garnish with tomato and remaining Parmesan cheese.
- Nutrition Facts
- Per Serving:
- 366.1 calories; protein 12.8g 26% DV; carbohydrates 29.8g 10% DV; fat 22.6g 35% DV; cholesterol 76.9mg 26% DV; sodium 727.7mg 29% DV.

344.   Tortilla Casserole Recipe

Serving: 6 | Prep: | Cook: 75mins |Ready in:

Ingredients

- 1 pound(s) boneless sirloin steak
- 6 tablespoon(s) lime juice
- 1/2 teaspoon(s) ancho chile pepper powder
- 1/4 teaspoon(s) salt
- 1 large red onion, cut into 1/2-inch slices
- 2 ear(s) (about 1 1/4 cups) fresh corn
- 2 tablespoon(s) olive oil
- 1 can(s) (15-ounce) black beans
- 1 can(s) (15-ounce) kidney beans
- 2 jalapeño peppers, seeded and sliced seeded into 1/8-inch rounds
- 1 teaspoon(s) chopped chipotle pepper
- 1/4 cup(s) low-sodium chicken broth
- 1/2 teaspoon(s) lime zest
- 6 corn tortillas
- 2 cup(s) monterey jack cheese, shredded
- 4 tomatoes, cut into 1/4-inch slices
- 1 1/2 teaspoon(s) chopped oregano

Direction

- Preheat grill to medium-high heat.
- Marinate the steak with 2 tablespoons of the lime juice, Ancho powder, and salt for 30 minutes.
- Toss the onion and corn in olive oil. Grill onion until tender, corn until golden brown, and steak to rare.
- Cut steak into 3/4-inch pieces, chop onion, cut kernels from the cob, and transfer all to a large bowl.
- Preheat oven to 400 degrees F.
- Toss beans, both peppers, chicken broth, remaining lime juice, and lime zest with the steak.
- Place 2 tortillas in the bottom of a 9-inch by 13-inch casserole dish and sprinkle with 3/4 cup of the cheese.
- Spoon 1/3 of the steak and bean mixture evenly over the cheese and top with 1/3 of the tomato slices and 1/2 teaspoon of oregano.
- Repeat to complete 3 layers, cover with aluminum foil, and bake for 20 minutes.
- Bake, uncovered, for 10 more minutes.
- Serve immediately.

345. Tyler Florences New York Strip Steak With Brandied Mushrooms And Fresh Thyme Recipe

Serving: 4 | Prep: | Cook: 15mins | Ready in:

Ingredients

- 4 New York strip steaks, each about 1 1/2 inches thick
- extra-virgin olive oil
- kosher salt and freshly ground black pepper
- 2 pounds wild mushrooms, trimmed, brushed clean with a towel and stemmed, caps left whole
- Leaves from 2 sprigs fresh thyme
- 2 cloves garlic, chopped
- 1/4 cup brandy
- 1/2 cup heavy cream

Direction

- Heat 2 tablespoons oil in a large sauté pan over medium-high heat until smoking.
- Sprinkle the steaks all over with salt and pepper.
- Put the steaks in the pan and cook, turning to brown all sides completely, until medium-rare, 8 to 10 minutes depending on how thick the steaks are.
- Remove the steaks to a platter with tongs and cover loosely with a tent of aluminum foil to keep the meat warm while you make the sauce.
- Put the sauté pan back over medium-high heat and add 1/4 cup olive oil.
- When the oil is smoking, add the mushrooms and cook, stirring, about 10 minutes, until golden brown.
- Then add the thyme and garlic, and season well with salt and pepper.

- Toss a few more times to cook the garlic, then dump the mushrooms out onto a platter.
- Take the pan off the heat, add the brandy, and cook until almost evaporated.
- Add the cream and cook that down 2 to 3 minutes until reduced by about one-half and thickened.
- Return the mushrooms to the pan with whatever juices have collected on the platter and simmer the whole thing another 2 minutes until thickened again.
- Season with salt and pepper.
- Slice the steak thin against the grain. Taste the sauce for salt and pepper and serve.

346. Tylers Ultimate Flank Steak Fajitas And Guacamole Recipe

Serving: 6 | Prep: | Cook: 9mins | Ready in:

Ingredients

- marinade (Mojo):
- 1 orange, juiced
- 2 limes, juiced
- 4 tablespoons olive oil
- 2 garlic cloves, roughly chopped
- 3 chipolte chiles, in adobo sauce
- 3 tablespoon roughly chopped fresh cilantro leaves
- 1 teaspoon ground cumin
- 1 teaspoon salt
- Fajitas
- 2 1/4 pounds skirt or flank steak, trimmed of fat cut into thirds or 8-inch pieces
- salt and pepper
- 2 red bell peppers, thinly sliced
- 1 large onion, thinly sliced
- lime juice, olive oil, optional
- 12 flour tortillas, warm
- guacamole, recipe follows
- Good quality store bought salsa
- Guacamole:

- 5 ripe hass avocados
- 3 to 4 limes, juiced
- 1/2 small onion, chopped
- 1 small garlic clove, minced
- 1 serrano chile, chopped
- 1 big handful fresh cilantro leaves, roughly chopped
- kosher salt and freshly ground black pepper
- Drizzle olive oil

Direction

- In a small 2 cup measuring cup, or something similar size and shape, combine all the marinade ingredients. Using a blender, puree the marinade until smooth. Transfer to a re-sealable plastic bag and add the steak, seal and shake to coat. Refrigerate the beef for 2 to 4 hours to tenderize and flavour the beef.
- Preheat a ridged grill pan on high heat.
- Drain the marinade from the beef.
- Lightly oil the grill or grill pan.
- Season liberally with salt and freshly ground black pepper.
- Grill the steak over medium-high heat and cook for 4 minutes on each side and then transfer to a cutting board and let rest. Depending on the size of your grill pan you may need to cook in batches.
- Once the beef is off the grill pan and resting, add the bell peppers and onions tossed with lime juice and olive oil, if using. Grill the mixture for 7 to 8 minutes until the vegetables are just barely limp.
- While the peppers and onions are cooking, heat up the tortillas. Turn any free burners on a medium low flame. Place a tortilla on each flame and let it char about 30 seconds to 1 minute, flip the tortilla and repeat on the second side. Once heated and charred remove the tortilla to a clean tea towel and wrap to keep warm. Repeat until you have warmed all of your tortillas.
- You can also heat your tortillas in a microwave, lightly dampen a tea towel with some water, wrap the tortillas in the damp towel and heat in the microwave for about 1 minute. Check to see if they are warm, if not repeat the heating at 1 minute intervals until they are warm and pliable.
- Thinly slice the steak against the grain on a diagonal.
- Guacamole:
- Halve and pit the avocados.
- With a tablespoon, scoop out the flesh into a mixing bowl. Mash the avocados with a fork, leaving them still a bit chunky.
- Add all of the rest of the ingredients, and fold everything together.
- Lay a piece of plastic wrap directly on the surface of the guacamole so it doesn't brown and refrigerate for at least 1 hour before serving.
- To serve:
- Spread some guacamole on a tortilla, top with a few slices of steak, peppers and onions, and salsa. Roll up the tortilla to enclose the filling.
- May also be served with sour cream, ripe olives, chopped tomatoes and shredded cheese.

347.   Upside Down Shepherds Pie Recipe

Serving: 6 | Prep: | Cook: 20mins | Ready in:

Ingredients

- 2 pounds yukon gold potatoes, cut in chunks
- 2 tablespoons milk
- 2 tablespoons butter
- 1 teaspoon salt, divided
- 1/2 teaspoon fresh ground black pepper, divided
- 1 pound ground sirloin
- 3/4 cup chopped onion
- 2 garlic cloves, minced
- 1 tablespoon all-purpose flour
- 1/2 cup corn kernels
- 1/2 cup beef broth
- 1/4 cup ketchup

- 1 tablespoon worcestershire sauce
- 1/3 cup shredded white cheddar cheese

Direction

- In a large pot of salted water, add potatoes - bring to a boil and cook until tender, about 15 minutes. Drain off water and place potatoes back in the hot pan to evaporate some of the excess water. Add milk, butter, 1/2 teaspoon salt and 1/4 teaspoon pepper - mash until desired consistency. Scoop the mixture into a 2 quart casserole dish lightly coated with non-stick spray. Spray to an even thickness - use damp fingers to form a little lip around the edge to hold in the meat mixture.
- Meanwhile, in a large skillet over medium-high, add beef and onions - cook until the beef has cooked through and the onions soften, about 5 to 7 minutes. Add garlic and cook until fragrant, about 1 minute. Sprinkle with flour and continue to cook, stirring, for 2 more minutes.
- Stir in corn, stock, ketchup, Worcestershire, remaining salt and pepper. Reduce heat to medium and cook, stirring often, for 10 minutes.
- Preheat broiler.
- Scoop the meat mixture over the potatoes and scatter the top with cheese. Place under the broiler until the cheese is bubbly and melted.

---

348. Uvich Spanish Rice Recipe

Serving: 4 | Prep: | Cook: 60mins |Ready in:

Ingredients

- 4 bone-in pork chops about 3/4" thick
- 1 cup uncooked white rice (not converted)
- 1 yellow onion, chopped
- 4 cloves garlic, minced or crushed
- 2 celery stalks, diced
- 1 15 oz. can tomato sauce

- 1 small can diced tomatoes with juices
- 1 teaspoon Italian seasoning
- sprinkle of crushed red pepper flakes, or to taste
- salt and pepper to taste
- 1 15 oz. (tomato sauce can) of water
- 1 tablespoon butter
- 1 tablespoon vegetable or olive oil
- (or preferably two tablespoons Ghee to replace the butter and oil)

Direction

- Pre-heat oven to 350
- In a Dutch oven, heat butter and oil or ghee.
- Generously salt and pepper both sides of all chops. Brown the chops on both sides in the butter and oil (or ghee) slowly on medium heat. After they are golden brown on both sides, remove chops from pan to a large plate. Add onions, celery and garlic to Dutch oven and sauté until soft and just starting to brown, scraping any browned bits up while stirring.
- Pour in rice, tomato sauce, and diced tomatoes with juices, water, Italian seasoning, red pepper flakes, salt and pepper. Stir.
- Return chops to Dutch oven, pushing them into the rice mixture gently.
- Cover tightly and cook in the oven for one hour.

---

349. Vivacious Saucy Steak Skillet Recipe

Serving: 4 | Prep: | Cook: 30mins |Ready in:

Ingredients

- 1 pound boneless round steak
- 1/4 cup all-purpose flour
- 1 tablespoon vegetable oil
- 1 large white onion chopped
- 1/4 cup catsup
- 1 tablespoon worcestershire sauce
- 1 bell pepper diced

- 1 teaspoon salt
- 1/2 teaspoon dried mushrooms
- 1 package frozen green beans
- 1 jar sliced pimientos drained
- 2 potatoes boiled reserving liquid

Direction

- Coat beef with flour and pound into meat then brown in oil in heavy skillet.
- Push beef aside and cook and stir onions in oil until tender.
- Drain.
- Add enough water to potato liquid to measure one cup then mix with peppers, salt, Worcestershire sauce, marjoram and pepper.
- Pour over meat and add onions then heat to boiling and reduce heat.
- Cover and simmer until beef is tender.
- Rinse beans under running cold water and separate.
- Add potatoes, beans and pimentos to skillet then heat to boiling then reduce heat.
- Cover and simmer until beans are tender.

---

350.   W W Smothered Steak With Mushrooms And Onions Recipe

Serving: 4 | Prep: | Cook: 25mins | Ready in:

Ingredients

- 1 lb ground sirloin
- 1/2 C plain breadcrumbs
- 1/4 tsp salt
- 1/4 tsp pepper
- 1 (8 oz) pkg fresh mushrooms, sliced
- 1 lrg onion cut in half vertically and then sliced
- 1 envelope of brown gravy mix (Knorr Classic Brown is best)
- 1 cup of water (1 1/2 Cups if using Knorr)

Direction

- Combine first 4 ingredients in a bowl and mix well
- Divide into 4 equal portions and shape into 1/2 thick patty
- Heat a large, non-stick skillet until hot. Add patties; cook until done, turning once
- Remove from skillet; set aside
- Increase heat to medium high
- Add mushrooms and onions to skillet; sauté 10 minutes or until very tender
- Combine gravy and water, whisk together well. Add gravy mixture to skillet and cook until thickened, about 3 minutes, stirring constantly
- Return patties to skillet; cook 2 minutes or until heated through
- Serving is 1 patty and 2/3 C gravy
- 6 points
- Diabetic exchanges; 1 starch, 1 veg. 3 L meat
- 268 calories

---

351.   Wacky Ingredients But Oh So Good Pork Chops With Savory And Tangy Gravy Recipe

Serving: 4 | Prep: | Cook: 60mins | Ready in:

Ingredients

- 4 pork chops (1 or more per person depending upon hunger-meter and size of pork chop)(Can be bone in, or boneless pork chops)
- kosher salt and Fresh Cracked ground pepper
- 3/4 cup flour
- For Sauce: here goes anything wacky in your fridge
- 5 tablespoons ketchup
- 5 tablespoons grape jelly (yes jelly - can be strawberry or any jelly you have in fridge)
- 3 tablespoons low sodium soy sauce
- 3 tablespoons mustard
- 1 tablespoon dry mustard

- 2 tablespoons worcestershire sauce
- 3 fresh garlic cloves minced
- 2 tablespoon herbes de Province
- (if you don't have herbs de province then add 1/2 teaspoon dried time, 1/2 teaspoon dried tarragon, 1/4 teaspoon rosemary and up your pepper)
- 1/2 to 1 cup water
- 1/2 cup red wine (optional)
- 2 tablespoons olive oil & 1 tablespoon butter
- Equipment needed: Deep skillet with lid, 2 bowls: one for sauce and one for mixing up season flour.

Direction

- Take pork chops out of fridge, let come to room temperature and sprinkle generously on both sides with salt and ground pepper - set aside for now.
- Take one bowl, add dry mustard and a dash of salt and pepper to 3/4 cup of flour and mix till incorporated. This is to be used to dredge your pork chops in.
- With other bowl, add ketchup, grape jelly, soy sauce, wet mustard, Worcestershire sauce, minced garlic and all herbs as listed.
- Add 1/2 cup water to sauce and mix till blended well. It maybe that some of the jelly didn't break down - that's ok, it will while cooking.
- Grab the heavy-duty skillet of yours, turn on the heat to a medium-high beneath the skillet and let get quite hot.
- While skillet is getting hot, grab those pork chops and dredge in seasoned flour, shake off excess.
- Put olive oil in skillet first, then add butter. If pan is ready, place pork chops into skillet.
- Do not move, (no, not you, the pork chops of course, let them get caramelized on one side - it may take up to five minutes)
- Turn pork chops over and let them brown for three minutes.
- Take 1/2 cup of wine and carefully pour into skillet to deglaze. If not using the red wine (or

instead simply drinking it, just skip this step and go to next - no one will know)
- Then add sauce from bowl directly into skillet, turn down the heat from under skillet to be on low heat and let simmer at least 45 minutes
- Put lid on skillet while your dish simmers. This dish only gets better as the more time you simmer the dish, the tenderer your pork will be. I usually let it simmer for 1.5 hours.
- When ready, serve over egg noodles (1st choice) or penne (2nd choice) or rice. Reserve sauce for when you may reheat dish for the next day - delicious!

352.   Walking Tacos Recipe

Serving: 24 | Prep: | Cook: 10mins |Ready in:

Ingredients

- 1½ pound ground sirloin
- 1½ pound ground chuck
- 3 (1.25 ounce) packages taco seasoning mix
- 3 cups water or beef broth
- 24 INDIVIDUAL SIZE bags of tortilla chips
- TOPPING INGREDIENTS:
- 3 (15 ounce) cans black beans, seasoned or regular
- 6 cups finely shredded lettuce
- 3 cups salsa and/or taco sauce
- 3 pints sour cream
- 3 cups guacamole
- 6 cups grated Mexican Four cheese (or any other cheese)
- 3 cups finely diced tomato
- 3 cups finely diced onion
- 2 cups sliced black olives
- plenty of sliced jalapenos

Direction

- Fry ground meat in a large skillet.
- When meat is browned, add taco seasoning mix and water or broth.

- Simmer for about 10 minutes, until liquid is reduced down.
- This is where the fun begins!
- Keep the meat mixture hot in a crock-pot.
- Have all the topping ingredients next to the crockpot, so each person can make their own "walking taco".
- Instruct everyone to crush an individual size bag of taco chips for themselves, then open it up and start adding in all the toppings they want (or can get in the bag), starting with the meat first.
- When they have their toppings in the bag, fold over the top and shake vigorously. Open the bag, grab a fork, and walk around with your meal in your hand!

353.   Weiner Schnitzel Recipe

Serving: 6 | Prep: | Cook: 5mins | Ready in:

Ingredients

- thin veal cutlets (you can use skirt steak or pork)
- egg
- heavy cream or half and half
- all-purpose flour
- seasoning salt
- pepper
- cooking oil of choice (I use vegetable)

Direction

- Pound your cutlets flat with the raised side of your meat tenderizer. I usually pound three times on each side, covering the whole cutlet.
- Mix eggs and cream (the amounts depend on how many cutlets you have, I had 12, so I used 6 eggs and about a cup of cream) in large bowl and set near cooking area.
- Mix seasoning salt into flour in large bowl until it has a pinkish cast, add pepper to taste, and set near cooking area.

- Preheat oil in large skillet. You will need enough oil to cover the cutlet, or you can use a deep fryer.
- Dip cutlet in flour, coating both sides, then the egg and cream mixture, coating both sides, and then again into the flour, covering it. Drop into oil immediately after coating.
- If you are using good veal cutlets, you really only have to let the coating get golden brown on both sides (about three minutes) before removing from the oil. For lower grades of beef or for pork, you want to let them go about five or six, but it doesn't take long because they're very thin.
- My mother made a mushroom Paprikash sauce for me to pour over them, they are good with burgundy mushroom sauce as well, and can also stand alone without any sauce.

354.   Whiskey Pork Chops With Glazed Apples And Onions Recipe

Serving: 4 | Prep: | Cook: 30mins | Ready in:

Ingredients

- 1 tablespoon brown sugar
- 1/2 cup apple cider
- 1-1/2 teaspoons Dijon mustard
- 2 tablespoons whiskey
- 1 teaspoon grated lemon rind
- 1/8 teaspoon red chili flakes
- 2 tablespoons cider vinegar
- 1/4 teaspoon dry rubbed sage
- 4 thick cut loin pork chops
- 2 tablespoons olive oil
- 1/2 teaspoon salt
- 1 medium granny smith apple with skin cored and thinly sliced
- 3/4 cup thinly sliced red onion
- 3 tablespoons whiskey
- fresh sage leaves for garnish

Direction

- Place brown sugar, cider, mustard, whiskey, rind, chili flakes, vinegar and sage in plastic bag.
- Add pork chops then seal and shake around to distribute marinade.
- Refrigerate several hours.
- When ready to cook remove pork chops from marinade and reserve marinade.
- Heat 1 tablespoon olive oil in large non-stick pan over high heat.
- Season pork chops on each side with salt then place in pan and brown well 4 minutes per side.
- Place pan of pork chops in oven and continue cooking at 375 for 20 minutes.
- Remove chops to platter and keep warm.
- Meanwhile pour any juices from chop pan into reserved marinade.
- Place pan back on stove and heat remaining olive oil over medium high heat.
- Add apple and onion then cook stirring often about 5 minutes.
- Add whiskey and marinade then increase heat to high and cook 2 minutes longer.
- Remove from heat then serve spooned over chops and garnished with fresh sage.

---

355. Wienerschnitzel Breaded Veal Cutlet Recipe

Serving: 4 | Prep: | Cook: 45mins | Ready in:

Ingredients

- 4 thin boneless pork chops or veal chops (veal chops are better)
- 1/2 c. oil (I use olive oil)
- 3/4 c. fine bread crumbs
- 2 eggs
- salt & pepper
- 2 lemons

Direction

- Heat the oil in a large skillet at medium high heat. Place each chop between two sheets of plastic and pound with the smooth side of a meat tenderizer until thin (1/4" - 3/8"). Beat the two eggs in a bowl that is wide enough to dip the meat into. Spread the bread crumbs onto a plate or flat surface. Take each cutlet, season with salt and pepper and dip both sides of meat into eggs to coat. Then coat the entire cutlet with the bread crumbs. Place in hot oil and cook on both sides until golden brown. It only takes about 1-2 minutes per side. Serve each cutlet with half a lemon on the side. Some people go ahead and squeeze the lemon onto the schnitzel before serving. I prefer to squeeze the lemon juice onto the meat just before I eat it. I prefer to serve with half a lemon, rather than wedges, because it is not as messy when you squeeze it. (Which you would appreciate if you have paper cut)!
- ** Some people serve this with a fried egg placed on top of the schnitzel.

---

356. Wild Mushroom And Emmentaler Stuffed Pork Chops Marinated French Green Beans Asian Pear Chutney Recipe

Serving: 4 | Prep: | Cook: 25mins | Ready in:

Ingredients

- For Asian pear Chutney:
- 2 Asian pears (or Bosc or Bartlett), cored and diced small
- 1/2 cup fresh cranberries (or sub canned whole berry cranberry sauce if you can't find fresh)
- 1/2 cup Medjool dates, pitted and coarsely chopped
- 1/2 cup water (omit if using canned cranberry)
- 1/2 cup rice wine vinegar
- 3 tablespoons sugar (or more to taste)

- 1 tablespoon minced fresh ginger
- 1 cinnamon stick, broken in half
- 1/2 teaspoon cloves
- 1/2 teaspoon ground cayenne pepper
- kosher salt, to taste
- Pork Chops:
- 4 boneless, all natural pork loin chops-1" thick with pockets for stuffing
- kosher salt, white pepper
- 2 tablespoons unsalted butter
- 1 cup canola oil (or light olive oil)
- Filling:
- 1 cup shredded Emmentaler swiss cheese (or gruyere if you prefer)
- 2 tablespoons butter
- 1 shallot, chopped
- 2 cups assorted wild mushrooms (or just cremini mushrooms)
- 3 sprigs fresh thyme leaves
- kosher salt, white pepper to taste
- Breading:
- 1 1/2 cups all purpose flour
- 2 eggs plus 2 tablespoons water, beaten
- 1 1/2 cups panko (Japanese bread crumbs)
- Marinated French Green Beans:
- 1 pound French green beans, stem end removed
- 1 shallot, finely sliced
- 1/4 cup extra virgin olive oil
- 1 tablespoon champagne vinegar (or white wine vinegar)
- 2 tablespoons lemon juice
- 1 tablespoon sugar
- 1 teaspoon lemon zest
- 1 teaspoon Dijon mustard
- 2 tablespoons fresh tarragon, chopped
- kosher salt to taste

Direction

- Chutney: Combine all ingredients in a saucepan over medium heat. Cook for 20 minutes, stirring frequently, to blend flavours. Remove from the heat, cool and remove cinnamon stick.
- Stuffed Pork Chops: Preheat oven to 350 degrees. Make pockets in chops and lay them out on cutting board. Cover loosely with plastic wrap and with a mallet (or rolling pin) pound out the chops until 1 inch thick. Season with kosher salt and white pepper on each side.
- Melt butter in non-stick sauté pan; add mushrooms and shallots, Sauté until mushrooms are slightly caramelized. Season with thyme, salt and white pepper. Allow to cool slightly then add grated cheese.
- Stuff each pork chop pocket with about 1/4 cups of stuffing. Coat each one with flour, dip in beaten egg then panko, pressing chops down with your hand so the breadcrumbs adhere. Refrigerate for at least 30 minutes.
- Melt butter and canola oil in large skillet over med-high heat. Add pork chops and brown on each side, about 3-4 min per side or until golden brown. Transfer pork chops to lined baking sheet, bake for 15 minutes in oven or until the cheese starts to ooze out.
- French Green Beans:
- Cook beans in large pot of boiling salted water until crisp-tender, about 1 1/2 to 3 minutes. Drain. Transfer to bowl of ice water to cool. Drain and dry well with a clean towel.
- Combine the shallots, olive oil, vinegar, lemon juice, zest sugar, Dijon and tarragon in a small bowl. Toss the beans with the vinaigrette in a bowl, refrigerate until serving.
- To plate: Cut each pork chop in half at an angle, place on serving plate with side of French Marinated Green Beans and Asian Pear chutney

357.   Winey Ribeyes Recipe

Serving: 2 | Prep: | Cook: 20mins |Ready in:

Ingredients

- 2 ribeyes
- 1/2 cup red wine
- 1 tablespoon vinegar
- 1/4 cup grainy mustard

- 1/4 cup grated white onion
- 1 teaspoon crushed garlic
- 1/4 cup dark brown sugar firmly packed
- 1 teaspoon salt
- 2 teaspoons freshly ground black pepper
- 1 teaspoon worcestershire sauce
- 1 teaspoon cayenne pepper
- 1 cup mushrooms sliced
- 1/4 cup chopped white onions
- 1 tablespoon butter

Direction

- Combine wine, vinegar, mustard, onion, garlic, brown sugar, salt, pepper, Worcestershire and cayenne pepper and blend well.
- Marinate ribeyes in marinade in the refrigerator at least 2 hours.
- Remove from marinade and grill 8 minutes on each side.
- Sauté mushrooms and onions in butter.
- Top ribeyes with mushroom mixture right before serving.

358. Wood Smoked Tri Tip Beef With Sicilian Herb Sauce Recipe

Serving: 6 | Prep: | Cook: | Ready in:

Ingredients

- • 3 tablespoons fresh thyme leaves
- • 2 garlic cloves, peeled
- • 1 1/2 teaspoons dried oregano
- • 1 teaspoon coarse kosher salt or coarse sea salt
- • 2 tablespoons fresh lemon juice
- • 1/2 cup extra-virgin olive oil
- • 1 well-trimmed 2 1/2- to 2 3/4-pound tri-tip beef roast
- 3 cups oak, mesquite, or hickory wood chips, soaked in water 1 hour and drained

Direction

- Blend thyme leaves, garlic cloves, dried oregano, and coarse salt in mini processor until garlic is finely chopped. With processor running, gradually add lemon juice, then olive oil. Season herb sauce to taste with pepper and transfer to bowl. DO AHEAD Can be made 1 day ahead. Cover and chill. Bring to room temperature before using.
- Sprinkle roast generously on both sides with salt and freshly ground black pepper. Let stand at least 30 minutes and up to 2 hours.
- Prepare barbecue (medium-high heat).
- If using gas grill:
- Wrap wood chips in foil; pierce foil all over with fork. Remove top grill rack, place foil packet directly on burner, and replace grill rack. Place roast over packet and grill uncovered 6 minutes (wood in foil will begin to smoke). Turn roast over. Move to spot on grill where heat is indirect and medium-hot. Cover grill and cook until thermometer inserted into thickest part of roast registers 128°F to 135°F for medium-rare, turning roast occasionally, about 13 minutes.
- If using charcoal grill:
- Sprinkle wood chips over coals and place roast on rack. Cook roast uncovered 7 minutes. Turn roast over. Move roast to spot on grill where heat is indirect and medium-hot. Cover grill and cook until thermometer inserted into thickest part of roast registers 128°F to 135°F for medium-rare, turning roast occasionally, about 13 minutes.
- Transfer roast to platter. Let stand 10 minutes. Thinly slice roast across grain. Serve, passing sauce separately.

359. Zucchini Casserole Funeral Food Recipe

Serving: 10 | Prep: | Cook: 55mins | Ready in:

Ingredients

- 6 small to medium zucchini, scrubbed sliced in coins
- 1/2 tablespoon of oil
- 1 medium onion, chopped medium
- 2 cloves of garlic, minced
- 1 tablespoon of worchestershire sauce
- 1/2 teaspoon of dried oregano
- 1/2 teaspoon of dried basil
- 8 to 10 passes of a fresh nutmeg on a microplane or rasp
- 2 tbsp. of flour
- 1/4 cup of beef broth
- 1 lb. of ground sirloin or chuck (drain it well)
- 2 lbs. of small curd cottage cheese, drained well
- some grated lemon rind
- 1 beaten egg
- 1/2 teaspoon of pepper
- 1/2 teaspoon of salt
- 2 tablespoons of chopped parsley
- 8 ounces of sharp cheddar cheese

Direction

- Prep veggies as directed above.
- Nuke the sliced zucchini in a microwave safe bowl for 50 percent power for 2 minutes. (You only want to par-cook them, alternately you could blanch them in boiling water for 40 seconds and then plunge in ice water.) Cool and reserve.
- Drain the cottage cheese in a coffee filter lined colander in the refrigerator for at least 20 minutes. Mix in a beaten egg and salt/pepper, parsley and lemon rind. Reserve.
- Brown ground beef and DRAIN THE FAT VERY WELL.
- Remove from pan.
- Add oil to pan and sauté the onion and garlic, sauté till soft and limp. Add seasonings, including Worcestershire and cook for a 45 seconds to a minute. Add flour and cook stirring constantly. Add hamburger back to the pan and mix well. Add the broth and cook over low heat until it thickens.

- Assembly:
- In a 13 x 9 pan, layer a single layer of zucchini coins, side to side as full as you can. Cover with the ground beef mixture. Top entire pan with the cottage cheese mixture. Top with another layer of zucchini coins, side to side to cover the whole pan. Can cover tightly and freeze at this point. (I do this for the families we take it to in a double layered disposable foil pan, tightly covered in foil and a baggie of shredded cheese on the side.) Instructions for cooking:
- Defrost overnight in the refrigerator and bake for 55 minutes in 350 degree oven 40 minutes covered, 15 not covered. Pull out of oven and top generously with the grated cheddar cheese and continue to heat until the cheddar is bubbly and hot, probably another five minutes or so. Let rest at least 10 minutes to set up before serving.
- If cooking directly without freezing, cook 20 minutes covered, 10 uncovered and five minutes with the cheese.

---

360. Baked Cubed Steak Smothered In Brown Gravy And Onions Recipe

Serving: 6 | Prep: | Cook: 3774mins | Ready in:

Ingredients

- 6 pieces of cubed steak
- 1 onion
- 1 package of SM old fashioned brown gravy (2.75 ounces)
- aluminum foil

Direction

- Cover baking pan with aluminum foil
- Separate cubed steak and place it in the baking pan on top of the foil
- Cut up onion and spread it all over the cubed steak

- Prepare the old fashioned brown gravy and pour on top of cubed steak and onions
- Bake at 375 for about 45 minutes
- Stir gravy if necessary

361. Round Steak Stroganoff Recipe

Serving: 4 | Prep: | Cook: 30mins | Ready in:

Ingredients

- 1 1/2 # round steak (tenderize meat)
- 1/4 cup butter or margarine
- 2 tbsp. flour
- 1 cup beef bouillion
- 1/2 cup dry red wine
- 1 tbsp. instant minced onion
- 1 can (4 0z) sliced mushrooms
- salt & pepper
- 1/2 cup sour cream
- Hot buttered noodles or rice

Direction

- 1) Cut steak across the grain into thin strips 1/2" X 2"
- Sprinkle with tenderizer, let stand
- 2) Melt 2 tbsp. butter in a skillet over medium heat. Add steak & brown gently. Remove meat from skillet
- 3) Melt remaining butter in skillet. Stir in flour to make a smooth paste. Stir in bouillon, red wine, & onion. Drain mushrooms & add mushroom liquid. Cook over medium heat, stirring constantly, until smooth & thickened. Season with salt & pepper (according to taste)
- 4) Return meat to sauce. Add mushrooms
- 5) Cover. Lower heat & simmer gently about 30 min. (or until meat is tender.
- 6) Stir in sour cream & heat, (But do not BOIL)
- 7) Serve with hot noodles or rice
- 8) Makes about 4 servings

362. Saltimbocca Recipe

Serving: 4 | Prep: | Cook: 10mins | Ready in:

Ingredients

- 8 veal top round or round steak 1/4 inch thick (about 1 1/2 bounds)
- 1/2 cup all-purpose flour
- 8 thin slices prosciutto or fully cooked ham
- 8 thin slices (one ounce each) mozzarella cheese
- 8 fresh sage leaves
- 1/4 cup butter
- 1/2 cup dry wine or chicken broth
- 1/2 tesp. salt
- 1/4 tesp. black pepper

Direction

- Lightly pound each veal steak with meat mallet to tenderize to flatten slightly.
- Coat veal with flour.
- Shake off excess.
- Layer one slice each of prosciutto and cheese and 1 sage leaf on each veal slice.
- Roll up veal and tie with butcher string or secure with toothpicks.
- Melt butter in 10 inch skillet over medium heat.
- Cook veal rolls in butter for about 5 minutes.
- Turning occasionally until brown.
- Add wine and sprinkle rolls with salt and pepper.
- Cover and cook over medium-high.
- Heat about 5 minutes or until veal is no longer pink in center.

363. Smothered Pork Chops Recipe

Serving: 4 | Prep: | Cook: 45mins | Ready in:

Ingredients

- 4 Thick cut pork chops (I used 3/4-1" center cut boneless)
- 1 (10.75 ounce) can condensed cream of mushroom soup
- 1 Packet onion gravy mix
- 2 Cups water
- 1 Med. onion, chopped
- 2 cloves garlic (minced)
- 5 Tbsp. butter (divided)
- 1 tsp. season salt
- 1 tsp. black pepper

Direction

- In a deep, or electric skillet melt 3 Tbsp. butter
- Add pork chops, brown on both sides (about 4 min per side)
- Meanwhile, in separate bowl, mix together soup, gravy mix, and water. Mix well! Set aside.
- Add remaining butter, onion, and garlic to skillet.
- Season chops and onions with season salt and pepper.
- Brown & soften onions (about 2 Min.)
- Add soup/gravy mix, covering chops bring to a boil. Cover, reduce heat and simmer med-med/hi 45 Min.

---

364. Stuffed Pork Chops Recipe

Serving: 4 | Prep: | Cook: 30mins | Ready in:

Ingredients

- 4 thick cut pork chops
- 1 cup crushed saltines
- 1 teaspoon white sugar
- 1/2 teaspoon ground black pepper
- 1/2 teaspoon salt
- 1 teaspoon garlic powder
- 7 tablespoons melted butter, divided

- 1 small yellow onion, chopped
- 2 tablespoons dried parsley
- 2 cups chicken broth

Direction

- Make slits in pork chops to form a pocket in fat end.
- Combine saltines, sugar, pepper, salt, garlic powder, 5 tablespoons of the melted butter, onions, and parsley; mix well.
- Stuff chops generously and skewer shut with toothpicks.
- Heat the remaining 2 tablespoons of melted butter in a skillet.
- Brown chops slowly over medium heat for 5 minutes on each side.
- Add chicken broth and simmer over low heat for 30 minutes until tender, turning chops at least once.
- Uncover turn heat to med. high, and boil 2 min. or until liquid has thickened/reduced.
- Remove toothpicks and pour pan juices over pork chops before serving.

---

365. Svickava Czech Beef In Sour Cream Sauce Recipe

Serving: 8 | Prep: | Cook: 160mins | Ready in:

Ingredients

- 1 boneeless beef roast (sirloin tip, eye of round) about 4#'s
- 2 slices of bacon,cut into thin strips
- 2 lasge onions,chopped
- 1 large carrot, diced
- 1 cup diced celery
- 8 pepper corns
- 4 whole alspice
- 1 large or 2 small bay leafs
- 1/4 tsp. thyme
- 1 tsp. salt
- red wine vinegar and water
- 2 Tbs. flour

- 2 cups sour cream

Direction

- Push a knife through roast, several times. Use a larding needle and lard roast with the bacon, tie roast with string and place in a crock or kettle; add everything except flour and sour cream.
- Cover with equal parts of vinegar and water, marinate for 24 hours, turning several times.
- Spoon vegetables into a baking dish and place meat on top, add liquid.
- In a preheated oven at 325°F, roast for about 35-40 minutes per pound, to desired doneness.
- Remove roast from pan and cover to keep warm.
- Strain liquids and put into a sauce pan, stir in flour with a whisk, cook slowly, stirring until thickened, stir in sour cream and heat through, don't boil.
- Slice meat and serve covered with sauce.
- This meat has a pleasant sweet-sour taste.

Index

Conclusion

Thank you again for downloading this book!

I hope you enjoyed reading about my book!

If you enjoyed this book, please take the time to share your thoughts and post a review on Amazon. It'd be greatly appreciated!

Write me an honest review about the book – I truly value your opinion and thoughts and I will incorporate them into my next book, which is already underway.

Thank you!

If you have any questions, **feel free to contact at:** *author@fetarecipes.com*

Paula Stone

fetarecipes.com

Printed in Great Britain
by Amazon